When Young Children Need Help

When Young Children Need Help

Understanding and Addressing Emotional, Behavioral, and Developmental Challenges

DEBORAH HIRSCHLAND

Redleaf Press®
www.redleafpress.org
800-423-8309

Published by Redleaf Press
10 Yorkton Court
St. Paul, MN 55117-1065
www.redleafpress.org

First edition 2015
Cover design by Elizabeth Berry MacKenney/berrygraphics
Cover and interior photographs by Sage Sohier. Originals in color.
Interior design by Erin Kirk New
Typeset in Sentinel and Cronos
Printed in the United States of America
22 21 20 19 18 17 16 15   1 2 3 4 5 6 7 8

Library of Congress Cataloging-in-Publication Data
When young children need help : understanding and addressing
emotional, behavioral, and developmental challenges / Deborah
Hirschland. -- First edition.
     pages cm
     Includes bibliographical references and index.
   ISBN 978-1-60554-238-6 (paperback)
   ISBN 978-1-60554-273-7 (ebook)
1. Problem children--Education, Elementary. 2. Behavior disorders in children. 3. Emotional problems of children.
4. Behavioral assessment of children. 5. Early childhood education.
6. Educational psychology. I. Title.
   LC4801.H54 2015
   371.9--dc23
                    2014037385

Printed on acid-free paper

To

Libby Zimmerman, who helped forge the path,

Loretta Wieczner, who walks it by my side,

and

My grandson Avi, who is teaching me about early

childhood in a most wonderful new way

Contents

Preface ix

Acknowledgments xiii

Introduction xvii

Part 1 *Getting Specific Before Getting to Work* 1

    Chapter 1 From Reflection to Action: Looking Closely, Thinking Clearly, Intervening Effectively 3

    Chapter 2 Generating "Maybes": Observing with Depth, Breadth, and an Eye for Surprises 17

    Chapter 3 Spotlight on Development: Understanding the Building Blocks of Early Childhood Mastery 31

    Chapter 4 Spotlight on Causation: Considering the "Whys" behind Worrisome Behavior 39

    Chapter 5 Developing Child-Specific Portraits: Making Sense as the Foundation for Making Progress 53

    Chapter 6 Pathways to Growth: Joining Big-Picture Thinking with Practical Strategies 65

Part 2 *Connection Is Key* 83

    Chapter 7 Spotlight on the Three Cs: Connection, Communication, and Cue Responsiveness 85

    Chapter 8 Getting to Work with Hannah: Helping a Child with Dark Moods and a Dark Past 97

    Chapter 9 Getting to Work with Hannah, Continued: "Seeding the Day with Connection" and Other Strategies 111

Chapter 10   Getting to Work with Jenny: Helping an Intensely
Shy Child 127

Chapter 11   When Home Has Been Hard: Helping Children Climb
(or Re-climb) Developmental Ladders 139

Chapter 12   When Language Is Limited: Helping Two Boys Who Struggle
to Communicate 155

Part 3 *Addressing Problems in Self-Regulation* 171

Chapter 13   Getting to Work with Gabrielle: Helping Out When Energy
Is High and Focus Is Low 173

Chapter 14   Getting to Work with Brian: Helping an Easily Frustrated
Child 193

Chapter 15   Getting to Work on "Big Feelings": Helping Children Who
Get Swamped by Anger or Anxiety 211

Chapter 16   Spotlight on Parenting: Helping Families Set Effective
Expectations at Home 231

Part 4 *Putting It All Together* 247

Chapter 17   A Letter about Sam: Helping a Child with Multiple
Challenges 249

Chapter 18   When Young Children Need Help: Big Changes Start with
Small Steps 265

Appendix A   Seeking Clarity—Useful Forms 271

Appendix B   Staying on Track—Principles for Intervention 283

Appendix C   Learning More—Tools and Resources 289

References 295

Index 299

Preface

Many years ago my daughter's preschool director asked if I'd come to her early childhood association and present a workshop on supporting children with challenging behaviors. The question was sensible enough. She knew I was a professor at a local school of social work who taught courses in child development. Sensible to her at least. Not to me, whose initial but unspoken reaction was, "You must be joking!" What did I know that could be helpful to preschool staff? My children's teachers were the people I turned to when I was stuck, not the reverse. I'd get shown the door. But while this inner voice was telling me to decline without delay, I heard myself saying, "Sure . . . what a wonderful opportunity. I'd love to."

The evening of the workshop arrived. Just before I was about to begin speaking to an intimidatingly packed room, my city's beloved early childhood consultant walked in and found a spot at the back. Judy Medalia—who was at that time about the age I am now—came to my children's preschool once a month for a "parent coffee." I tried not to miss a single one of those gatherings, at which a group of us would literally sit at Judy's feet as she helped us figure out how to deal with bedtime troubles, sibling troubles, "you're not the boss of me" troubles, and more. Our questions were varied and many, and she'd comfortingly offer us ways to understand whatever was going on. Then she'd suggest approaches to handling our children's difficulties with good sense and good cheer. Judy was my hero.

So there I was, about to present for the first time to a group of early childhood educators, when once again something came out of my mouth I didn't expect: laughter. "Oh, Judy. I'm so glad you're here! I can't possibly offer these teachers anything approaching what you know. Why don't we switch places and I'll happily listen to what you have to say." For whatever reason, the group of teachers and directors who were assembled in that room laughed with me and not at me. I relaxed. These were not people who were out to show me what I didn't know. We could spend an interesting few hours together. And we did.

As we settled into the workshop, some of the participants shared war stories from their programs: stories about children who had major explosions for seemingly minor reasons, who hit to hurt, or who ransacked their classrooms when upset. Others described kids who were worrisomely active and unfocused or painfully withdrawn. I offered some stories as well, both from my life with my husband and two daughters and from my experiences as a child and family therapist. As our conversation deepened, I began weaving in perspectives from the theories I explored with my graduate students, in the hopes that those perspectives would help teachers more fully understand the most challenging youngsters in their classrooms. Then, after working together to come up with pictures of why particular children might be behaving in problematic ways, we shared ideas about what staff could do to help those kids begin to thrive. We talked about how to collaborate with families too.

When the workshop ended a few hours later, all I knew was that partnering with its participants had been deeply satisfying to me and seemed to have worked well for them too. What I didn't know was that the experience of being in conversation with those teachers and directors would ignite a passion for the work of consulting with early childhood educators. I didn't envision either that I'd begin spending increasing amounts of time in preschool, Head Start, and kindergarten classrooms, nor that I'd eventually leave my position at the school of social work where I taught in order to focus more fully on early childhood issues. I certainly couldn't have imagined that years later I'd take such pleasure in writing about home- and classroom-based intervention for the young children that parents and teachers worry about the most.

My first book, *Collaborative Intervention in Early Childhood*, targeted mental health practitioners, early childhood educators, and graduate students in a range of disciplines. Even as I worked to complete it, I imagined writing another one for teachers alone, with their experiences in their classrooms placed center stage. *When Young Children Need Help* is that book.

The structure and content of *When Young Children Need Help* harken back to my experience sitting at Judy Medalia's feet during those long-ago parent coffees and to the workshop I gave with her smiling and nodding from the back row. Why did those coffees feel useful to so many of our preschool's parents? I suspect it was partly because Judy took the time to notice that we were sometimes quite unhappy with ourselves about how we were reacting to problems at home. But that's not all. Judy also helped us tease out just what our children were doing, offered insight as to why they were doing it, and gave us practical ideas about how to make things better. My guess is that the workshop I ran for teachers and directors felt useful to its participants for much the same reasons. We took a look at some children behaving in problematic ways. We commiserated about how challenging kids can leave teachers feeling like unpleasant adults. We worked to develop a clear picture of what those kids were doing. Then we considered the reasons behind what was going on and—out of those provisional understandings—came up with practical ideas for supporting growth.

This progression from observation to reflection to action lies at the heart of our ability to help the hardest-to-reach kids in any classroom. The intent of this book is to give you tools and insights that will allow you to move through it more easily when you find yourself stumped by a particular child or a challenging group. If after reading it you have both a deeper understanding of what lies behind the behaviors that concern you and a toolbox filled with strategies that can make things better for everyone involved, it will have done its work successfully. Should that be the case, what is passed along will be mainly due to guidance I've received from Judy and many other mentors, and to wisdom gleaned from the wonderful teachers and parents with whom I've collaborated throughout my career. I am grateful to each and every one of them. And I'm grateful to the children themselves, who—if we remember to observe and listen to them with care—teach us so much of what we need to know to help them grow and thrive.

Acknowledgments

This book couldn't have been written without the company, support, and help of many along the way . . .

Thanks to the wonderful teachers, child care providers, and program directors who have been willing to talk and partner with me even when I feel as uncertain about how to move forward as they do. Your work inspires me endlessly. My grateful appreciation as well to the many families who have allowed me to join them in their efforts to understand and help with their children's difficulties. I feel fortunate, indeed, to have been welcomed into your lives.

Thanks to the extraordinary colleagues whose work I trust, intellectual company I treasure, and advice I rely upon, some of whom offered tremendously valuable feedback as this manuscript was in process: Joan Abramson, Connie Adkins, Amy Bamforth, Mitchell Baum, the staff of the Cambridge Human Services Preschools and Creative Start Child Care Centers, Mary Watson Avery and my partners on the advisory board of the Connected Beginnings Training Institute, Donna Fromberg, Jeffrey Fine, Margaret Hannah and the Freedman Center for Child and Family Development, fellow members of the Guild of Accessible Practitioners, Deborah Haynor, Judith Kneen, Betsy Leutz, Lizzie McEnany, members of the Newton Early Childhood Association and Newton's early childhood community, the clinicians of the Preschool Outreach Program and their director Paul Creelan, Fran Roznowski, Candace Saunders, Susan Stone, Loretta Wieczner, Kathy Wilcox, Rob and Andy Wizer-Vecchi, and, in memoriam, Adrienne Asch and Libby Zimmerman.

My heartfelt thanks to my circle of amazing friends, who have offered unstinting support throughout the journey of birthing this book and have graciously tolerated my absence during long stretches spent in my "writing cave." I won't list you by name, but you know who you are. A special shout-out to my friend and fellow writer Susan Goodman, without whose support and skillful help I couldn't have made it through, and to Sage Sohier, whose wonderful photographs grace these pages and whose willingness to enter and document my world has been an incredible gift. Thanks too to Sage's assistant Kent Rodzwicz, who worked tirelessly and skillfully by her side throughout this project.

Thanks to my extended family, who have offered such loving support throughout this process: my brother David, with his good cheer and thoughtful advice; my sister Madi, pillar of encouragement and insightful editor-at-a-moment's notice; my brother Richard, who always puts the stresses in his life aside to ask about what's going on in mine; and my mother, whose commitment to making a difference in the world is such an inspiration and whose belief in this project and eye for good (and not so good) writing helped me stay the course. Gratitude also to my father, who if he were still alive, would be cheering me on, and to Janet Hirschland, whose interest and humor has buoyed me up in innumerable ways.

Many thanks to the staff at Redleaf Press: Kyra Ostendorf, who rolled out Redleaf's welcome mat so warmly; David Heath, who believed in this project from the beginning and shepherded it along with a wonderfully intelligent and humor-filled touch; Laurie Herrmann, who kept me and the manuscript excellent company in its later stages; and Jim Handrigan, Erin Kirk New, Alyssa Lochner, Ashley Robinson, and Doug Schmitz, whose contributions were so important throughout the pre-publication process. And a very special thanks to my amazing editing partner Elena Fultz: her eye for structure, willingness to read, read, and read again—and her tolerance of my need to hammer out the details until we got them just right—made this a far better book than it would have been otherwise.

Finally, with love and deep appreciation . . .

Thanks to my daughters, Sarah and Shoshanna Fine, who in the midst of their very busy lives have showered me with incredible caring, support, and (wonderful writers both) editing help whenever needed. Thanks also to their partners, Micah Perlin—with his thoughtful questions, friendly advice, and skillful tech support—and the inimitable and kind Laurel Gabler, who always found time in the midst of her hectic schedule to ask how things were going. Thanks to little Avi, who won't understand these words until he is older, but whose presence in my life has brought an even deeper meaning to the endeavor of helping young children and whose ineffable spirit is one of my greatest joys. And last but certainly not least, thanks many times over to my husband, Jeffrey Fine—co-parent and grandparent, partner and close friend of over forty years, and favorite colleague. You have kept me company throughout this endeavor in so many ways: with support for my early morning risings and late night crankiness; with home-cooked meals and thoughtfully planned nights out when I needed a break; with an ever-present willingness to consider a word choice, hear a paragraph, discuss an idea, or thrash out thorny questions of substance; and with a love-filled belief that this work of writing about my ideas was very much worth doing, even when it took away from our time together. I am so lucky to have all of you by my side.

Introduction

This is a book about young children who are hard to understand, hard to help, or both. If you're a teacher or child care provider, you know how stressful it can be to work with kids like this: they're often the ones you focus on the most yet sense you're reaching the least. You may feel relieved as you say good-bye to such youngsters at the end of a long day. But when you get home, you can't stop thinking about them. You care about them, fret about them, and truly don't know what to do about them. You see their gifts peeking out from behind their vulnerabilities but can't seem to help those gifts shine more fully.

When teachers feel this stumped, an early childhood consultant is sometimes called in to take a fresh look at what's going on. I've been such a consultant for many years now. This book tells the stories of some children I've met along the way and the caring adults who worked to help them. Through those stories, it offers a picture of how we can understand children's difficulties without losing sight of their strengths. It looks at how to generate step-by-step goals for growth. And it provides many practical and child-friendly ways to foster that growth for a range of challenges.

Just who are the kids I'm describing as hard to help? What do they do? Some of them make the lives of everyone around them exceedingly difficult. Perhaps they respond to little problems in big ways—sobbing or punching, hurling insults or toys, and upsetting the children around them over and over again. Perhaps they wiggle and cruise their way through each part of the school day, annoying their buddies during circle time and making it difficult to get out to the playground without mishaps along the way. Maybe they refuse to listen—or listen but can't make use of what they hear. Maybe they do a lot of these things at once.

Not all hard-to-help children are disruptive, however. Some have trouble communicating and, tired of trying to make themselves understood, quietly lose their zest for friendship and their passion for learning. Others react to the world of their classroom as if it's terribly unsafe, hovering on the edges of play and clamming up in response to friendly overtures from classmates and teachers alike. Then there are the kids who respond to both people and activities with a kind of dazed disengagement. Such children can be gently propelled through their days in school and don't make life difficult for others. But as easy as it is to have them in a classroom, they may be just as hard to reach as kids who lash out regularly.

These descriptions capture only a few of the ways young children show us that they aren't feeling comfortable in themselves and confident in their worlds—and aren't developing the skills they'll need to succeed as friends and learners in the years to come. Whatever the particulars, such difficulties often lead staff to ask a set of questions. If it hasn't happened already, is it time for a child to undergo an assessment process? Might some outside services—or even a different school placement—be helpful? What about what's going on at home? Should a referral for child or family therapy be made?

These are good questions, and their answers often help us help kids. However, while assessments can offer valuable information, they don't always capture the fullness of who a child is and how his difficulties are nested in the worlds of his family and classroom. They usually don't clarify how teachers can support that child's growth in a moment-to-moment way either. And while supplementary services can be very useful, most hard-to-help kids remain in their classrooms for many hours each day.

All of this means that even after assessments are complete and extra supports are in place, teachers still have a big job: To use whatever information is at hand to understand the most worrisome children in their care. To come up with their best guesses as to what approaches will support growth, and to start using them as skillfully and compassionately as possible. To keep a close eye on how those approaches are working, tweaking and revamping them as needed. And to partner with children's parents whenever possible, so that the most important people in a child's life are collaborating on how to move forward with hope.

When Young Children Need Help delves deeply into the progression just described—one that goes from making meaning to making progress. It does this, however, without suggesting that if a child does *this,* then teachers should do *that.* As young children learn and grow, they're supremely and uniquely themselves. That's what can make working with them such an adventure and such a pleasure. Hard-to-help kids are no exception, and the approaches we use to assist them must be tailored to who they are. There's another ingredient to add to the mix too: the strategies a teacher uses to support growth have to be a good fit for that particular child. Approaches to intervention work well only when the people using them find ways to make them their own.

My intent, then, isn't that you'll finish this book knowing exactly what to do when a particular child is having difficulties. You will find plenty of strategies you can add to those you already like and use. But, just as importantly, you'll encounter some perspectives that may help you think more clearly about the challenging children you teach, and allow you to come up with your own creative approaches to supporting them and their families.

When Young Children Need Help is organized as follows. The chapters of part 1, "Getting Specific Before Getting to Work," take a close look at the process of observation, reflection, and action planning. Then the book moves on to examine specific approaches used to target specific difficulties. The six chapters of part 2, "Connection Is Key," highlight the nature of work with children who struggle to connect with pleasure and communicate with ease. The chapters in part 3, "Addressing Problems in Self-Regulation," put a spotlight on how we support kids who have trouble slowing down their bodies, focusing their minds, managing their feelings, and controlling their impulses. Part 4, "Putting It All Together," begins by taking an integrative look at intervention through the story of a hard-to-help child with a mix of developmental challenges. Then the book's final chapter celebrates the little steps that lead to big changes as it looks back on what has been explored and forward to new possibilities.

It is my hope that the ideas you'll find throughout *When Young Children Need Help* will make those little steps easier to take and those big changes easier to believe in. I hope, too, that the children whose lives and struggles fill its pages will bring those ideas to life. All of these youngsters—and their families—have been heavily disguised. Their issues, their classrooms, and the interventions used to help them, however, are absolutely real.

Anyone who writes about young children and their caregivers runs into a problem: it's hard to find an efficient yet inclusive language with which to describe early childhood work. In this book, I use the word *teacher* to stand in for toddler, preschool, and kindergarten teachers, program-based child care staff, and family child care providers. *Parents* stands in for mothers, fathers, grandparents, aunts and uncles, foster parents, and any other adults who anchor life at home. Finally, *classroom* and *school* represent all early care and education settings. In addition, I generally alternate the pronouns *he* and *she* from chapter to chapter to offer gender-neutral language without having to repeatedly use *he or she* and *his or her*.

One last note before these explorations begin. It is my good fortune to have as a dear friend a wonderful photographer. Sage Sohier heard about this writing project early on and very generously agreed to take photos of some of the classrooms where I consult. The kids whose photographs you'll find throughout this book, including on its cover, are not the hard-to-help youngsters I describe in its chapters. Rather, they're children going through their days in school, experiencing the joys of play, learning, and friendship—and the challenges of being little in a big and sometimes complicated world. I'm indebted to Sage for capturing the nuances of their experiences so beautifully. I'm indebted as well to their parents and teachers for being willing to share Sage's photos of life in school.

Getting Specific
Before Getting to Work

It's easy to say that helping a youngster successfully requires us to understand her in all her uniqueness. And it makes sense that understanding her in this way helps us create a child-specific approach to intervention. But what do these statements actually mean? What do they look like in action? The following six chapters take a close look at the answers to these two questions. In chapter 1, a teacher's overwhelmed request for help sets the stage for an overview of the process we go through any time a child is struggling. Then, chapters 2 through 6 break down that process by following the story of Alain, an endearing but highly challenging four-year-old. Chapter 2 hones in on observation. Chapters 3 and 4 feature aspects of the field's knowledge base that help us understand what we've observed. Chapter 5 explores how we come up with a nuanced portrait of a child in her world. Finally, chapter 6 illuminates how we use the reflective process to come up with a detailed action plan.

Because Alain serves as a kind of "stand-in" for any child parents and teachers worry about, his story is explored from many angles of vision and in great detail. By following his team's efforts to help him from beginning to end—that is, from the endeavor of observation and reflection on to the work of action planning and intervention—these chapters offer the book's fullest picture of what is involved in "getting specific before getting to work."

Rainbow Ants

1 From Reflection to Action
Looking Closely, Thinking Clearly, Intervening Effectively

It's a Monday afternoon in early November. A group of teachers, many with some much-needed coffee in hand, settle into their chairs as they prepare to begin one of their program's lead teacher "drop-ins." These monthly groups carve out time for the head teachers of a large preschool program to seek advice from each other, get support, and think about new ways of approaching their work when things in their classrooms aren't going as well as they'd like. Often, they end up seeking help in regard to children they're finding particularly challenging.

As the program's early childhood consultant, I'm in the room too, sipping my own cup of coffee. We all exchange greetings, grumbling good-naturedly about the fact that the season's first snow is forecast for later in the week. Then Julia, the lead teacher of a prekindergarten classroom, asks whether she can start us off. The group willingly agrees: she's one of the program's most admired teachers and is more likely to offer help than request it. Her colleagues know she must be feeling on shaky ground if she's asking to take the floor. With a nod of thanks, Julia begins to speak.

"I really need to talk about Gabrielle. Things are getting worse. Well, not totally. She's not bolting out of the classroom like she was, and that's a huge relief. But she keeps grabbing the toys kids are using during free play or shoving their arms away if she wants something they're reaching for. And she's constantly telling them what to do and what not to do. So even though they know Gabby has fun ideas, most of the children won't play with her anymore. When they leave her alone, she does okay. She's a terrific artist. She loves the dramatic play corner, too. If she's there by herself, she'll pretend to be a mom, and you can hear her telling these long stories about what her doll babies need and how she's helping them. But we can't ask the other kids not to share the area with her, and then things fall apart immediately.

"It doesn't get any better either. Gabby roams around the classroom during cleanup—it's almost impossible to get her to help out. And now she's starting to push back big time about coming to circle at all. Even if we can get her there, she probably sits for less than a minute or two most days before she starts cruising the room and creating a big distraction.

"Then there's the playground. That's been a nightmare. I got there just in time the other day when Gabby was so focused on being first down the slide that she almost pushed little Jie-ling off the ladder. And you know how hard we've been trying to help Jie-ling feel safe here."

Julia has said a lot already. But before anyone has a chance to offer support or ask questions, she barrels ahead. Her stress and concern fill up our meeting room like this girl's energy and impulsivity fill up her classroom.

"Gabby does pretty well at snack and lunch though. When she's focused on eating, she seems to settle down, and then she can be really sweet and funny. You know, even though she does all these outrageous things, I don't think she's actually all that aggressive. She just does whatever comes to mind to get what she wants right then. When she's calm, she can be truly kind. Yesterday, one of the girls forgot her lunch, and Gabby offered to share her sandwich even though she was starving. She's really smart and curious too . . . when she's not being so difficult, you can see what a neat kid she is.

"The thing is, I know she's getting to me. I've become so frustrated with how she doesn't listen and how much time she's taking away from the other kids that I'm sure she can tell I'm more and more annoyed with her. I noticed this week that when I come close to her, it seems like she assumes I'm going to tell her she's doing something wrong. And she turns away even more than she used to.

"Here's something else. I know I didn't do a good job talking with her mom yesterday. I had the feeling Beth was doing everything she could not to cry when I told her what Gabby's day had been like. She just stood there looking sort of shell-shocked with her baby's nose running and her two-year-old tugging at her sleeve and Gabby ready to tear out the door into the parking lot like she did last Monday. I think Gabby's dad might be out of the house, too. I'm not sure what's up there."

A number of teachers nod. This is a family that has been on the program's radar since shortly after Gabrielle arrived some months back, and Julia isn't the only one who wonders how things are going at home. Julia, though, isn't quite ready to step back and begin reflecting on either Gabby or her family. She has more she needs to get out.

"I do feel so bad for Beth. But then I watch how she just lets Gabby run wild when they first get here. I mean, yesterday, Gabby literally climbed on a table right next to Beth. And Beth didn't say a thing! Then I hear how Gabby talks back to her mother at pickup time, and I sort of feel like these parents really shouldn't have had three kids so close together. I start judging Beth and feeling so angry with Gabby that I find myself wishing we could just kick her out. And you guys know me, right? That's not like me, it's really not who I am at all."

Now it's Julia who looks close to crying. Her openness isn't a surprise: the group has worked to create a nonjudgmental atmosphere that everyone has come to trust. These teachers aren't just seeking to "vent" during our meetings, however. Their hope, like Julia's, is to return to their classrooms with new perspectives and fresh ideas for intervention. That's a weighty agenda for sure. But not only do the teachers and I find our time together full of learning, we laugh a lot as well. Sometimes, even more than some interesting new ideas, it's that laughter that allows a teacher to take heart, regroup, and move forward.

It's clear, though, that it's going to take some sharing around the table before Julia can regain a sense of humor about Gabrielle. And even though some friendly laughter will help lighten her load, this teacher also needs our company in taking a closer look at her student's experience.

From Reflection to Action: An Essential Progression

What our drop-in group does, month after month, involves a set of steps. First we outline what we already know about what a child is doing and feeling, and add information about her inborn nature, history, and life at home. Then, using the information we've gathered, we consider the reasons behind what is going on and identify specific areas in which a child needs help. Finally, based on our understanding of these first two steps, we generate ideas about how to support growth. Framed more simply, we progress from reflection to action by answering three questions: *What do we see? What do we think? What should we do?*

This three-step progression is useful far beyond the work of our monthly drop-in group: it is central to understanding and helping any youngster whom teachers and parents are worried about. Taking the time to move through it fully can make all the difference when a child isn't thriving and the adults who care about her can't figure out what to do about it. That's because the keys to change often lie in observing what is going on even more carefully in order to get a better feel for why a child is struggling. It is only then that a sensible and child-specific action plan can be put in place to move things forward.

As we progress from seeing to thinking to doing, we need some "anchoring" ideas to keep us on track. A number of them, listed here, are rooted in widely shared beliefs connected to our field's knowledge base:

- The worrisome behaviors of hard-to-help kids are filled with information about *developmental skills* they're having trouble mastering and *troubling feelings* they're experiencing. Helping them to thrive involves paying attention to both.

- Understanding the reasons for those skill deficits and emotions means having to think about the mix of a youngster's constitutional nature (what we sometimes call "hard wiring"), the family situation into which she was born and lives, and difficult experiences she's had during her childhood.

- The nature of early relationships has a huge impact on how kids learn and grow. If a child's early and ongoing connections haven't been filled with trust and ease, a focus on positive relationship building is going to be central.

- When a child is struggling at home or school, adults often react in ways that make things worse, even though that's not their intention. Changing those patterns is another element behind successful intervention.

- Parenting is hard work—especially parenting in the face of life challenges or a child whose medical situation, constitutionally based vulnerabilities, or temperament makes her harder than usual to care for. Finding ways to partner with and support the parents of hard-to-help kids is often an essential piece to moving things forward.

- All kids have a core need to be loved and appreciated. When things aren't going well, a mix of support, affection, and optimism can go far in setting the stage for change.

Gabrielle's teacher, Julia, believes strongly in these ideas and frequently uses them to come up with thoughtful and compassionate approaches to all of the kids in her care. That's why she's highly respected by her colleagues and why so many parents feel good about dropping their children off with her each day. Even the best teachers can feel overwhelmed by particularly challenging kids, however. That's what has happened here. When a child's difficulties leave teachers feeling as concerned as Julia and her team are, it doesn't mean that the progression from reflection to action has lost its usefulness. It does suggest that we'll need to look even more closely and think more deeply before figuring out what mix of strategies (and, at times, outside supports) might make a difference. It also tells us that if possible, finding a way to partner successfully with a child's family will be an important piece of the puzzle.

Looking more closely at a child's experience isn't always as easy as it sounds. It requires pulling together a range of information about what's going on, and that can feel overwhelming when a youngster is on the complicated side or taking up a great deal of energy already. Luckily, we often have much of the information we need on hand. Our job is to assemble what we know in useful form.

Consider, for example, the plea for help that opens this chapter. Julia plunges into her description of classroom life with more desperation than organization. Even so, her keen observations touch on many of the areas our teacher drop-in group will have to sort through to make sense of what's going on. First, Gabrielle's behaviors can be very problematic. A number of them suggest that she is lacking some of the developmental skills kids need to do well—things like the ability to slow down her body, focus her mind, and control her impulses. Second, Gabby may be weighed down with some troubling feelings. Her way of pulling back from her teachers and talking back to her mother indicate that she may be both angry with others and feeling bad about herself. Third, the quality of her relationships with adults has become filled with tension, as her teachers get increasingly annoyed and her mother's eyes fill with helpless tears. In addition, Gabby is "starting to push back big time" and "turns away even more than she used to." It appears that the back-and-forth between how this child behaves, how people respond, and what she does next as a result—what we might call *interactive patterning*—may be causing her worrisome behaviors to become more extreme rather than less so. Finally, things at home don't seem to be going any better than things at school.

Certainly there's a lot to be worried about. We also learn, however, that Gabrielle isn't always as difficult as she appears at first glance. She's better at snack and lunch than at other times. She has some interesting play ideas on which she contentedly elaborates when no one is around to get in her way. In addition, she has genuine empathy for others when she's not at the mercy of her impulsivity. She is smart and curious, too, and has a great sense of humor. In fact when Gabby's strengths shine through, she is, in Julia's words, a "neat kid."

Behavior, developmental skill, emotional well-being, adult-child relationships, interactive patterning, life at home—all of these are at the core of what we need to understand about Gabby's struggles. Times when things go better or worse, the capacity for play, the ability to feel for and reach out to others, and strengths that peek out from under difficulties—these, too, are of great importance in our efforts to make sense of what is going on. Now, how do we take such broad-ranging areas and organize them systematically? How do we use them to progress from reflection to action in a thorough yet efficient way?

"Three-Part Flips": Using Observations to Set Goals and Consider Strategies

What do we see? What do we think? What should we do? How might we assemble the information we gather in answering the first question to help us reflect on the second? And how can our answers to that second question generate ideas in regard to the third? There's a lot to keep in mind, and the "three-part flip" framework that follows can help. It gives us a way to organize the information we have on hand by providing categories for consideration. And it encourages us to take what we've noticed and learned about a child and family, think about where we'd like to head, and use our hopes for change to ask questions about intervention. In that sense, it adds some "meat" to the bones of the "see → think → do" progression.

Here, then, are a number of exploratory "three-part flips" (with credit given to my colleague Loretta Wieczner for her central role in developing them). In each one, we first ask what we see that we're worried about. Then we flip our initial query on its head to consider what we *don't* see that we hope to foster instead. Finally, we pose some questions that ask us to start brainstorming about how to head toward that growth. These flips ask us to consider questions about:

Behavior and Developmental Mastery

- What is the child doing that concerns us?

- What isn't she doing that we'd like to see instead?

- How can we teach her the developmental skills she'll need in order to move in that positive direction?

Emotional Well-Being

- What is the child feeling when he is behaving in problematic ways?

- What feelings do we hope he will start experiencing more of instead?

- What can we do to foster those positive feelings?

Adult-Child Connections

- How are we feeling toward this child? (Is she "getting to" us as Gabby is getting to Julia?) How is she feeling toward us?
- What feelings, on both sides, do we hope might develop instead?
- What can we do to foster more feelings of pleasurable connection in both directions?

Interactive Patterning

- Are there things we do when interacting with this child that seem to be leading to more rather than less problematic behavior, even though that's not our intent?
- What kind of "he does → we do → he does" exchanges do we hope to get going instead?
- What can we do during our part of these patterns to help the child begin having different responses on his end?

Life at Home

- Are there things about this child's home life that may be contributing to what we see?
- What changes in the way her parent(s) interact with her might help her feel better and act differently? Might those changes also help family members feel more positive about their relationship with her?
- How can we forge a partnership with this family so that we offer support and mentoring around issues they're experiencing at home, while they help us become more successful at school?

These first five flips help us use our observations to come up with sensible goals, which then serve as a springboard for thinking about effective approaches to classroom-based support and home-school partnerships. But these flips don't give us the complete framework we need to organize the information we have at hand. Nor do they ask us to pay attention to all aspects of intervention. That's why we need to look at some additional categories, each one of which—like those just offered—involves a series of questions. The following question sets continue to ask about what we see and hope to see. They help us frame goals for getting to work as well. This time, we consider:

Triggers for Difficulty and Setups for Success

- What times of day, what situations, and which people seem to set off behaviors of concern?

- At what times of day, in what situations, and with which people does the child fare better?

- How can we use the answers to both these questions to shoot for more situations that help him to thrive? How can we use them to support him differently through periods of predictable difficulty?

Challenges "Playing Out in Play"

- How does the way in which this child plays (or doesn't play) reflect her vulnerabilities?

- What would her play look like if she was beginning to master her challenges successfully?

- What kind of classroom-based play support can we provide to help her gain the mastery she needs?

Family Culture and History

- What is this family's heritage? Are the norms at home different from those the child experiences in school? Did this family come to this country recently or under duress?

- How might we reach out to this child and his family? How can we help the family build a comfortable bridge between the child's experience in his home culture and his time in school?

- How can we convey the respect this child and family deserve, support his growing mastery in our classroom, and create an inclusive experience classroom-wide?

Outside Supports of All Kinds

- Does this child appear to have developmental challenges and/or emotional issues that could benefit from assessment or outside support? Is the family struggling with financial, housing, mental health, or other issues that make it hard for them to provide the basics their kids need?

- What kinds of assessment, support services, and/or advocacy might be useful?

- How can we reach out to this family successfully, especially if they are hard to engage? How can we help them begin to access the help they and/or their child need in a way that feels safe and supportive to them?

Getting Specific Before Getting to Work

If the answers to question sets like these were easy to come by, books like this wouldn't be necessary. Each one requires exploration, and each is discussed in the following chapters. Attending to their content starts us down the road to change, helping us "get specific" about a youngster's overall situation and "get to work" with approaches that are tailored to her unique needs. That's what starts to happen after the drop-in group's meeting about Gabrielle.

As is so often the case at the beginning of the progression from reflection to action, our drop-in group notes information connected to many of the categories just listed. But as is also common, a few content areas take precedence in our discussion. In this case, we focus partly on key areas of developmental mastery with which Gabrielle is struggling, and how teachers can find effective ways to teach her the skills she lacks. We also take note of some worrisome interactive patterns that have emerged in response to her skill deficits. Those patterns, we surmise, appear to be putting her emotional well-being at risk: she's starting to see herself as an out-of-control "bad girl" rather than a delightful child with some important things to learn. The group poses many questions about life at home as well, and Julia leaves with a commitment to reach out further to Gabby's mother, Beth.

I have a chance to visit the classroom about two weeks after that meeting. Julia tells me that she's become even more aware of what a big role Gabrielle's trouble regulating energy plays in what has been going on. As a result, she and her team have come up with some new ideas about how to break down and teach that developmental skill, step by step. As just one example, they've been running some group games that help children use their minds to direct their bodies to slow down. Gabby and her classmates have been moving to music using big, fast motions and then little, small ones. They've played games in which they dance and then freeze, or run fast and then walk slowly. They've pretended to be quick-moving eels alternating with leisurely sea turtles, too.

The teaching team hasn't just been working on energy regulation. They've also realized that Gabrielle's oppositional behavior stems in part from the fact that she has been feeling more nagged than appreciated. To change that dynamic, they've been "seeding the day with connection"—seeking Gabby out for brief moments of pleasurable engagement throughout her hours in the classroom. (See chapter 9 for more on this multifaceted strategy.)

Now it's circle time, and Julia is working to help the group settle in.

Gabby has shown up without too much fuss—a wonderful change—and is squirming on her mat next to her classmate Susannah. Julia, smiling at Susannah and then at Gabby, calls out, "I like the way Susannah is sitting!" She appears to be hoping that Gabby will use the encouraging cue to imitate her friend. Gabby turns to look at Susannah, who is sitting "crisscross applesauce." Barely able to sit at all, Gabby glances toward her teacher with genuine puzzlement. "How does she *do* that?" she asks.

It is a sweet and telling moment. The (problematic) interactive patterning that the drop-in group noted earlier has begun to shift. Gabrielle is trying, not balking. She's looking to Julia and asking for help rather than shutting her out. In addition she's starting to engage in some self-observation, a precursor to impulse control. As she does this, she notices that she's not managing to do what is expected. Gabby, however, doesn't know how to do what her teacher wants: her mastery of the skills connected to regulating energy and sensory input are still very low. Julia is right there with her student though. With the team's increased emphasis on both connection and developmental mastery, this teacher uses the moment beautifully.

Julia smiles at Gabby again and says out loud, "Great question!" Then she tells her that one of the other teachers, Maryanne, will be right over to lend a hand. Maryanne takes the cue and moves to sit behind Gabby. She places her large hands on Gabby's spindly upper arms with a bit of friendly pressure, giving her student some of the sensory "diet" the team has noted she needs. Maryanne also offers Gabby some whispered instructions that help her settle a little more. Not as fully as Susannah, but as fully as she is capable of at this point. With a "thumbs up" directed Gabby's way, Julia briefly stops the story she's relating to the group. She smiles at her wiggliest classroom member one more time. "I like the way Gabrielle is sitting!" she says. Gabby grins back.

There is a lot going on here, though what these teachers are doing looks quite simple. Julia and her team have come up with a picture of where

Gabrielle's vulnerabilities lie. With that picture as a guide, they have agreed on a set of goals. They're working on relationship building, on skill development, and on boosting Gabrielle's experience of well-being and confidence. They are also trying to change the back-and-forth patterning that was leading Gabrielle to become increasingly oppositional. And they're doing all this while still making sure that circle time continues apace for the other children in their classroom. It's impressive teaching that reflects what Julia, her colleagues, and I call "thinking big but acting small."

The work that Julia's team does to support Gabby and her mother serves as a case example of the approaches we use to help the kids I call "the wiggly ones." Other features of that work are explored in chapter 13, but there are a few additional points worth noting here. The first is that being aware of what's going on for a child always means considering life at home, not just in school. The second is that we can't underestimate the importance of staying open to new information. Sometimes, it's that information that helps us envision the best pathway to mastery for a child or family.

The Importance of Staying Open and Curious—with Kids and with Their Families

As lead teacher, Julia has witnessed Beth's close-to-tears concern and her seeming lack of response to Gabby's impulsive behaviors. However, as is so often true, there is considerably more to discover about what is going on. Julia and I reach out to Beth over a number of meetings. We quickly learn that she's well aware that Gabby is not in good control, and very willing to accept some support and guidance. The problem for Beth is that one of the few things Gabby responds to when she's misbehaving is loud yelling. But this mother hates yelling and for good reason. Beth, it turns out, grew up with a father who had a terrifyingly violent temper when he'd had too much to drink. And he drank a lot.

When Beth became a parent she promised herself she wouldn't scare her kids. However, trying to stay calm at all costs has caused a different kind of problem. Gabby has been so energetic, so wild, and so unwilling to listen when her mother speaks softly that Beth ends up locking her in her room when she has behaved especially badly. Gabby hates that, and it makes Beth feel awful too. Sometimes, though, it seems to be the only thing that works, at least in the moment. Longer term, Beth knows that what she is doing isn't really helping. Gabby is just impossible in the grocery store and embarrassingly out of control when she's picked up at school. In addition, Beth has been wondering something: Has Gabby been running out of the classroom because she has been locked in her room regularly and now can't stand feeling closed in? It feels as though the whole business of trying to parent with gentleness has backfired.

As Julia and I talk with her more, this soft-spoken woman tearfully reveals that she married a man who has turned out to have a temper not unlike her father's. Her husband works all the time, she notes. In some ways, given what he is like when he's home, that can be a relief. In fact, Beth is so unhappy in her marriage that she has been thinking about divorce. But she feels stuck, she tells us. She and her husband have three young kids and not enough money to support two households.

In our ever-deepening conversations with Beth, the first layer of observation leads to a second and even a third. And what Julia and I learn about underlying issues leads directly to hopes for change. The categories behind our three-part flips come in handy, too, as we brainstorm with Beth about goals she has for getting support, for gaining control over Gabby, and for changing the back-and-forth between them that is leading her daughter to become less and less compliant. As we move from what we all *see* to what we *think* to what Beth can *do*, the three of us do some role playing. Beth tries out what a firm but reasonable "voice of authority" might sound like (see chapter 16). We talk about how she can set effective limits at home. In addition, we consider how she and the team can partner to help Gabby learn to "pop up and tune in" (an attention-related skill examined in chapter 7). With help, Beth becomes far more effective with Gabby and far more confident in herself. Watching this mother start to experience a sense of empowerment is a pleasure.

Shooting for an Ideal While Living in the Real

There is much to celebrate as Gabby moves through her final year of preschool. But Gabby and her family's story isn't one with a perfect ending. Like so many children with challenges, this girl makes wonderful progress. Yet she heads off to kindergarten in a way that has everyone holding their breath. Not surprisingly, Julia gets a call from Gabby's new teacher before the end of September. He wants advice as to how he can help his most challenging student stay focused and calm when he is on his own in a classroom with twenty kids. It is a great credit to the preschool team that Julia has many strategies to suggest. At the end of their conversation, Gabby's kindergarten teacher thanks her profusely: her way of understanding Gabby, he says, is truly helpful. Will what Julia has conveyed lighten the task the new team faces in supporting this lovable yet still-challenging girl? Julia hopes it will. Gabby has a long way to go.

2 Generating "Maybes"
Observing with Depth, Breadth, and an Eye for Surprises

"Claudia and Nancy asked if you'd come observe in their classroom—they're really worried about the mix of kids they have this year. There's one child who's been hurting his classmates so often that parents are upset. And a bunch of other kids with issues too. It's a difficult group for this team to manage, and that says something . . . things usually run smoothly in their room, even when they have a number of children with challenges. How about if you spend tomorrow morning with them and then do a follow-up meeting after lunch?"

It is mid-October and I'm on the phone with Robin, the director of a large early education program where I offer regular consultation. This is the time of year when teachers are starting to have a good feel for the work ahead. Who is eagerly diving in to opportunities for learning and socializing? Who is still settling in or holding back? Are there some puzzlers, youngsters who are hard to understand? Any who are especially challenging?

Often, there are a few kids who set off alarm bells. That usually spurs teachers to observe their most worrisome students even more carefully. Sometimes, as in this case, they'll request an "extra set of eyes" to observe as well. But what do teachers and specialists look for, and how do they use what they see? Such questions lie at the heart of this chapter's explorations of the process of observation. Those explorations unfold, in part, by tracking my thoughts as I observe the most challenging child in the room, the one that Robin is worried about. I arrange for a short meeting with Claudia and Nancy, the room's teachers, first thing in the morning on the day of my visit. It quickly becomes apparent that they are frantic: this is by far the most difficult start to a year they can remember. Claudia, the lead teacher, lets out a big sigh before launching in.

"It's a good thing you're here. We have to figure out what to do about Alain—he's so tough. He hits kids and then runs around and kicks things over when we call him to talk about what happened. He kicks us too if we try to stop him. He grabs what he wants, and it seems like wherever he is, some child gets upset. We feel like we're shadowing him constantly. Even so, he just missed another boy's eye when he threw a marker yesterday. I feel bad saying this, but we don't even try that hard to get him to come to circle because he almost always knocks kids aside as he insists on the seat he wants. Then we end up having to comfort whomever he's hurt and to deal with him. By the time we're done, the other kids have gotten restless and it's hard to rein them back in."

Claudia falters, as if there is so much to say that she doesn't know where to head next. She looks at Nancy, who takes over, her face etched with concern.

"The bottom line," Nancy says, "is that we're really wondering if Alain can stay here. I think Robin is starting to wonder the same thing. But that's an awful question to be asking. We love him—it's hard not to with that huge smile he gives us, even right after we've had to be stern with him. It's like he's asking, 'Is everything okay now? Can we still be friends?' And what will happen to him if he has to leave? He only has this year before going to kindergarten, and we don't know where else we could send him. Not only that, his mom is young, and she's on her own here. Her family is back home in Haiti. He needs us and she does too. Here's what makes the whole thing even worse. Alain is not the only one with challenges. He's so difficult that sometimes we feel like we can barely pay attention to the other children. And we have *a lot* of kids who need extra help."

Now, I begin to hear about some of the other children in the class. Emilio, a child whom Nancy describes as an "odd little butterfly," floating his way aimlessly through the day. Isabel, whose family has recently faced some unexpected setbacks, a sweet-tempered child who seems sad and lost in a way she wasn't when the school year began. And Jonathan, whose difficulties understanding and using language make it hard for him to hold his own with the other boys at the train table—the only place he likes to play.

There are more children to discuss and more to be said. But it's time to start the day. I watch Nancy and Claudia brace themselves as they see Alain barrel his way into the classroom, dragging his mother by the hand. His mother looks none too pleased. But Alain's whole face lights up as he responds to Claudia's "Good morning, Alain!" with one of those irresistible smiles Nancy just described. Then he takes off for the block corner.

"Deep Seeing": Observing, Wondering, Observing Some More

I'm lucky that my role as consultant allows me the freedom to stand back and observe children at length. I can zoom in on the raised shoulders and worried gaze of a reserved boy as he enters his classroom. I can note how he seems to pull further into his shell when his mom gently tries to get him to say hello to his teacher. Then I can wait to see whether he eventually relaxes into his day or continues to carry his caution with him like a cloak. I can watch how another child plays alongside others with friendly gusto until things don't go her way, and then suddenly lets out a loud scream of frustration. I can stay put as I note whether she is able to accept the help her teachers try to give her. I can observe whether she eventually finds a way to solve the problem at hand or storms away for good. Then I can see how long it takes before she regroups . . . and how long before she gets stuck once again.

Teachers observe such things all the time too. If that's your role, your challenge isn't so much to notice the details as it is to find the time and mental space to assemble a full picture of what you see. After all, to do your job well, you have to be "on" all the time. You work to offer learning-filled activities at a range of levels. You wipe noses and tables, offer hugs and Band-Aids. You rush to the block corner to mediate a tussle that otherwise may turn to outright war. And much more. But whether it's a consultant like me doing a focused observation over a few hours or you collecting even more information throughout your weeks in the classroom, our job is the same. We take the kinds of questions posed in the last chapter's three-part flips. We look closely at a child over time. Eventually, we fill in our answers with just as much specificity as we can.

As this chapter focuses in on the process of observation, I need to elaborate on my earlier description of how we go about filling in those answers. Overall it's true that observation (*What do we see?*) leads us toward understanding a child's difficulties (*What do we think?*). It's also correct that the way we make sense of those difficulties propels us toward effective intervention (*What should we do?*). But the truth is that even as we begin observing, we filter what we notice through our knowledge about child development. Doing so allows us to come up with a set of early hunches about the meaning of what we're seeing. Then we check out those hunches (and sometimes throw them out) as we watch some more. Thus, there is a "two-way street" quality to how we approach the task of observation. We turn to questions about what we think might be going on in order to see with more depth. That "deep seeing" eventually helps us come up with our best guess as to what's up.

Seeking Patterns and Purpose

As the kids in Claudia and Nancy's class come trooping in behind Alain, I am aware of just how challenging the task of deep seeing can be. Even before they've all settled in, Alain has already cruised from one corner of the room to another. And he's left cringing and crying children in his wake. How am I going to collect the information I need in the midst of such relentless misbehavior, I wonder? And if I'm feeling this overwhelmed already, what must it be like to be Claudia and Nancy?

I make a quick decision: during this visit, I'll focus mainly on Alain. If my observations help us get a better feel for why he is having such trouble, we'll have a chance of coming up with an effective approach to helping him manage himself more successfully. If he can even begin to do that, it will be easier to pay attention to some of the classroom's other worrisome children the next time I'm in. More important still, Claudia and Nancy will have the opportunity to give those kids more of the attention they deserve.

Claudia took a deep breath before telling me about her concerns. Now it's my turn. I give myself the same pep talk that I offer teachers when I am running workshops about challenging behavior: Kids want to do well, I remark to these often weary educators. When they don't, there are always reasons. If we look and think carefully, those reasons can be discovered. Patterns can be discovered too—having to do with what and when, how long and what next. There are moments of success buried in every mess . . . flowers growing amid the weeds. We can do our best to notice those flowers. And we can figure out how to clear out those weeds, leaving room for more flowers to grow. Kids want our help—and our love—even when it doesn't look that way, I say. It's our job to figure out what that help is, and how to offer that love in a way that they can receive.

Sometimes, when a group of teachers and I have connected well during a workshop, I see nodding heads and thoughtful faces as I end our time together with such words. At this moment, however, my mental cheerleader is having a hard time getting my attention. I'm too busy watching Alain wreak havoc everywhere he goes. *But is it everywhere? And is wreaking havoc actually what he's after?* I continue to observe, curious about what's to come.

Jonathan is at the train table, where teachers have told me he's the most comfortable. And Alain has, temporarily, come in for a landing right next to him. Jonathan may be a bit worried. He's not leaving the area. But he is determinedly hanging on to his line of trains and has quickly put some space between himself and his classmate. Alain takes a single train and starts it down the track with some energetic "choo-choos." As it speeds up, he catches Jonathan's eyes and grunts a friendly-sounding "Uh-oh!" Then his train crashes into Jonathan's locomotive. The two boys grin at each other.

This is interesting, I find myself thinking. I have been told that Jonathan struggles with language processing. And Alain hasn't said more than a word or two since he arrived—is there something going on with his communication skills too? If so, is Jonathan an easier person for him to play with as a result? It's striking that he made eye contact with Jonathan before the crash and that as they looked at each other, Alain offered his upbeat "Uh-oh!" Might that be his version of "Want to play?"

I keep watching and wondering. Will Alain do something that leads the train play to fall apart entirely? Will he and Jonathan just keep crashing into each other repeatedly? Or will these boys be able to allow their play to "go somewhere"—to develop a story line that has some depth and progression? Will there be any more than a "choo-choo" and an "uh-oh" language-wise?

Alain is staying with train play for longer than just a few seconds, I note. Not only that: although he did crash into Jonathan's locomotive, he hasn't tried to grab it. It's another interesting moment, and not what I thought would happen given how the morning has progressed so far.

As I consider what all this might mean, Emilio drops in. And Alain offers him a train—the first instance in which I've seen him willingly share a toy he values. Emilio, Nancy's "odd little butterfly," seems to be a sweetly spacey youngster: is it possible that he hasn't noticed how aggressive Alain can be? He certainly doesn't seem to be pulling back. He hasn't even put a little space between himself and Alain like Jonathan just did. Is that why Alain is being generous for the first time this morning? What must it be like to be a child that kids and adults alike are overwhelmed by and afraid of?

Perhaps my mental cheerleader is having some effect after all, I note with relief. I'm starting to observe with questions in mind, going down the "two-way street" of deep seeing.

Linking Observations to Categories of Importance

Kids don't organize their behavior and their feelings so that we can make sense of their challenges in a systematic way. They just behave and feel through their days, bringing all of who they are into the worlds in which they live. It's up to us to observe them carefully. Yet, at the same time, *we need to keep part of our minds free to link our unfolding observations to the categories laid out in chapter 1's three-part flips.* Doing this isn't always easy, and in Alain's case, I find myself going in and out of feeling overwhelmed by his frenetic behavior. All the same, I try to focus on deep seeing and reflection, and to consider how what I'm noticing may connect to the categories I lean on so often.

With those intentions guiding my time in the classroom, the mental process of linking observations to specific categories begins. Alain is dragging his mother in the door, and she looks mildly exasperated. Is this mix of his dominance and her helpless annoyance common for them? *Life at home.* Alain gives Claudia a lovely smile in response to her greeting. *Adult-child connections.* But he doesn't add a "hello" or "hi." And he only uses a few single words or phrases with Jonathan. Is he struggling with language processing? *Developmental mastery.* His play with Jonathan is, so far, pretty simple for a four-year-old. And he doesn't give Jonathan a lot of room to say "no" if a train crash isn't of interest. Does he know how to initiate play with a buddy, stick with play, elaborate on play? *Play skills.* He has happily offered a train to Emilio, one of the few children who does not seem fazed by him. What does it feel like to be a child who sets off distress in others so frequently? *Emotional well-being.* Does Alain behave differently when a child or adult's way of responding to him is inviting rather than reluctant? *Interactive patterning, triggers for difficulty and setups for success.*

Making Guesses (Not Decisions) and Joining Forces (Not Going Solo)

Linking observations to questions and categories has given me a place to start. Now, as always, I need to remember the importance of staying open and curious. That's to say, I should make guesses, not decisions, about what is going on with Alain. I'll also need to combine my observations with those of Alain's teachers—they know far more about him than I do. Joining forces in this way is always important. The more angles of vision we adults have about a particular child, the better chance we have of understanding why he is having a hard time.

Such perspectives partly come from any teachers who work with a particular child regularly. They can come from supervisors, directors, and specialists, too. Finally, whenever possible, they also come from family members. For example, input from Alain's mother, Carole, is going to be crucial to helping Alain. The team won't consult with Carole before doing some initial brainstorming, however. Things have gotten too extreme to wait, and we'll meet right after my morning's observation. That means I'll need to mine my time in the classroom for as much data as I can.

Tracking the Details behind Shifts in Behavior

Though I'd wondered if it might, Alain and Jonathan's play doesn't progress past a couple of crashes. And Emilio floats away shortly after being offered a train. Then Alain plays contentedly on his own for about five minutes, assembling a line of trains and accompanying its journey down the tracks with an assortment of enthusiastic noises. It's a good and focused stretch for him, I note. Does it help that Jonathan is the only other child in the area right now and that he is not all that interactive? Does Alain do better when there are fewer kids sharing a space with him? I have another question, too. The train table offers a concrete way of defining that space. Does that make things easier as well?

Watching the way children respond to the spaces they're in can be enormously useful. It can also be important to note how their behavior shifts when the number of children around them is higher or lower. Being aware of such details helps link what we see to the category of "triggers for difficulty and setups for success." Some children, for example, need lower numbers and more clearly defined territories in order to succeed, at least at first. Alain may be one of those kids. Other youngsters are highly reactive to the level of movement around them. This boy may be one of those easily overstimulated children too. I make a note to pay attention to when Alain is calm versus when he is active and impulsive. I'll also need to watch for how he manages the normal bustle of transition times, and whether his behavior worsens when he wanders into areas that have more than one or two other children.

Noting Developmental "Basics": The Capacities for Connection, Caring, and Communication

Alain abandons the train table to cruise the room. After moving past the dramatic play corner, he stops in the block area just long enough to kick over another boy's carefully constructed tower. Then he saunters over to watch Claudia put a Band-Aid on Isabel's finger. He stands next to his teacher—the first moment of the morning I have seen him entirely still. "Hurt!" he says worriedly. Claudia meets his eyes. "Yes, Isabel has a little boo-boo on her finger," she replies. Alain nods. Isabel is crying, her grief-stricken face reminding me of what the teachers mentioned earlier: things in her family are difficult, and she is far less buoyant than usual. Alain stares at Isabel gravely. He offers her a gentle pat, his face almost as sad his classmate's.

I notice myself feeling relieved and heartened. Alain seems to sense Isabel's deep unhappiness and is showing real interest in her well-being. Even more, he has offered a caring response to her distress—which feels huge for a child who so often causes harm. In addition, he has made comfortable eye contact with Claudia. It is clear that at least some of the time he feels connected to his teachers and sees them as allies. He is using words to express himself too. Actually, not a lot of words for a four-and-a-half-year-old, only one. But still, it's the right one. And he is nodding in response to Claudia . . . it seems like he understands at least some of *her* words. That's good. If he has some challenges in language processing, it looks like the basics may be there to work with.

A youngster's abilities to connect with others, feel for others, and communicate with others all loom large as far as healthy development goes. (See chapter 7 for an in-depth exploration of this important terrain.) As we observe children, it's vitally important to watch for situations that illuminate how they're doing in regard to these abilities. Thankfully, Alain's concern for Isabel and his interactions with Claudia demonstrate all three. However, in regard to communication, there is more to consider because Alain speaks Haitian Creole at home. I make a mental note to ask the teachers if they have checked with Carole about whether he speaks with ease there. Given that he's a second-language learner, we need to be careful not to jump to conclusions about processing challenges. Instead, it's going to be important to find out if he is struggling in both languages or only in English. Maybe he is just a child for whom learning a second language is taking a little longer than usual.

Generating "Maybes": Making Connections between Observations

Alain heads over to the puzzle table, where his classmate Kevin is intently working. He leans heavily on Kevin's shoulder and watches for a moment. Then he snatches a puzzle piece from Kevin's hand. Hmmm, his face looks interested, not angry. Is this aggression, I wonder? Or does it stem from a kind of cluelessness about how to join Kevin in assembling the puzzle? And what about this "leaning thing" he's doing, is it connected to how he was pressing his belly into the train table earlier? How is he feeling in his body? He does seem to have a lot of energy and is so often on the move. Is there any chance that he's one of those kids who craves sensory input and bangs, runs, kicks, and leans on anything available to get it?

Kevin practically falls off his chair and lets out a loud "no!" Now Alain's face does look angry. He slaps Kevin's arm, hard. Kevin begins to wail. Puzzle piece in hand, Alain takes off, glancing at Nancy. Is he looking to see if she's noticed? She certainly has. There is some mix of a sly grin, a "catch me if you can," and just perhaps, a bit of dismay on his face as he sees his teacher grimly head his way.

This is not the first time Alain has acted impulsively when his intent may have been to join another child in play. Nor is it the first time he has done the "leaning thing." As we notice patterns, repetitive behaviors, and inappropriate actions that suggest a child is trying to solve a problem (not make one), we can begin to generate "maybes." Doing this connects to our attempts at deep seeing, that all-important work of moving between observations and what they may suggest about what's going on. *Maybe* this behavior is connected to that one. *Maybe* he is doing this because he needs that. We keep these hunches as just that: hunches. But we pay close attention to them all the same. Our goal is to see whether they are confirmed through further observation . . . or not. Thus, keeping my maybes in mind, I continue to watch Alain.

It is circle time. Alain, as predicted, barges his way toward the seat he wants, pushing any number of children over. Then he hits Claudia as she tries, with admirable patience, to rein him in. She tells him firmly that hurting others is not okay, directs him to his designated spot, and then begins running the group. Alain squirms his way through the daily calendar activity. When it's over, he leaves the circle to wander the room while other kids discuss the weather and listen to a story. Then, hearing that his classmates are preparing to sing "The Wheels on the Bus," he eagerly returns to his seat. He sings all the words, knows all the motions, and is at his most focused—which is how he remains while the group continues singing some other songs that include gestures he knows well.

Alain is beaming; he clearly loves to sing and move. And the combination of familiar melodies, well-known words, and rhythmic gestures seems to help him feel relaxed and focused. Why is that, I wonder? I find myself musing over what I have seen so far. If it's true that Alain is having trouble finding the words he wants, *maybe* it's a relief to know which ones are coming in a much-repeated song. If he's a child who often satisfies his sensory needs by hitting and kicking, *maybe* being able to move while he sings helps him manage his body state—and his impulses—more successfully.

As I begin thinking about how these hunches might help us come up with new approaches to intervention, things fall apart once again. It's time for a trip to the bathroom, and Alain whacks another child on the arm in order to take over the front of the line. This time, Claudia takes his hand firmly. She gives him a sharp reprimand and removes him from the line. She gets a hearty whack of her own in response. Then Alain wiggles out of her grasp. He begins running around the classroom, kicking things over as he goes.

Each time Alain lands a firm kick, he checks to see if a teacher is watching. His face conveys that same mix of sly grin, "catch me if you can," and possible distress that I noticed earlier. Why, I wonder? What is he looking for at times like this? How is he feeling? I tell myself to keep an eye on upcoming moments of misbehavior to see if any patterns become clear. I remind myself to watch as well for times of success. One of those happy surprises is about to take place.

It is time for lunch. Alain takes his designated spot without shoving anyone else aside. Then—with just a little prompting from Nancy—he waits his turn for the milk pitcher. He says please and thank you at just the right moments, too, and carefully passes communal dishes of food to the child sitting next to him. He even watches for the cues that tell him it's okay to help himself to seconds. Most impressive of all, he manages to sit fairly still all the while. Nancy, who has looked increasingly tense through the morning, relaxes into the meal and begins to enjoy Alain's good cheer. The other kids do too.

What is it about mealtime that makes it easier for Alain to be calm and organized, I wonder? Certainly, he's doing something he enjoys—he's eating with great gusto. In addition, what's expected is clear. His place mat tells him just where to go, so there is no need to push anyone over. The rectangular table defines the space for him and also offers some room between him and the kids next to him. Furthermore, Alain knows he won't get his food until he is sitting in the spot he has been given, nor before he has waited his turn. In short, it's apparent that Claudia and Nancy have some well spelled-out and steady routines for lunchtime. Perhaps, I think to myself, there is some wisdom we can build on here.

My observation time is almost done: it's pickup time. Alain's mom, Carole, arrives and gets a wide smile from her son. She shines a smile back his way, pats his head, then timidly glances at Claudia. It's clearly a "How was his day?" kind of look. Claudia returns her gaze compassionately and shrugs. "The same as usual," she replies without words. Alain shoves another child aside as he lunges for his cubby to get his coat. "No, Alain!" Carole's voice is stern. Alain slaps her arm, but gently, and begins running through the classroom. She makes her way toward him and takes his hand. Alain protests briefly. Then he settles down and stands quietly by his mother's side.

I perk up. This is the first time I have seen Alain this compliant and calm after being corrected for misbehaving. What's going on? My mental radar on alert, I watch to see what is coming next. Less than a half minute later, I find out. With his mother distracted as she begins chatting with Claudia, Alain wiggles out of her grasp. He goes to the library area, where other children are reading as they wait for their parents. Then he begins hurling books. Looking up, Carole calls out another "No, Alain!" This time she sounds less sure of herself. She turns back to Claudia, her eyes radiating confusion. Alain looks her way as he begins to run, just as he did with his teachers earlier. After hesitating, Carole heads toward him. Once again, Alain allows her to grab his hand. And, once again, he protests mildly and then calms down.

I take a quick peek at Carole's face and sense that she is feeling embarrassed, perhaps even mortified. I know she has asked Claudia and Nancy for advice: Nancy found a few minutes earlier in the morning to fill me in about how things are going for this mother and her younger son. Apparently, Carole was quite upset as she shared that Alain's behavior at home is often as difficult as it is in at school. She made clear, though, that she has tried very hard to teach Alain and his brother to become polite and respectful children. She believes strongly in this, she told them. It's how she was raised in Haiti.

As Carole's attention wanders, Alain squirms away one more time, and the pattern repeats. *Misbehavior. Reprimand. Running with an eye to see who is watching. Hand-holding followed by calm.* This is something worth puzzling over. What is Alain looking for when he misbehaves, then immediately glances at an adult he knows is watching? Does he hope for some attention? Is he interested in what he can "get going," sort of like throwing a pebble in the water and watching ripples extend out in a circle after it hits the surface? Is he yearning for someone to stop him? All of these at once?

Considering Interactive Patterning, Cultural Norms, and Life at Home

Tracking how a child's behaviors are embedded in interactive patterns is an important focus of observation. When a child is behaving less than desirably, what do adults do in return? What happens next? Do adult responses lead to more behaviors of concern, either in the moment or over time? Are there situations when the reverse is true? These questions have great relevance in regard to Alain. It appears that Carole is able to stop her son quickly when she is fully attentive to what's going on and firmly takes his hand. And he lets her do it. It's only when she loses her focus that he wiggles away. Furthermore, her "No, Alain!" sometimes comes across as comfortably firm in a style that is typical of many Haitian parents. Sometimes, however, she sounds more uncertain. Is it hard for Carole to trust her instincts with Alain when she is on her own? She's young too. Does she sometimes offer Alain the kind of "stop messages" he responds to but at other times, either not know what to do or not have the energy to do it?

I wonder if it is especially hard for Carole to be in the United States without family here. Kids in Haiti are often raised by close-knit extended families with ample help from the community at large. Thus it wouldn't be surprising if parenting solo feels quite foreign and overwhelming to her. More maybes. However, one thought doesn't feel like a maybe. Rather, it just seems true: Carole was brought up to be polite and respectful in a way that is deeply entrenched in her culture. And Alain, when calm at lunch, is just that. She has clearly conveyed to him the values she holds dear. But Alain is a handful. Perhaps our team can give Carole some of the support she may not be getting elsewhere, and help her find a good mix of love and firmness to offer her wonderful but impulsive son.

Landing on an Observation-Based Picture: What's Up? Why?

As the kids head home, the hunches I have been generating through the morning begin to merge into a larger picture. I have some initial thoughts about how Alain's strengths and challenges are playing a role in what is happening. I have a feel for when it's easier for him to be successful and when not. And I have some guesses about patterns that may be going on at home, patterns that may connect to what teachers are seeing in school. In addition, I have some questions. Given that this program doesn't allow time-outs (a philosophy I fully support), are Claudia and Nancy lacking some version of firm control that Alain needs and craves—the kind of control that infuses Carole's culture and that, sometimes, she's able to offer him successfully? What about the fact that I have now observed numerous instances when Alain behaves unsafely (throwing toys or kicking people, for example), and gets a reprimand but nothing else?

In the face of Alain's combination of limited language and trouble thinking before acting, does he need clearer and more consistent responses to unacceptable behavior? Are the patterns that involve what he does and what happens next actually leading to more rather than less of the behaviors Carole and the teachers are so worried about? If so, might there be a way to shift those patterns for the better? How could we do that, though, without turning punitive or harsh? Finally, how might we keep support and skill development as our most central goals if a different approach to limit setting is in order? I'm glad it's time to sit down with Claudia and Nancy. My observations will give us a lot to think about.

3 Spotlight on Development
Understanding the Building Blocks of Early Childhood Mastery

With the children gone, a welcome calm pervades Claudia and Nancy's classroom. The three of us sit on child-sized chairs around a low table, waiting for Robin to arrive. As the program's director, she wants to be a part of our discussion given how many families have called with concerns about Alain's aggression. Their kids are getting hurt regularly, she's been hearing. It is frightening for them to be in a classroom that doesn't feel safe. If the program can't figure out how to make things better, why hasn't Alain been asked to leave?

Claudia and Nancy need a plan, and quickly. It's at a point like this that teaching teams are tempted to launch headlong into brainstorming about strategies. In fact, that's often what happens when a child is particularly challenging, because everyone involved is desperate for a change of course. But taking a close look at what is going on—and why that's the case—has to come first. It's the "think" step of the see→think→do progression that allows teachers to create action plans that have a good chance of succeeding.

That step works best when informed by ideas that come from our field's knowledge base. It is a knowledge base that is both deep and broad. There is information about the brain, about child development, and about families and communities. There is research about loss and resilience, learning styles, and the impact of trauma. And those topics are just a beginning. In fact, as reflected in the title of the groundbreaking book *From Neurons to Neighborhoods: The Science of Early Childhood Development* (Shonkoff and Phillips 2000), our early childhood lens needs to be very wide indeed as we work to understand the experiences of young children in their complex worlds.

Where to begin when there is so much to consider? Often the best place to start is by establishing how a child is faring in regard to core aspects of developmental mastery—in other words, to come up with that youngster's "developmental profile." As it follows the beginning of our team's meeting about Alain, this chapter explores some of what teachers need to know about development in order to create such profiles. The meeting begins with Claudia and Nancy sketching out a picture of what they have been dealing with from day one of the school year.

Pooling Observations about Behavior

Robin has arrived. We start by making a list of the behaviors Nancy and Claudia are most concerned about. Alain hits, kicks, pushes, and grabs. He is often on the go during free play, wiggly and restless during group time, and revved up during transitions. He uses few words and doesn't seem to understand many more. He always wants to be first. His solo play is limited, and his cooperative play ends up in fights. He listens poorly, sustains attention poorly, and doesn't stop inappropriate behavior when asked. Instead, he runs away. Robin's expression is one of deep concern. Things sound even worse than she had feared.

Our team knows the danger of describing a child just in terms of his struggles, and we quickly turn to areas of competence and well-being. Alain has a loving bond with his mother and warm connections with his teachers. He shows genuine concern for other kids' distress when he isn't the one who has hurt them. He wants to play with friends, though he doesn't know how. And there are activities he loves—train play, singing and moving, eating and cooking—during which he shows signs of being organized, calm, and attentive. Finally, when his body is relaxed and his mind is engaged, he can be a polite and considerate child—a child with a smile so sunny that kids and adults alike, including those he has hit or kicked, can't help but respond with some sunshine of their own.

Now that we've pooled our observations, we start linking them to questions about Alain's development. What do the behaviors we've noted tell us about where he is struggling with developmental skill deficits? In what areas does he show signs of mastery?

Placing Developmental Mastery Center Stage

With these questions, our team uses a focus on development to begin narrowing in on what's going on for Alain. Throughout this book, I've placed development in the hub position as well. The decision to do so is a practical one. When family members and teachers are getting increasingly worried about a child's well-being, there is usually a relatively short list of things they wish were different. Those things are often directly connected to developmental skill. Such adults want a child to hit less, engage with others more, focus for longer, or do what she's asked without a fuss. They want a youngster to make his thoughts and needs known more easily, to cry less often, to slow down more successfully, or to be able to reach out and branch out with confidence. They want a child to feel good about herself and be kind to others. Or to share, take turns, and wait. Sometimes they wish for a number of these items all together.

In short, these adults want their children or students to master a set of developmental basics. It would be useful if our field had an agreed-upon list of what those are. However, theorists, researchers, and specialists in both developmental medicine and early childhood mental health have studied aspects of developmental mastery for many years. And because of how complex development is, there is no one list on which everyone agrees. This situation gives us some flexibility though. It's possible to take the issues experts have explored over time, combine them with the things family members and teachers most wish to see, and come up with a practical list that embraces both perspectives. Years back, I made just such a list. I call it the Seven Building Blocks of Development.

The building blocks outlined on the next page don't cover every aspect of development needed to understand every child. However, more often than not, they get at the heart of what we see and worry about, and are a useful guide as we work to make sense of children's difficulties. They're easy to keep in mind too.

Seven Building Blocks of Development

1. *Feeling safely and warmly connected:* The building block that supports them all—experiencing trust, interest, and pleasure in relationships.

2. *Tuning in:* Being able to harness and sustain attention, and to focus on people, ideas, requests, and expectations.

3. *Communicating effectively:* Understanding others and making others understand, both verbally and nonverbally.

4. *Regulating energy:* Being able to shift from one energy level to another; having the capacity to slow down and stay calm.

5. *Regulating feelings:* Managing small difficulties without large reactions; being able to regain composure after getting upset; maintaining self-control in the face of frustration.

6. *Changing tracks and being flexible:* Being able to adapt reasonably to change and to the needs of others; knowing how to share space, materials, and ideas; having the ability to end one activity when it is time to begin another.

7. *Feeling capable and confident:* The building block that follows from the rest: having a sense of resourcefulness, competence, and optimism (Hirschland 2008, 17).

In some ways, separating these seven building blocks doesn't make sense: development is a far more complex and intertwined process than any itemized list can capture. Furthermore, this list doesn't highlight empathy, impulse control, and problem solving, all of which are tremendously important to kids' success as friends and learners. The problem is, for any developmental framework to be comprehensive, it's going to be long—and in the heat of the moment teachers need something short that they can work from with ease. That's why, since empathy, impulse control, and problem solving stem from building blocks I have included on the list (for example, connection and emotional regulation), I have left them off. You may decide to use a different and more extensive set of building blocks. Or you may go with mine. Which direction you choose isn't so important. What *is* important is to have an organizing framework that helps you see the big picture of where a child is thriving and where she's lagging, developmentally speaking.

Climbing the "Ladders of Mastery"

No matter what framework works best for you, there's a point worth keeping in mind: developmental mastery in any particular area unfolds slowly. There isn't a dividing line under which a child does not have the skill of tuning in or managing feelings and over which she does. In fact, each of the building blocks might be thought of as connecting to a developmental pathway—or what we sometimes call a "developmental trajectory" (Aber et al. 2003, 3). Children come to have a sense of safety in connection over time, learn to package up their attention and to communicate over time, and gain the skills of frustration tolerance and flexibility over time, too. They start gaining mastery in these areas when they are very young. Thus, a toddler who is flailing around in the grocery store because her dad has said she can't have a box of the sugary cereal she loves isn't necessarily flunking out on emotional regulation. In fact, her tantrum (very possibly one of many she has had in the last month) may be part of how she is learning to hear the word "no" from the outside and stay steady on the inside.

The idea of developmental pathways runs through the literature upon which our field relies. Using an image offered by two of its experts, Stanley Greenspan and Serena Wieder, it can be useful to picture each pathway as a ladder (1998, 71). That image, combined with what we know about children's growth and learning, leads to a useful metaphor for supporting growth. We know that children develop at different rates. We know, too, that many of those rates are perfectly normal. Sometimes, however, where a child is on one of the ladders seems worrisomely delayed. Then it's important to figure out just where she is located on that particular ladder *so we can help her climb her way up, rung by rung* (Greenspan and Wieder 1998, 121).

With this metaphor in mind, Claudia, Nancy, and I need to think through some questions. Which ladders is Alain having trouble climbing? Which ones are easier for him? How might his ability to climb the easier ones help him make his way up the others? Or, in more classic language, how can our team use Alain's strengths to help us work on his challenges?

Charting Areas of Strengths and Challenge

Claudia, Nancy, and Robin know from experience that framing a child's developmental profile often illuminates possibilities for supporting "rung-by-rung" progress. They know, too, that their program has helped plenty of challenging kids make such progress in the past. At the moment, though, they're feeling alarmed rather than hopeful. I'm concerned too. At the same time, things I saw and thought about during the morning's endeavor of deep seeing have left me curious and optimistic. Perhaps that energy helps us with the next step of our reflective process, as we use the behaviors we laid out at the beginning of our meeting to come up with a developmental profile for Alain.

As should always be the case, Alain's profile charts both strengths and challenges:

- *Connecting:* The affection running in between Alain and his mom is clear to all. In addition, he grins at Jacob as their trains crash together and pats Isabel's arm when she is in pain. He's always happy to see Claudia and Nancy in the morning, too, and loves the praise he gets when he is doing well. It's certainly true that once he's having trouble, Alain's empathy and desire to please are hard to locate. But we all agree that this boy's capacity for warm and pleasurable connection is solid.

- *Tuning in:* This one is harder for us to puzzle out. When Alain is doing something that helps his body feel calm and his mind get organized, he can tune in to what is going on around him. At other times, though, it's difficult to make eye contact with him. In those moments, it is hard for Alain to respond to a cue that says "stop, look, and listen." The team ends up guessing that this building block's variability is connected to other areas of challenge. When Alain is struggling to understand and use language, to manage his energy or sensory needs, or to handle frustration, his ability to tune in is affected. Given that these other challenges come up frequently, tuning in has become a problem in its own right.

- *Communicating effectively:* It's clear to all of us that Alain has trouble understanding and using language. What we don't yet know is how much those difficulties are connected to second-language learning and how much to challenges in language processing. Some testing may be in order, we agree. But whatever the balance, Alain's challenges in this area seem to be contributing to his limited play repertoire, his low frustration tolerance, and his struggles to get along with others. What must it be like to have to use single words to convey what he has in mind when some of his classmates seem to talk in paragraphs? How must he feel when he wants something and doesn't have the words to ask for it?

- *Regulating energy:* This appears to be another area of vulnerability. Alain's natural energy is high, and his body seems to crave sensory stimulation. It's going to be important to figure out how to help him feel more calm and organized in his body. We have a related question: Can we help Alain learn to get the sensory input he needs without crashing into kids, kicking toys, and knocking over furniture?

- *Regulating feelings:* For a child who can be so aggressive, Alain doesn't seem deeply angry. The team ends up thinking that he is a cheerful child who has a lot to be frustrated by—especially his trouble communicating. With a limited capacity to stay calm when things are tough for him, and to engage in what is often called *self-soothing* once he is upset, his frustration hijacks his efforts to do well. If Alain could manage his feelings more competently, we believe, he'd be far easier to have around. That would allow him to accept support in other areas of challenge too. Right now he's so often frustrated that it's hard to offer him the help he needs to learn and grow. In fact, Claudia and Nancy report, they mostly end up making their way from crisis to crisis, managing him through his days. That bothers them a lot. They're wondering something. Is there any way to focus more on mastery than on management? Can they do something to reduce these moments of frustration so they can begin teaching him the many skills he lacks?

- *Changing tracks and being flexible:* Claudia and Nancy have an easy answer for this one—Alain hasn't yet mastered this building block. Perhaps once he gets better at using words and staying calm, it will come along on its own.

- *Feeling capable and confident:* Alain may be a cheerful boy at heart, but none of us see him as a confident one. How could he feel confident when so many things he tries to do end up with him in trouble? We all agree, though, that this last building block rests on the others. If we can help Alain communicate his ideas, focus his mind, and regulate his energy and emotions, he may end up feeling far better about himself too.

It is probably evident that even as our team works to come up with a developmentally based picture, we're already considering questions about intervention. How can we help Alain get stronger in *this* area so that *that* one will come along too? How can we use our understanding of the mastery he lacks to come up with a skills-based agenda for learning? In other words, *how can we shift our focus from problems to possibilities?*

If asked at this point, we'd all agree that the answer to this last question will be central to our action plan for Alain. Yet before we can create that plan, there are more factors for us to consider. Creating developmental profiles, though important, is only one aspect of what teachers do to understand hard-to-help kids. They also need a sense of why those kids struggle the way they do. It is the "whys" behind worrisome behavior that are featured in the next chapter.

4 Spotlight on Causation
Considering the "Whys" behind Worrisome Behavior

It is for good reason that I've decided to make Alain the top priority during my first visit to Claudia and Nancy's room. Even so, knowing that there are other children needing extra help too, I find myself very aware of his classmates. They are an interesting and vivid bunch. Some are full of energy and curiosity, eager to connect and explore. Some chat animatedly to their teachers in English, while talking with their friends in Spanish, Creole, or Portuguese. A number of them have impressively detailed play ideas and fold those ideas into things their classmates have in mind for a princess story, a building project, or a pretend meal being cooked up in the dramatic play corner. Others, however, play with far less skill. Like Alain, Jonathan is in the latter group. Contentedly and repetitively running his beloved trains back and forth along their track, he plays more like a toddler than a preschooler.

During my observation I note other things as well, some of which point to possible areas of concern. A few of the group's members, for example, are strikingly self-contained. Yet the "feel" of that quality varies. In little Maria, it looks comfortable—like a coat that fits just right. In four-year-old Jenny, silent and stiff, it looks more like a prison. But it's not just the quality of self-containment that varies across kids. Children's ways of focusing do too. Emilio, a cheerful free spirit flitting here and there, is distractible in a way that has Claudia and Nancy worried. His classmate Adam, on the other hand, displays a lack of focus that seems reasonable given his age (just three) and energy level (high).

Finally, there are a few children whose ways of being leave me feeling worried and saddened. One is Hannah, grave-faced and isolated, needy and provocative. Another is Isabel, whose unhappiness radiates quietly through the room. Kevin is the third. He is a sweet and cuddly child, seemingly easy to love and care for. But he's tremendously hard to manage through the day with his inability to take in where he should be in line and what is about to happen next.

Even from my first few moments observing in Claudia and Nancy's vibrant classroom, it's clear that none of these children looks anything like Alain as far as behavior is concerned. They don't look like each other either. That's not a surprise. They each have different inborn natures and families, along with widely divergent histories and everyday experiences—all factors that have likely contributed to how they feel and act. With our initial focus on Alain, how can Claudia, Nancy, and I identify the factors that may be at play in his case? When that focus eventually shifts to other worrisome kids in the classroom, how will we identify the factors behind what is going on for them? These two questions lead to a third: how can teachers use such underlying issues to understand any child they're worried about? This chapter touches on Alain's story as it offers some answers to these questions, in part by exploring a number of "causal factors" that can fuel early childhood challenges. And because no one story or child can illustrate the range of factors that lie behind such challenges, a few of Alain's classmates are introduced as well. In each of their cases, the situations touched upon here are explored more fully in later chapters.

Looking Back at the Past and Closely at the Present

One way to think about the "whys" behind worrisome behavior is to divide them into two categories. The first category relates to past events or factors that have been present from early on in a youngster's life. It bears on the importance of both "nature and nurture" and can be separated into three main areas: hard wiring, hard starts, and hard times. The second category includes two factors related to how children's difficulties play out in the here-and-now landscapes of home and school. Interactive patterning is one of those factors. The other involves the bigger picture in which behaviors are nested—both what triggers those behaviors and what follows them.

Each of these categories and the elements they involve can have a profound influence on the way children experience themselves and their worlds—and on their behaviors as well. These explorations begin with the first element of the first category: hard wiring. It's one I encountered on a deeply personal level after I became a parent.

Considering Nature and Nurture

Hard Wiring

When my older daughter was born, I believed that my husband's and my love for her, along with the experiences she'd have with us and others, would shape her into the person she'd become. Then along came her sister—such a different kind of child right from the get-go. It was as if I had to learn how to parent all over again. Both now adults, my "girls" are good friends. But although their interests have much in common, their styles of being don't. What I've come to understand firsthand, of course, is that children enter the world with different ways of being: what we call "temperament" has a powerful effect on who they will become. In addition, I now know that they are born with brains that have varying styles of (and capacities for) taking in and making sense of the information they encounter day and night. That information is seen and heard, tasted and touched, people based and idea based. This second area is often referred to as *information processing.*

In our computer- and technology-saturated world, many of us now refer to qualities connected to a child's genetics as his "hard wiring." This phrase encompasses both a child's temperament and his approach to information processing. Given how each one can have a profound impact on a youngster's experience of himself and his world—and on his behavior too—anyone working with young children is well advised to have an understanding of both. Here, a look at temperament comes first.

Temperament

Most of us in the early childhood field are familiar with the multifaceted aspects of temperament. These hard-wired qualities first became widely known through a study done in the 1960s (Thomas, Chess, and Birch 1968). Then they were elaborated on by, among others, Stanley Greenspan, author of many books, including (with Serena Wieder) *The Child with Special Needs* (1998); and Stanley Turecki, author of *The Difficult Child* (2000). Each temperament-based quality is best thought of as ranging from one end of a continuum to another. We look at children's levels of adventurousness versus their inborn caution. We consider their natural flexibility versus their need for predictability. We take note of their easygoing natures or, conversely, their emotional intensity. We notice their lower or higher energy levels, too, and their tendencies toward focus or distractibility.

These aspects of temperament aren't familiar just because they play out in our classrooms. Most of us experience them in the day-to-day textures of our friendships, too. Or they can drive us crazy in our partners or siblings. When that's happening, it may be because those individuals are different than we are in one category or another. Perhaps, though, it's because they're actually (and sometimes annoyingly) very much like us.

Information Processing

Although most teachers are familiar with the idea of temperament, not all are as aware of the different types of information processing every human being relies upon through his days. Nor is it as widely known how children's brains are equipped with a range of abilities (or vulnerabilities) related to each one. A list of four important types of processing is presented here, along with some comments about how they bear on children's development. (For further elaboration and study, there are some excellent resources listed in appendix C.) Briefly stated, information processing includes the following:

- *Processing sounds, sights, and sensations:* In more technical terms, this type involves auditory processing, visual-spatial processing, and the all-important sensory processing. Each of these is relevant to children's development. The last comes up repeatedly when we are thinking about our most active and impulsive children.

- *Storing and retrieving information:* This capacity plays a role in children's abilities to understand and use language. It also helps them to play successfully with their peers and to take in and remember new facts and ideas.

- *Focusing in and screening out:* These intertwined abilities are closely connected to the quality of temperament that involves attentiveness and distractibility.

- *Organizing, sequencing, and conceptualizing:* Whether organizing and sequencing language, ideas, or physical actions—or building bigger units of meaning from smaller ones—this final category has broad implications for how children talk, move, play, and learn.

Recognizing the "Contribution of Constitution"

I like to call the role of hard wiring in children's development "the contribution of constitution." Keeping its far-reaching implications in mind can help us understand the specifics of why children are struggling in just the ways they are. That's certainly true in regard to Alain. As our team moves from charting out his developmental profile to thinking about the reasons behind his difficulties, we find ourselves guessing that hard wiring is one of the factors at play. As we've seen before in our program, the combination of a naturally high activity level, some intense sensory needs, and vulnerabilities in language processing can be challenging for kids to manage. What must it be like, we wonder, for Alain to have a body that needs to move so quickly and a mind that can't keep up? Might those factors account, at least in part, for how often he's impulsive or frustrated? If so, there are important implications for how we should offer him classroom-based support.

The contribution of constitution also looms large in relationship to Alain's classmate Jenny. It turns out that this girl's intense reserve made its appearance when she was very young, and is probably connected to a particularly cautious temperament. Claudia and Nancy are in a bind with Jenny: nothing they have tried to date has had much effect on the way she holds back. They'll need to brainstorm about an approach that takes her "get me out of the spotlight" responses into account without abandoning her to her isolated state. The plan they come up with—explored in chapter 10—grows directly out of an understanding of her hard wiring.

Then there's Jonathan, Alain's buddy at the train table. Unlike Jenny, Jonathan is by nature a contentedly sociable child. Also unlike Jenny— who speaks easily when she's in the safety of her own home—this boy has some significant challenges in language processing. As a result, he'll need steady doses of straight-on friendly connection coupled with simple language. How his teachers provide such help is covered in chapter 12.

There are many reasons for early childhood educators to keep hard wiring in mind. Certainly, as in Alain's case, we may be more apt to pick up information processing issues that have been masked by misbehavior. Or, as in Jenny's, our understanding of temperament-driven behaviors can lead to possibilities for different (and more effective) responses to worrisome behaviors. Perhaps most important of all, being aware of the power of hard wiring sometimes allows us to have more compassion for children we find hard to help and hard to like.

The contribution of constitution has implications for work with families as well. As we open up conversations about temperament or information processing with our parent partners, important shifts in their feelings and behaviors may result. They may develop a deeper appreciation for why their children have been challenging—something that ends up being true for Alain's mother, Carole. They may also be more willing to experiment with some new approaches to intervention at home. (That turns out to be the case for Carole as well.) In fact, I've seen enough changes along these lines that I now believe educating parents about the contribution of constitution can be transformational.

Hard Starts

Few would argue with the idea that the qualities a child brings with him from the moment of birth have a big impact on his unfolding experience. But the people he joins from that moment on play just as central a role. We know, through research on attachment, how important his relationships with those people will be to his well-being. We know, too, that there are many reasons why his earliest connections with caregivers may end up being less than ideal. Perhaps, as an infant, a child is cared for by a mother flattened by postpartum depression or parents numbed by the death of a beloved relative. Perhaps his older siblings are so clamorously needy that his weak cries get lost in the fray. Or maybe one of his parents is seriously ill, and the other is ricocheting between home and a dreary hospital room.

The consequences of these and other hard starts aren't a foregone conclusion. Research confirms what we know intuitively: children's resilience in the face of adversity varies widely, as does that of families. That said, if situations of the sort just described set the stage for significant difficulties, it helps us to be aware of what has gone on. In regard to their classroom's children, Claudia and Nancy don't have information suggesting that Alain had a particularly hard start in life. But they know that Hannah and Kevin did: both were removed from their homes when very young. How the team ends up working with these two children (see chapters 9 and 11, respectively) stems directly from this knowledge of their early histories.

It is important to note that relational "misses" can happen in the context of other kinds of hard starts, too. Some babies are more difficult to connect with than others, whether it's because they're easily distressed, hard to soothe, or more inner-focused than other-focused. Sometimes, what we call the "goodness of fit" (Landy 2002, 49–53) between a child and a primary caregiver is off, and that impedes the development of a healthy attachment. (Think of a slow-moving father with a hugely energetic son, for example. Or a rough and tumble mom paired with a constitutionally timid daughter.) On occasion, it is the circumstances preceding adoption or an infant's struggle with a severe medical problem that gets in the way of pleasurable connection. In yet other situations, a parent is struggling with substance abuse or chronic and exhausting physical issues. There are many additional possibilities as well—too many to list here. Whatever the situation, knowing the particulars of a child and family's hard start can help us get to work successfully.

Hard Times

Is there anyone in our field who hasn't worked with a family where marital conflict regularly erupts into intense arguments? Or where there have been significant financial issues, a serious car accident, or an unexpected medical diagnosis? Many early childhood educators have experienced such hard times themselves—we're human beings after all, and life can have its share of hurdles. But whether our own experience has included hard times or not, we know just how much young children can be affected by the distressing events unfolding around them.

Alain is one of these youngsters. There have been periods when money has been so tight and Carole so desperately lonely for her relatives back home that life in the family has become fraught with tension. Add to that the high-energy temperament that can make Alain such a handful, and hard times have sometimes felt like horrific times to Carole.

Isabel, who Nancy and Claudia tell me spent the summer smiling through her days, is another such child. About two months ago, this girl's father lost his job, and the family—which had struggled to make ends meet all along—plummeted into a state of financial crisis. Just a week or so later, Isabel's beloved abuela (her mother's mother) had a stroke. Currently, Isabel's father is working three different jobs in order to support the family, and her mother is distractedly trying to balance caring for both her children and her mother. Hard times, indeed, and in response Isabel has appeared increasingly sad and isolated. Claudia and Nancy are worried: they've been trying many different ways to offer Isabel extra support, but she hasn't responded to their efforts. She appears almost frozen with distress, and they aren't sure what to do next.

Isabel's situation offers an excellent example of how the combination of hard wiring and hard times can cause unexpected difficulties. It turns out that she has historically been an easygoing and friendly child. Highly valued for those qualities in her family, she never learned to ask for help in the face of difficulty. Now that hard times have hit, she doesn't know how to reach out for what she needs. The story of how the team learns to support this child successfully is featured in chapter 11. Here, it's worth noting that her situation is just one example of how nature *and* nurture can play a role in children's unfolding difficulties.

Taking Stock of the "Here and Now"

One part of examining the whys behind worrisome behavior may involve taking stock of the dynamics that fuel problems in the present. That is certainly true in Alain's case, though the teachers and I (along with Alain's mother) have some work ahead to figure out exactly what's at play. The first question worth addressing in situations like his—and other children's too—is how a youngster's challenging behaviors are nested in everyday interactive patterns.

Problems and Patterns

As we put a close eye on the patterns connected to a youngster's problems, we often see something like this: The child acts in unwelcome ways. Adults respond with actions of their own, actions that unintentionally reinforce the problematic behaviors in question. Over time, the child's difficulties increase.

The situation just described is one that most teachers know well. How often have you heard a colleague say something like, "It seems like he's hooked on negative attention, and it's only getting worse"? (This is certainly a dynamic Claudia and Nancy wonder about in regard to Alain.) How many times have you worried about offering extra support to a child who has multiple outbursts every day? You know that he is genuinely distressed, and you want to help out. Yet you wonder, "Am I reinforcing the very behaviors that concern me?" (Alain comes to mind again here.)

How frequently have you noticed a parent, say a father, relenting in the face of a child's unreasonable demands at dismissal time? You understand that it is embarrassing for this man to hold the line in public. You know that his child is not only tired by the end of the school day but also intense by nature. Even so, it's abundantly clear that his reactions are causing his child's stridency to increase by the day. Furthermore, your sense is that it isn't just at pickup time that such interactions take place. Have you found yourself thinking (with irritation you try to keep from showing), "What will it take for this father to put his foot down?"

Such observations and questions are important, though it's sometimes easier to *notice* patterns than to *change* them. The endeavor of stepping back and reflecting is a good place to start. In doing this, we base our thinking on an understanding of some basic principles of reinforcement. Those principles include the following:

- When adults take pleasure in, praise, or reward children's behaviors, those behaviors tend to increase.
- When adults give (unwelcome) consequences for or ignore unwanted behaviors, those behaviors tend to decrease.
- Variability in expectations—sometimes certain behaviors are framed as unacceptable and sometimes not—can lead to an increase in those behaviors.
- Inconsistency in adult responses—sometimes a caregiver relents in the face of undesirable behaviors and sometimes not—can lead to an increase in those behaviors, too.

In summary, as early childhood educators know well, clarity about and consistency of expectations are important. When children understand the specifics of what adults would like them to do, know what will happen if they do or don't comply, and have learned that those consequences will be the same from day to day, they meet expectations more often. That's especially true if those expectations are reasonable given their age and temperament.

Actions on the Surface, Feelings Underneath

Identifying problematic interactive patterns is often a first step to understanding children's behavior. Yet behavior isn't only a surface phenomenon involving action. *It is also a kind of communication connected to feelings.* Another way of saying this is that children's behaviors don't just reflect what they have been reinforced for doing or not doing, but also grow out of their deepest experiences of self and world. A child like Alain, for example, may be enormously frustrated by not being able to express his needs in words. Then he ends up lashing out at others who don't have the same problem. Another youngster may engage in challenging behavior because he spends many hours in the care of a less-than-compassionate nanny and feels chronically angry. Yet a third has heard arguments between his parents that are terribly disturbing to him—behaving poorly may be the only outlet he has for letting the people around him know that he is overwhelmed.

The adult end of interactive patterns can be saturated with feelings too. A child has gotten to his teacher. She feels cornered by the child's rigidity the way she felt dominated by a parent years ago. Finally, she's had enough. She gets annoyed. She gets rigid herself and loses her usual warmth. The child in question senses what is going on even if he doesn't understand why. Then he becomes even more dug in.

Teachers are human. Humans regularly get mired in difficult feelings. Sometimes those feelings are actually more about the past than the present. That's why if you find yourself caught up in a familiar but problematic pattern as an early childhood educator, it may help to picture behaviors running back and forth on the surface and feelings rumbling around underneath. Getting to know why those feelings are coming up—and seeking support from others when they're getting the better of you—can help a lot.

This picture pertains to many parents, too. You might see it playing out at a school function. An easily overstimulated child begins pushing back against his mother's urgent "behave yourself" message in the midst of a throng of kids and adults. You watch this mother getting more and more unnerved and insistent. At the same time, you see the child becoming increasingly out of control. What is underneath the mother's part in this unfortunate exchange? Most likely, there are terrible feelings of shame as, aware of being watched, she experiences her identity as a good parent to be on the line.

What happens over time in situations like those just described? Very likely the relationships between adults and children become frayed. Feelings of irritation, of "you don't care about me or you wouldn't act this way," of frustration or guilt or sadness begin to take up the space that everyone would rather have occupied by affection. As a result, children's behaviors often worsen. Adults' behaviors sometimes go downhill as well. The way this happens takes many forms and inevitably requires some attention. When ill feeling permeates the bonds between a struggling child and the adults who care for him, finding pathways to warm connection is almost always a top priority.

Triggers and Troubles: The ABCs of Behavioral Analysis

My morning in Alain's classroom has made something clear: although his behavior is problematic *much* of the time, that's not the case *all* of the time. In fact, he does well when he's singing, when he's sharing communal food, and at the train table when there aren't too many kids crowding him in. I've also noticed that even when he's done something truly unsafe, not much happens by way of consequence other than a verbal reprimand. It doesn't look, at least to me, like such reprimands have the kind of impact teachers hope they will.

These observations lead to one more factor worth exploring any time a child is struggling: the before-and-after context of problematic behavior. We ask: Are there particular times of day or particular situations in which a child behaves poorly? What does he do when he's having trouble? And what happens once he has behaved in the way that concerns us? We can pose these questions in reverse too. When does a child seem to do especially well? Are there particular times of day, situations, or sorts of activities that lead to success? What does his behavior look like then? What happens as a result?

A full look at before-and-after context points to a few additional questions worth considering. Do adults interact with pleasure when this child is doing the best he can? Or do his more positive behaviors go relatively unnoticed? (If the latter is true, it may be because those adults are relieved to attend to the many other things—and children—they have to take care of. That's understandable but also a problem.)

Using language from the world of behavioral analysis, the questions above can be framed as a set of ABCs. First we consider a behavior's **A**ntecedent, what happens just before it occurs. Then we look at the **B**ehavior itself. Finally we examine the behavior's **C**onsequence, what it results in from the child's point of view (Minahan and Rappaport 2013, 32). Doing such an ABC analysis often helps us pinpoint at least some of the triggers for difficulty and setups for success. It's also common to discover that children are regularly getting rewarded for unwanted behaviors by getting something they want or avoiding something they don't want. Sometimes we become aware, to our dismay, that kids don't receive much positive reinforcement when they are doing as well as they're able.

Next Steps

This chapter's content roams widely, from constitutional issues to troubling events in family life, from patterns of interaction to predictable triggers for difficulties. Understanding the way these factors play a role in a young child's life can anchor our efforts to make sense of the particular way he's struggling. But whether it's Alain or another youngster, there is one more step we need to attend to before we can move on to brainstorming about how to support growth. We must combine our observations with our knowledge base and come up with the most comprehensive understanding we can about what has been going on for him. That effort then allows us to move into the terrain of goal setting, action planning, and intervention.

What do we see? What do we think? What should we do? In regard to Alain, Claudia and Nancy are eager to join me in answering the second question if they feel that doing so will help with the third. Which brings these explorations back, in the next chapter, to the substance of our team meeting about him.

5 Developing Child-Specific Portraits

Making Sense as the Foundation for Making Progress

What can be done about Alain? As our meeting continues, the team is in full alert mode. We know that this boy's being able to stay through the year is at risk. Is there the possibility of a new start for him, for us, and for his overwhelmed mother?

At a moment of crisis like this, it can be hard to pause and put together a detailed picture of what is going on for a child. It takes time to develop such a picture, and time often feels as though it's running out. Yet stepping back in this way is exactly what is needed. Otherwise family members and teachers continue to use strategies that aren't working well, or they keep switching approaches from hour to hour and day to day, depriving children of the consistency they need to learn new ways of coping. Claudia and Nancy have been doing some of both.

Our team has already started engaging in this kind of reflection by sketching out Alain's developmental profile (see chapter 3) and considering some of the issues that may be contributing to his difficulties (chapter 4). Now we need to assemble what we've learned into a child-specific portrait. This last step is crucial; it is the details contained in such portraits that point the way toward fresh approaches to intervention.

Creating Narratives out of Complexity: The Limits of Labels

Just what do I mean by a child-specific portrait? *Portrait*, after all, isn't a word we generally use in the world of education. I use it intentionally though; it suggests the idea of creating narratives that touch on the fullness of children's experiences. Such narratives allow us to see the richness behind what is going on with a particular youngster in a way that medical/mental health diagnoses and educational assessment criteria don't.

One could certainly talk about Alain, for example, as a child with sensory issues or even with sensory integration dysfunction. Such descriptions, however, wouldn't answer an important question: how are his sensory-seeking behaviors embedded in the context of family and classroom life? It wouldn't be unusual to add that Alain has hard-wired receptive and expressive language processing vulnerabilities. But would that statement capture the ways in which those vulnerabilities leave him feeling about himself? Would it offer insight into how they're reflected in his interactions with kids, and how they affect his play? Finally, one might describe Alain as a child who seeks out negative attention in a fashion that suggests a diagnosis of "Oppositional Defiant Disorder." But would such a diagnosis do justice to his young age, his developmental profile, and the complexity of his life at home?

Creating child-specific narratives, a process I call "storying," can be helpful in answering these questions, moving educators and parents beyond the information that diagnostic assessments can offer. It's important to note here that diagnostic assessments aren't dangerous in and of themselves—they often give us valuable information. But the labels that may accompany their results are rather fixed things. In consequence, they sometimes lead family members and teachers to believe that children can't or won't change. Furthermore, because diagnoses can place kids in broad categories, they sometimes result in our thinking that we know more about a youngster's difficulties than we actually do.

Creating child-specific portraits that go from the past to the present does two things that assessments frequently don't. First, such portraits keep children's many gifts and strengths in full view. Second, they allow us to take what we know—about constitutional issues, hard times and hard starts, and patterning that has developed in a family and classroom—and place it into the context of ongoing life as it has been lived and felt. Storying in this way encourages us to see with depth and understand with compassion, the precursors to getting to work with skill.

The Power of "Storying"

The power of creating these narratives came alive for me one morning over a decade ago as I was facilitating a monthly child-study group. Attended by a citywide collection of early childhood educators, the group's focus was on exploring various facets of development. In addition, on a regular basis, someone would present a child about whom they had pressing concerns.

That day, we were discussing Sophia, a particularly worrisome four-year-old. Sophia's family was often in crisis and had been so even before she was born. Currently, this girl's parents weren't getting along. In addition, one of her older brothers was struggling with some special needs, and her home life, though loving, lacked both structure and stability. Sophia's behavior was becoming increasingly challenging. However, with all the complexity she had faced from birth onward, it was hard for her teachers to get a handle on why. They felt almost as if the turmoil she experienced in her family was invading and clouding their thinking. As a result, "getting specific in order to get to work" felt truly hard to accomplish. Sophia's teacher addressed the group with distress: How could she figure out ways to help Sophia when she couldn't understand what was going on with her?

For whatever reason, I suddenly thought of an exercise that might help us make meaning out of the many different issues that were contributing to Sophia's difficulties. "How about if we try something," I suggested on a whim. "Anyone who feels like it can start a story, like this: 'My name is Sophia. I'm four. When I was little, my grandmother died. No one knew that would happen. She was fine and then, suddenly, she was gone. She was the one who took care of me when I was a baby . . .' Or you might say, 'My name is Sophia. Sometimes, after my dad gets home from work, he and my mom yell at each other. I never know if it's going to be one of those days.'"

"Here's another possibility," I added. "'I'm Sophia. My brother can get scary. Sometimes I go into the bathroom and stay there until I can tell he's calmed down . . .' Just go along until you run out of steam," I continued, wondering whether this idea would lead us to new perspectives or to a dead end. "Then another one of you can pick up where the previous person left off, or start an entirely new story line."

This exercise in whimsy turned out to be surprisingly constructive. Everyone dove in, and we got a number of story strands going. Each of these story lines touched on an aspect of Sophia's experience. One captured her inner confusion. Another spoke to her relentless need for attention. Yet a third illuminated the ways in which even a hint of disorganization or additional noise during transition times could trigger anxiety about what was to come. That one helped us understand why transitions made Sophia intensely anxious even though in her classroom, unlike at home, there wasn't anything in particular to be feared. There were other story strands as well. When the exercise came to its end, we felt we had an overall narrative that helped us understand Sophia's situation far more clearly. At that point, it was much easier to brainstorm about ideas for intervention.

Our study group began to use this exercise regularly, and I have returned to it many times since. Claudia, Nancy, Robin, and I don't use it formally to make sense of Alain's situation during our team meeting. However, storying his experience in this way is a useful way to begin capturing the portrait we eventually develop for this boy. Here are some of the story strands the team might have come up with, had we tried telling them from his perspective.

An Exercise in Meaning Making: Storying from the Child's Point of View

My name is Alain. I'm four. I live at home with my mom and older brother, Stephane. Mom comes from Haiti, and she misses *her* mom and dad and sisters a lot. Sometimes she gets really lonely.

Mom loves me, I know she does. I like to hug her, and she pats my head, and it feels so nice. But she gets upset when I'm bad, and sometimes she cries about me. She really wants me to be a good boy. Mom tells me that Grann and Grandpè love me a lot too, even though they're far away. She says *they* want me to be a good boy too. I try to, really I do.

I have a lot of energy, I always have. Even when I was a baby. Stephane is way calmer than I am—he's a good boy, and I'm not. I think mom loves him more than me. But she sure pays attention to me when I'm naughty.

Sometimes I just *have to* run and jump and hit and kick—it feels really good. Mom gets frustrated with me because I'm too wild. She always tells me to stop. But she's quiet, and I'm strong. It's easy to get the better of her! I feel bad, though. Mom looks really sad after I'm naughty. So after a bad time is over, I give her a hug, and she smiles at me.

People are always saying a lot of things to me, but I don't usually get more than a word or two. I have a lot to say too, but it doesn't come out right, and then no one knows what I mean. So I don't try to talk very often. And sometimes I kick kids when they talk fast—it makes me mad when they do that! Why don't they wait to hear what I have to say?

I really, really like school. My teachers are so nice. And I love to sing and dance and play and eat. But sometimes kids take my toys. They take the place I want to sit in too. So I have to stop them. That makes my teachers upset with me, but what am I supposed to do? I *want* my toys, and I *want* my seat.

It's hard not to do the wrong thing—I just do something bad and then get in trouble. And besides, when I do naughty things, it can be interesting. My teachers run after me, and their faces get red! No one can stop me. I'm bad! (Can someone stop me? I'm not *really* bad.)

I think some of the parents don't like me. They take their kids' hands when I'm near, and they stare at me. Why is that? And why did Nancy look so tired today after I hit Kevin? I tried to give her a hug, but she didn't want one. Does she still love me?

Completing the Picture: Developing a Child-Specific Portrait

The story Alain "tells" here is rich with data. In fact, when paired with Claudia and Nancy's observations and my morning's deep seeing, it paves the way for the kind of child-specific portrait we always shoot for. What follows here is just such a portrait, a fleshed-out version of the way Claudia, Nancy, and I come to understand Alain's experience. Note that it loosely follows the lines of this book's "three-part flips," the set of categories teachers can use to organize their thinking about children's behavior and experiences (see chapter 1).

A Portrait of Alain

Behavior and Developmental Mastery
Alain is a cheerful and resilient boy—a lover of singing and train play, a gung-ho climber and runner, and an enthusiastic consumer of all things edible. His frequent frustration, impulsive behaviors, difficulty listening and attending, and way of cruising the classroom suggest a number of developmental skill deficits. Many of those skill deficits appear, in part, to be connected to issues of hard wiring. Alain's struggles to communicate, for example, probably stem from vulnerabilities in language processing paired with his status as a second-language learner. His motion-filled and impulsive behavior appears related to some hard-wired challenges in sensory integration, along with a high-energy, distractible temperament.

Emotional Well-Being and Adult-Child Connections
Alain's mother and teachers care for him deeply. However, his connections with these adults have become frayed; they're often frustrated by him, upset by him, and wearied by him. He senses those feelings and worriedly looks to reconnect after he has been in trouble. But Alain isn't

just concerned about the ways in which adults feel toward him. He's also conflicted about this whole business of misbehavior. On the one hand, he enjoys the power he gets from acting out. After all, he can get the world to move with misbehavior in a way he can't yet get it to move with language. On the other, he is afraid he isn't as loved and appreciated as his brother and his classmates. So, even as Alain yearns for power, he wishes that someone—anyone—knew how to rein him in. So far, however, there isn't a "someone" who's been steadily successful in doing so.

Interactive Patterning

A number of interactive patterns seem to be playing a significant role in what's going on:

- Alain does something he shouldn't. That's usually followed by a verbal reprimand, one that involves a lot of words. He probably doesn't understand many of those words, though he can tell something is amiss. In any event, whether he understands them or not, words rarely stop Alain from engaging in whatever he is doing. In fact, verbal reprimands often result in his behavior worsening. Alternatively, a firm scolding may set off a running episode.

- When Alain runs, his teachers attempt to stop him. But because they are not allowed either to use time-out or to physically restrain him against his will (both understandable policies), they often give up. When teachers do take his hand, Alain tends to kick or punch. Such behavior results in their letting him go, usually with another ineffective reprimand.

- If Alain's mother takes his hand when he is doing something she's unhappy about, Alain settles down quickly. But Carole tends to get distracted. Or, perhaps, she gets uncertain about whether what she's doing is acceptable in the eyes of others. Then she lets her son wiggle out of her grasp, and Alain often misbehaves further.

- Sometimes Alain's teachers and mother are able to redirect him successfully. That is a relief, allowing everyone to move on from whatever has taken place. However, redirection appears to have had little impact on Alain's learning to control himself over time. If anything, he has discovered that his negative behavior rarely leads to specific consequences. That learning may be leading to more misbehavior, not less.

- Furthermore, at least in school, Alain is getting far more attention when he is doing poorly than when he's doing well. When he is relatively calm,

Claudia and Nancy are relieved to be able to spend time with other kids and tend to leave him to his own devices. But Alain craves attention and looks for it wherever he can find it. If there's not positive attention to be had, negative attention may come in a close second. Maybe it is even starting to come in first.

Life at Home

Raised by a loving but timid mother living far from home and family, Alain was probably on the high maintenance side right from the get-go. In the face of her older son's easiness, Carole has been a capable and confident parent. In response to Alain's relentless activity level paired with his trouble using language, however, she has felt increasingly helpless. That helplessness has contributed to some strikingly oppositional behavior on Alain's part, and things at home are now quite out of control. Even so, Carole and Alain still have plenty of mutual affection to draw upon when family life hits moments of calm.

Triggers for Difficulty and Setups for Success

In school, Alain functions better when there are fewer kids around and when space and expectations are well defined. That is also the case when play themes are at a level that he can handle, when there is singing and movement involved, and during less verbally intensive activities like cooking or outdoor play. Alain does far worse during transitions and other periods when there is a great deal of noise and commotion.

Alain's troubling behavior is almost always triggered by something that is happening at a particular moment in time. He wants a specific toy or seat but doesn't have the language to ask for it or the frustration tolerance to wait for it. He grabs or pushes instead. He has a play idea that he can't fully express, and his classmates' play takes off without him. He lashes out. His sensory issues are set off during transitions—or when he's playing in a larger group of kids—and he quickly gets restless. If things don't settle down (and because of his rising activity level they usually don't), he kicks or hits. If he wants a teacher's attention but she is talking with someone else, he has little capacity to hold on until it's his turn. More hitting frequently ensues.

Play

Almost every challenge Alain struggles with can be seen in his play—both in what he *doesn't do* that is age appropriate, and what he *does do* that is of concern. For example, Alain's play is choppy and restricted. It's likely that his limited language makes it hard for him to extend a story line the way other four-year-olds often can. He dumps blocks and then, perhaps, makes a short tower. Task completed—no further building and no story to go along with his construction project. Similarly, he runs his trains on the track, but they don't seem to be going anywhere in particular. He drifts by the dramatic play area and, though he loves to cook in reality, rarely plays out even a limited cooking scenario in his imagination.

Alain's high energy, inattention, and low frustration tolerance are evident during his play, as is his impulsivity. He cruises from place to place, rarely staying anywhere for long. He grabs rather than asks for things and finds it hard to wait his turn. He lashes out rather than engaging in problem solving. In contrast, Alain thrives at the puzzle table. That may be because puzzles don't require an accompanying narrative, his visual-spatial skills are strong, and he doesn't have to negotiate with other kids in order to complete them.

Family Culture and History

Carole misses her family terribly yet stays in this country to make a better life for her sons. It's not easy. She is on the shy side, which leaves her even more isolated than she might be otherwise. In addition, she is parenting solo. That means that when Alain is difficult, she doesn't have the net of family support that is so central to life back home.

Carole has done everything she can to keep her culture's norms center stage though. Politeness is important to her, and appropriate behavior is too. When Alain is calm and organized, as he is during lunch, her work to foster both is well in view. In addition, Carole's way of invoking Grann and Grandpè's love and hopes for their grandson to be a "good boy" is consistent with her culture's style of disciplining children: in Haitian families, emphasizing the important pairing of family and community care—and family and community standards—is a common way to shape children's behavior (Ballenger 1992).

However, Grann and Grandpè aren't around to back Carole up. Nor is she connected to a Haitian community in this country. As a result, her entreaties don't have the impact they would have back home. Her anxious glances at Alain's teachers as her son begins to misbehave may communicate not just confusion (What should I do here?) but also a plea for help. *Will you be my family and community backup? That's what I need and what I remember from when I was a child. In fact, almost anyone felt free to call out their window or stop me on the street and remind me that they'd talk to my parents if I didn't start doing the right thing.*

Carole is shy, and it takes her a while to warm up to almost anyone new. But—given this way of thinking so deeply rooted in her culture—she is slowly coming to see Claudia and Nancy as part of her close-knit community in this country. In the past month, she has not just been glancing at them in distress when Alain is out of control, but also reaching out regularly for support and advice. If these teachers can come up with a new plan for working with Alain at school, she'll probably be more than eager to partner with them in putting something similar in place at home. To her, that may well feel not just familiar but also comforting.

Moving Along: Laying Out Goals for Growth

It has taken a number of chapters to land on this comprehensive portrait of one little boy. That's because Alain is the child I'm using to illuminate the full process we go through when we have serious concerns about any youngster's development. I want to note something here, however. Although exploring Alain's story takes up many pages in this book, the reflective process in his case actually unfolds relatively quickly. In fact, it takes only Claudia and Nancy's observations, their mostly on-the-fly conversations with Carole, plus my morning's visit and an afternoon team meeting for us to land on a picture of what is going on—and an approach to making things better.

That team meeting lasts just over an hour. By its halfway point, this portrait has emerged. Then we're ready to move on to goal setting. Our goal setting rests under the "thinking" prong of the see → think → do progression but serves as a bridge to its "doing" prong. We jot our goals down as we sketch them out, using categories from the three-part flips as a general guide. Those categories aren't followed in order, and not every category is employed. That is often the case at this point in the reflective process: no matter what child we're thinking about, we keep the categories in mind and use them in whatever way works best. As is frequently true, connection comes first for Alain—it is the foundation on which all our efforts will be built. Here is our list, expanded from the shorthand version we scribble down during our meeting:

Connections

We hope Alain will . . .

- have a growing confidence in how much adults care for him.
- trust that his relationships with those adults will stay strong and loving even when he's having trouble.
- take pleasure and gain skill in connecting with his classmates.
- feel like a valued and cherished member of the classroom.

Developmental-Behavioral Skills

We want Alain to learn to . . .

- use words and gestures to communicate what he thinks, wants, and needs.
- get the sensory input he craves in positive ways.
- calm his body, focus his mind, and pay attention for longer stretches.
- manage frustration and other strong feelings.
- wait with patience.
- think before acting.
- stay calm in the midst of transitions and other busy times.

Emotional Well-Being

We'd like Alain to feel . . .

- more confidence about and pride in his abilities.
- more certainty that he can be powerful and strong in positive ways.
- more of a sense of inner goodness (rather than "bad boy-ness").

Interactive Patterns

We'll aim for exchanges that involve . . .

- less seeking of (and receiving) negative attention for negative behaviors.
- more seeking of (and receiving) positive attention for positive behaviors.
- less time during which Alain does something unsafe or unwelcome, experiences a reprimand, and then ramps up further by running, kicking, hitting, or yelling.
- more consistency and effectiveness of adult responses to problematic behaviors.

Play

We want to support . . .

- more use of language during play.

- more happily shared play experiences.

- more successful problem solving during play.

- an ever-growing expansion of play ideas and play narratives.

Family Partnership

We hope to offer . . .

- times for conversation about how things are going both at home and in school.

- regularly built-in support for Carole in her role as single parent.

- ideas about what everyone can do to help Alain learn the skills of self-control.

- brainstorming about challenges in language processing—how to help and whether to look into the possibility of specialized services.

From Goal Setting to Action Planning and Beyond

Nothing on this list is surprising. Once teachers have a full picture of a child's strengths and challenges, goal setting usually flows easily, especially when we rely (in a flexible way) on an organizing framework like the three-part flips. Those flips ask: What do we see in each category of importance? What don't we see that we would like to foster instead? What can we do to achieve those goals? Claudia, Nancy, Robin, and I have worked our way through the first two questions. As we settle into the final portion of our team meeting, it's time to consider the last one.

6 Pathways to Growth

Joining Big-Picture Thinking with Practical Strategies

We're in a bind. Robin believes strongly in the program's rules about not using time-out or physically moving children against their will. Furthermore, Claudia and Nancy take great pride in running a learning-filled classroom where kids are supported and redirected rather than scolded or punished. At the same time, our conversation has left us wondering: Does Alain need a kind of steady firmness we haven't been offering?

"Let's think about this," I say. "We've come up with a great list of goals for growth. But the thing is, Alain is behaving so unsafely so often that it's going to be hard to get in there and help out. We may need some different ways to address the safety issue and the running away, attention-seeking stuff. If we can get those in hand, we'll be so much more able to give him the support he needs."

I turn to Robin. "Would you be willing to consider making a slight exception to the rules for now? Especially if we keep our main focus on support and skill development?" She looks both skeptical and interested. Claudia and Nancy do too. All three suggest that I take the floor and sketch out what I have in mind.

So that's what I do, with plenty of give-and-take along the way. Out of that spirited conversation comes a plan to which we all agree, though Robin thinks carefully before signing on. She wants to be sure—and rightly so—that what we do stays positive and nonpunitive.

Multifaceted Goals, Multifaceted Strategies

The plan we design for Alain has a number of parts: our goals for him are multifaceted, so the strategies we'll use to meet them must be too. Some of those strategies will help us boost Alain's experience of pleasurable connection. Others will anchor our work on skill development in areas of challenge and help him develop a growing sense of pride, belonging, and competence. Still others will allow us to provide effective "stop messages" for unsafe behavior while cutting down on negative attention seeking.

The plan focuses on our partnership with Alain's mother, too. Based on our fullest understanding of Alain's difficulties, the plan is anchored by specific, easy-to-implement ideas that the teachers can put to work right away. That marriage of big-picture thinking and practicality is the hallmark of effective action planning. It is also the foundation of successful intervention.

Running through the team's plan for Alain are principles central to work with many children, and each one is explained as it comes up in this chapter. (Because of their importance, these principles—along with some others—are compiled and reviewed in appendix B.) Note that each of the plan's prongs addresses a particular goal. The first prong involves safety. This focus on safety doesn't diminish our commitment to increased connection and developmental mastery as prime goals for Alain. But the teachers need space and time to work on those goals. And right now, unsafe incidents happen so often that it feels almost impossible to offer Alain the kind of warmth and skill-building help he needs. Safety comes first for another reason too: the classroom needs to be a trustworthy place for its other children, and right now it's not. Here is what the first prong looks like:

Starting Off: Safety Comes First

Targeting Extreme Behaviors and Attention Seeking:

- The team will have a "short list" of unsafe behaviors: hitting, kicking, pushing, and throwing toys. They'll introduce that list to Alain by using a simple visual chart. There, each of the four behaviors will be represented by a picture followed by a large stop sign. At the bottom of the chart will be the figure of a smiling child with hands and feet highlighted in bold colors. Underneath that figure will be the words, "I have safe hands and safe feet!"

- Without shadowing Alain too closely, Claudia and Nancy will regularly position someone in his vicinity. When he does something on the list, whoever is nearby will quickly take his hand. Keeping her words to a minimum and emphasizing safety, that teacher will firmly but calmly let him know his behavior isn't acceptable. (*"Alain! We have safe feet in our class!"*)

- Then, continuing to hold Alain's hand, the teacher will remove him to a spot a few feet away from whatever he has been doing. With a kind of relaxed steadiness, she'll say little if anything. And rather than looking

Alain's way, she'll keep her focus on other children. The overall idea here is that things will feel neutral rather than negative to Alain.

- Alain will have to hold his teacher's hand for a few minutes—until he's calm and the fact that he's not allowed to be part of activities has sunk in. Then, with hands still joined, that teacher will turn to him with warmth. She'll catch his eyes and ask (with similar words each time), "Ready to be with your friends?" There won't be any discussion of Alain's unsafe behavior during the initial stages of using the plan. Instead, he'll be encouraged to rejoin his peers. To support his success, he'll be given some friendly help as he settles back into the life of the classroom.

When I first suggest my ideas for promoting safe behavior, Claudia and Nancy glance at each other. Such strategies are unlikely to work on their own, they point out. Alain will start hurting them as soon as they take his hand. It's clear we need a second-tier response to safety issues. We decide not to use a classic time-out chair. That doesn't feel right to any of us. But we *will* set up a place for Alain to go when hand-holding doesn't allow him to regain control. We'll call that place the classroom's "safe space," we decide, and introduce it to the group as a spot all children can use when they need to calm themselves down, sort through some intense feelings, or just take a break from the fray.

There is a particular way the team envisions using the classroom's safe space for Alain. At first, it involves removing adult attention briefly. That's something we'd rather not do, given that he often acts unsafely when he's frustrated over his lack of skill. But now we have a picture of what has been going on in regard to attention seeking, and of the way he settles down quickly when his mother manages to be calm and firm in her hand-holding. Based on that picture, we'll give this a try. The teachers will, however, be sure to offer plenty of warm engagement and skill-building support shortly *after* Alain has pulled himself together.

Having a Backup Plan to Support Safety

- If Alain starts hurting his teacher upon removal from activities, she'll keep holding his hand. But instead of continuing to stand where they are, she'll guide him to the safe space. Should Alain resist going, she'll place her free hand behind his back and gently push him along so that he's not getting tugged or pulled in a way that hurts him. Once he's there, that teacher will position herself so he can't run out. (If he continues to lash out physically, she'll protect herself with a pillow the team will position nearby.) Claudia and Nancy may also choose to switch places at that point if it appears that doing so will help Alain regain control more quickly.

- After Alain has been guided to the safe space, whoever is there won't talk with him—except to gently remind him on occasion that it is his job to "relax and get safe." Instead, she'll nonchalantly chat with other children as he settles down. After a few minutes of calm and without any mention of his previous behavior, she'll do the same thing she'd do after a period of hand-holding: offer Alain some warm reconnection, an invitation to return to play, and the friendly help he needs to rejoin his peers successfully.

A Few Essential Principles

At first glance, the first prong of Alain's plan appears to promote safety alone. But there's considerably more to it than that. It also targets emergent frustration tolerance, impulse control, and self-soothing, all developmental skills the team hopes Alain will begin learning as he starts acting out less and calming down more. In addition, this prong aims to reduce reinforcement of escalating behaviors—the "throwing a stone in the water and seeing what happens" interactions that are making things so difficult. It also requires teachers to be neutral rather than irritated when Alain lashes out, and directs them to reach out with warmth and care when his time away from other children is over. In doing both, it looks to promote feelings of adult-child connection that are more steadily positive.

My fellow consultant Loretta Wieczner, who was a preschool teacher for many years, often reminds me that our approaches should have the "biggest bang for the buck." In other words, whenever possible, strategies should target multiple goals at once. For example, "Leo the Loud-Mouthed Lion," an adorable puppet who needs to learn that his voice can get too loud for his animal buddies' comfort, is one of Loretta's many sidekicks. Leo teaches children about modulating their voices—an aspect of developmental mastery—while also promoting literacy skills. How does he do this? Leo *loves* places (the lending library) and activities (licking lollipops) that start with the letter *l*.

The first prong of our team's plan is infused with this "biggest bang" principle, although literacy isn't one of its goals. Rather than merely targeting safety and attention seeking, it is also saturated with connection and skills-based learning. In addition, it asks teachers to be ready for what is coming (in this case, unsafe behavior targeting other children) and for what sometimes comes after that (unsafe behavior targeting teachers). And it requires them to have strategies ready to go that won't just manage what is happening in the moment but will, over time, promote the mastery they are hoping for. That's to say, the plan reflects another principle on which we build our work: it is proactive, not reactive (Greene 2008, xii).

There is yet another principle reflected in this prong: it builds on a child's strengths to help with his vulnerabilities. Note, for example, how Claudia and Nancy will use visual prompts to support Alain's understanding of what is expected. That's because he is great at puzzles and other visually oriented activities but not yet skilled in language use. This same principle can be seen in the way these teachers will keep Alain company when he's ready to rejoin his classmates. In such situations, they'll rely on his naturally upbeat nature resurfacing quickly after he has misbehaved. They'll partner with that good cheer (one of his most endearing strengths) and take advantage of his deep desire to reconnect with the people around him once trouble is over (another strength). Then they'll work to support him in finding successful ways to interact with his peers (an area of challenge).

These three principles lie at the heart of good teaching practice. The idea of being proactive, not reactive, is especially useful in the case of children like Alain, whose difficult behaviors can lead us to become more negative in tone and frustrated in spirit than we like to be. And the last of these principles reminds us that even the most easily frustrated (and hard to manage) kids have many strengths. Recognizing those strengths often points the way toward successful intervention.

Principles for Intervention, Part One

Whenever possible, we look for strategies that target more than one goal at a time, seeking the biggest bang for the buck.

It helps to be prepared for children's difficulties with mastery-focused responses that are "proactive, not reactive."

Building on children's strengths to help with their vulnerabilities not only feels better to them, it works better too.

Is This Doable? We're Exhausted Already . . .

Claudia and Nancy are aware that the strategies we've come up with so far aren't ends in themselves. In fact, if those strategies work as intended, they'll merely support Alain in getting his most extreme behaviors under control. Much more will be needed, we agree. We'll have to work on replacing his experience of negative attention with plenty of warm connection. We'll also need to provide steady opportunities for adult-supported play and step-by-step help in learning a range of developmental skills. As we begin thinking about how to incorporate these ideas into our plan, Claudia's and Nancy's faces convey uncertainty and exhaustion. They wonder aloud whether they can possibly give Alain any more time than he is already getting.

Their concerns are legitimate. They are the ones who will have to carry out our plan. Thus, whatever we come up with can't just be helpful to Alain—it has to feel doable to them. Luckily, based on my experience with other challenging children, I'm confident that we can design an approach that will take less of their energy, not more. I reassure them as best I can in this regard. And I note that if the kind of plan I'm envisioning works as intended, it will feel like a better and more pleasurable use of the time they *do* offer this boy. To their great credit, these teachers look at each other and then nod: they're ready for more brainstorming. Then, with their involvement and blessing, we lay out a set of strategies for supporting connection, communication, self-regulation, and play—and for offering Alain some of the sensory input he needs to stay calm and focused.

From Safety to Skill Development

Here are the strategies we come up with, which comprise the second prong of our action plan.

Fostering Pleasurable Connection:

- Teachers will offer Alain many opportunities for connection throughout the day. They'll drop by for moments of warm engagement when he's playing. They'll give him extra hugs and smiles. They'll invite him to help them with jobs he might enjoy, too. And they'll find his eyes from across the room and offer a friendly wave.

- In addition, Claudia and Nancy will work to pull one or two other children into their interactions with Alain. That way, we hope, he'll start connecting more with his peers, begin (with support) to learn the skills of give-and-take, and experience the pleasures of friendship.

Offering Opportunities for Self-Regulation and Sensory Input:

- Claudia and Nancy will provide plenty of the singing and movement activities that help Alain stay calm and attentive. Furthermore, they'll appoint him the group's song and movement leader for a few weeks, in the hopes of boosting his sense of competence and feeling of being a valued member of the classroom.

- They'll also find times for shoulder squeezes, push/pull games, heavy lifting, and the like. (See appendix C for resources on sensory-focused strategies.) For the most part, they'll offer these opportunities *before* Alain gets too revved up. Afterward, he's less likely to accept them.

Supporting Language and Play:

- Teachers will find opportunities to join Alain in play with other children before he has gotten frustrated. Then, staying by his side as they offer him skill-building support, they'll work to help him play with more depth, breadth, flexibility, and success. That may, at times, include offering the kinds of ideas other kids need to stay interested in playing with Alain. Later on, as Alain gains both language and play skills, they will slowly hand off the responsibility for generating ideas back to him.

- Teachers will help Alain use language to describe his play. They'll assist him in using words to solve problems, too, and to talk about what he thinks and feels. Furthermore, during play periods, snack, and lunchtime, they'll encourage other kids to slow down enough to listen to Alain's input.

- When Alain says something inappropriate ("Jonathan, you stupid!") or grabs a toy out of someone's hand, teachers won't remove him the way they will when he is physically unsafe. Instead, they'll focus on skill development by offering him the words he lacks. Then they'll warmly encourage him to repeat the phrases they've suggested, and stick around to help him through the negotiation at hand.

- Any time there are things Alain wants (food, toys, etc.), teachers will build in some friendly connection. In addition, they'll prompt him to use some simple language to ask for what he wants. That prompting will sometimes include giving him a scripted version of the words he needs. But they'll be careful to infuse these interchanges with pleasure rather than pressure.

Some Additional Principles

A number of additional principles guide the strategies in this second prong of our plan. The ways teachers will offer frequent opportunities for warm engagement, what I call "seeding the day with connection," reflects the first principle. That one reminds us that connection is key to children's well-being and should lie at the heart of all our efforts to help them thrive. A second principle can be seen in the strategies that aim to support Alain in using language to ask for what he wants, express his feelings, and solve conflicts of interest. Based on a "rung-by-rung" picture of how children learn and grow, this principle emphasizes that it's always useful to focus our work where children really are skill-wise, not at the level we'd like them to be. In close partnership with this second principle is a third one: the idea that we need to "chunk down" our goals for growth so that kids can be successful, one step at a time.

Principles for Intervention, Part Two

Warm connection should lie at the heart of all our efforts to help out when children are struggling.

The help children need should start from where they are developmentally speaking, rather than where we wish they'd be.

"Chunking down" goals for growth, and working step-by-step helps children feel—and be—successful.

Play as Medium, Scaffolding as Method

The second prong of Alain's plan doesn't include just a focus on language; it also puts play center stage. Action plans for other kids frequently put play in this central role too. And that leads to another principle: play can be a marvelous medium for intervention. Before teachers can use play as a vehicle for growth, however, they must answer two questions. First, how do a particular child's issues play out in play? (In regard to Alain, that question is addressed in chapter 5.) Second, how might we use play to help that child learn?

The specifics of play support vary from child to child (see chapter 7 for more). But overall, when adults have honed in on where a child's vulnerabilities lie and then connect to his play with pleasure, they can offer him some of the assistance he needs. The balance of offering that help without taking over can be tricky. That's certainly true in Alain's case, given how much trouble he has playing successfully and how quickly he becomes frustrated when things aren't going the way he wants them to. It will undoubtedly be important for Claudia and Nancy to accompany him in doing the things he can't yet do, while supporting him in learning those he's ready to master. At the same time, they'll need to give him plenty of room to shine in areas where he can. With this kind of artful balance—and with the joy of play providing fuel for growth—they'll be able to offer Alain "scaffolding for skill."

Scaffolding is a term early childhood educators hear a lot these days. It speaks to our way of identifying the growing edge of a child's learning in a particular area and offering the assistance he needs right at that point. Associated with the work of the influential Russian theorist Lev Vygotsky (1978), scaffolding has become a buzzword for child-friendly, learning-filled approaches to classroom support. That support can be focused on pre-academic and academic skills or on social-emotional ones. I sometimes call scaffolding that targets social-emotional skills by another name: "lending an ally."

When we lend an ally, we offer ourselves as an upbeat partner in learning, handing back opportunities for competent functioning just as soon as kids are ready for us to do so. It's just the kind of help Alain needs when he's playing, when he's trying to talk at snack and at lunch, and when he has to solve a conflict of interest with a buddy and doesn't know what to do other than hit.

Principles for Intervention, Part Three

Play is a wonderful medium for intervention.

Lending an ally to support learning—offering "scaffolding for skill"—is a prime tool for supporting growth, during play and in other contexts too.

Being Prepared for Predictable Difficulties

Our team meeting is almost over. Before it concludes, Claudia and Nancy want to be sure they have strategies in hand for periods that are predictably hard for Alain. They are particularly concerned about transitions and circle time. These teachers emphasize that they don't feel Alain is ready to fully comply with their usual expectations at these times, and Robin and I are quick to agree. It's not that our team doesn't want to encourage Alain in being successful at any level he can. But until he begins to master the developmental skills we're targeting, it's going to be more important that he stay calm and confident.

We decide that to help Alain manage transitions and normal classroom activity levels, Claudia and Nancy will offer a mix of previewing and success-focused support, and that they'll also provide positive alternatives at times when Alain needs a break. That way, they'll be able to foster his growing ability to manage predictably challenging activities but avoid the negative behaviors he has been using when he is overwhelmed.

The final prong of our plan includes the following strategies:

Providing Positive Options for Breaks:

- Claudia and Nancy will assemble a "fun for one" basket filled with things Alain likes to do, and set aside a special pillow to go with it. Alain will be able to request both when he notices (or teachers suggest) that he needs a break. He'll use them in a particular spot: the classroom's "book nook."

Providing Proactive Support for Times We Know Are Hard:

- The teachers will also make a set of classroom-wide job necklaces for cleanup time. They'll give Alain his necklace a bit early so he knows his assigned task. His jobs will mostly be carried out away from the fray, either on his own or with one other child. And they'll be jobs he especially enjoys, like sensory-friendly paintbrush rinsing or tabletop sponging.

- Teachers will start setting out the children's circle-time mats slightly earlier than usual, making sure that they show Alain his spot well before group time begins. Then they'll offer him an enthusiastic high five when he gets to that spot successfully.

- In addition, either Claudia or Nancy will go to Alain before a transition is about to happen. They'll connect warmly with him about what he's doing. Then they'll preview and plan out what's to come.

- Furthermore, instead of just using words, they'll make a visual schedule they can bring to Alain—like the one on the classroom's wall but smaller and with some extra pictures just for him. So they can have some flexibility based on what any particular day involves, they'll make sure the schedule's pictures are backed with Velcro. That will make it easy for each one to be attached or removed as needed.

Claudia and Nancy have a quick back-and-forth about this last strategy, making sure they have a good grasp on how to make it as connection saturated, visually focused, and Alain friendly as possible. Here is a quick sketch of what one version might look like:

Claudia drops by and kneels down on Alain's level. "Look at your trains Alain! What are they doing?" She smiles at Alain, waiting for him to use whatever words he can to share what he's up to. When it appears that he is done speaking, Claudia jumps in with a single word of her own, "Wonderful!" She smiles again, putting in a slight pause before she resumes speaking. She knows it takes Alain a while to figure out what is being said, and she wants to give him a chance to get ready for the next piece of input.

"Alain, I have something to tell you. I'm going to flick the lights to show that cleanup is coming soon . . . Look! Here's the picture of me flicking the lights." Claudia points to the visual chart, sees that Alain is glancing down at it, and then goes on. "And here's the picture of cleanup time." She points at the chart again. Then, directing Alain's attention to the job necklace she's brought along, she says, "This is your job necklace, Alain." Claudia shows Alain the necklace's picture of a child at the sink, before helping him place it around his neck. Pointing to the sink and waiting until she sees that he's looking there too, she remarks, "You can clean the paintbrushes today!"

Claudia goes on, reminding Alain (with the help of more visuals) that he'll have his special pillow to sit on during circle time. She lets him know, too, that his favorite song, "The Wheels on the Bus," will be on the docket. Alain perks up—it's clear he knows the song and is excited that it's coming.

"Now you can play some more, Alain. I'll come back soon!" Claudia says with enthusiasm. She waits for Alain's smile and returns it in kind before heading along.

A Rule to Live By: "Connect Before You Correct"

The ideas behind what Claudia is doing here—and behind the action plan's last prong—are probably clear. Her work is proactive, not reactive, with a big focus on previewing and planning. It is connection saturated, strengths based, and skill focused too. At its heart lies another central principle, one that has become a kind of mantra in Claudia and Nancy's program: *"Connect before you correct . . . or redirect."* That is to say, even when things aren't going well, it helps to begin our interactions with a dose of warmth and care. That way, children are far more likely to join us in our efforts to help them learn new behaviors and let go of old ones.

This "connect before you correct" idea sounds easy on paper. It isn't. When we're worried about what a child is about to do, or upset with what they have just done, our words may be kind. Sometimes, however, our body language and our tone of voice are not. That's why I often encourage teachers to slow down slightly before approaching a child who is having trouble. Then, I add, they might try kneeling down to interact at his level. As I approach my older years, I have a way of reminding myself about this last suggestion: "If my knees aren't cracking, I'm probably not doing the work." My younger teaching partners often laugh when I say this. Those who are close to my age know exactly what I mean. And what I mean leads to one last principle: it helps to meet a child not only at his developmental level, but also at eye level.

Principles for Intervention, Part Four

Whenever possible, we connect before we correct . . . or redirect. That is true whether we're asking a child to stop something he's doing currently, or offering some prompting for what's to come.

Remembering to get down on a child's level can increase the power of connectedness and the power of whatever help or support we have to offer too.

Finding the Right Mix of Support and Expectations

The plan is close to complete. It frames an approach that builds on strengths, aims for connection and mastery, and offers limits that will help Alain feel he can stay safe and in control. That sounds good to all of us. But Claudia and Nancy will be on the front lines, and they want clarity on when to do what. When should they offer Alain step-by-step help in learning new skills? When should they give him a chance to express and understand his feelings? When would it be best to set—and follow through on—firm expectations for behavior? I suggest thinking of the action plan as a kind of road map that will help them decide when to "lean in" and when to "lean out." They know this language—we've used it together before.

I came up with the "leaning in—leaning out" idea years ago when working with the parents of a particularly explosive child. It has turned out to be helpful not just to parents but to teachers as well. When adults "lean in," they give children the warm connection, support for learning, and opportunities for emotional expression they need. When those same adults "lean out," they set a bar for behavior and have a sensible plan for following through. The lend-an-ally support Claudia and Nancy will offer Alain qualifies as leaning in. The safety prong of the plan exemplifies leaning out.

Leaning in is full of warmth, not irritation. Leaning out is full of clarity, not frustration. The importance of this division is that when kids are being provocative, adults often end up feeling confused about whether to lean in or lean out and can end up offering a "sloppy mix" that includes some of both at the same time. Furthermore, no matter what they choose (and sometimes adults acknowledge they don't feel they're choosing at all, just reacting), strong and negative feelings often accompany their words. Cleaning up this sloppy, emotional mix helps kids a lot.

Finding an effective mix of leaning in and leaning out means having a picture of what each one looks like. That is why our team has to be very clear about just what Claudia and Nancy will do in carrying out the safety plan. There's another benefit to using this way of thinking: it helps adults take a quick moment to figure out which kind of response makes sense when a child is beginning to have difficulty. It may help Claudia and Nancy, for example, to remember to pause for a brief moment to figure out whether to lean in or lean out. When adults learn to do this in the face of a child's misbehavior, they can get their own feelings of reactivity out of the way. Then they're able to respond calmly and clearly. That way, children get an emotionally supportive experience of adult efforts to lean in. And they get a firm but not irritable experience of the leaning out part, too. Such changes almost always make a big difference in how things go. Claudia and Nancy certainly hope they will in Alain's case.

General Principles Are Important . . . but Specifics Matter

Each of the principles throughout this chapter holds true both for teachers and their family partners. These principles—along with the strategies that help us carry them out—are part of what we offer parents in regularly scheduled conferences. (We may also discuss them in those "we need to meet soon" brainstorming sessions that can follow a child's difficult weeks in his classroom.) Claudia and Nancy, for example, eventually share a number of this book's approaches with Carole. But as important as these ideas may be to Alain's progress, specifics matter. The ideas we share—and how Carole learns to use them—have to line up with who she is as a person and the culture from which she comes. In other words, the details of any plan must be tailored to each child, each teacher, and each family. There is no one route to change. The overall approach we embrace must make sense in terms of what we know about children and about development. But the specific strategies we use to implement it need to fit the child and adults in question.

A Final Step to Action Planning: Ironing Out Details

The team is ready to wrap up, just as soon as we finish discussing two final details. The first involves the safe space. Where will it be? What should be in it? Nancy and Claudia decide to relocate their book nook, currently off in the quietest corner of the classroom. That corner seems like the best spot for the safe space. They'll take down the posters that are currently decorating its walls because Alain is likely to rip them when he's upset. The book nook's comfortable pillows will stay put, though, with the addition of some soft toys that won't hurt anyone if they are tossed. Claudia and Nancy will also write a short, scripted story (see chapter 14) that reminds Alain of the things he *can* do when he's frustrated.

And they'll put up visuals depicting those strategies near, but not in, the space itself. (Such child-friendly self-soothing strategies—and the scripted stories we sometimes use to accompany them—are also explored in chapter 14.)

The second detail is as important as anything else in the plan: involving Alain's mother fully in what we are doing. Claudia commits to chatting with Carole the next day. In that conversation, she'll offer a quick description of what we are about to try and will set up a full meeting in the near future. At that point, she and Nancy will offer Carole some support. They'll also think with her about some home-based versions of what they will be trying in the classroom. These teachers are confident Carole will be an eager partner; she has already approached them numerous times to chat and seek advice.

Principles for Intervention, Part Six

There is no one route to change: the strategies we use to support growth have to make sense in terms of what is going on, but they have to fit the child and adults involved too.

Partnering with families is an essential ingredient in moving things forward.

Getting to Work with Alain: A New Journey Begins

Early on in our meeting, Claudia and Nancy express their fears that the plan for Alain will be all-consuming. It turns out that it isn't. To our great surprise and pleasure, the strategies targeting safety begin working fairly quickly. Not immediately though. In fact, before the meeting ends, I check in with these teachers because I am worried about whether they're ready for the ride ahead. "If this plan works," I say, "there may be a week or two of testing before Alain's behavior really improves. Is that okay with you? Do you feel you can stay steady so we can find out if what we have in mind will help?"

The teachers make clear that they're willing to carry through with what we've discussed. They may get a few bruises as Alain lashes out in response to their hand-holding. But if the plan has a chance of working, they're game. They truly care about this boy, and what we have decided to do makes sense to them. And they're afraid that if they don't do something different, Alain will be asked to leave within the month. It's a go.

I check in late the next day. If anything, initiating the plan has been even more difficult than we had imagined. Alain had to be taken to the safe space many times an hour and by midmorning was not only angry but bereft. Claudia and Nancy are shaken but committed. They make clear that they did everything they could to stay positive and to connect with Alain steadily throughout his day in school.

The following morning begins similarly. However, after about an hour and a half, Claudia and Nancy start noticing moments when Alain stops himself just before he is about to hit or kick. When he does do something unsafe, he is becoming less likely to fight the prospect of hand-holding. Instead, he begins pulling his teacher to the safe space. Then he sits down willingly. By lunch, Alain is smiling, not a push or a hit to be seen. The next day is even better—two minor kicks and a gentle push. Each time, Alain takes himself to the safe space completely on his own. When he sees one of his classmates push another child over by accident, he addresses that boy with great seriousness: "No Emilio. No push. Go safe space."

There is a long journey ahead. But Claudia and Nancy are ecstatic. Carole is too. Our hunch was right, and Alain seems relieved that he is being stopped every time he behaves unsafely. Now he is demonstrating that he can control himself far more than we had imagined he could. He adores the positive attention he has been getting when he is settled and calm, too, and is soaking in the play support he so badly needs. That said, while Alain's impulse control is improving daily, his communicational skills are even more limited than we had realized, and his social skills are equally marginal. In addition, he has significant trouble slowing down his body, harnessing his attention, and solving the many conflicts of interest he experiences as he tries to interact with friends.

As the year unfolds, the team continues to partner with Carole. She needs support in setting firm limits and guidance about how to lean in and out with clarity. Claudia and Nancy see immediate benefits from this partnership. The more Carole feels confident and skilled at home, the more quickly Alain makes progress. Claudia, Nancy, and Carole now have regular conversations about how to help Alain use words comfortably, slow down and focus successfully, and solve problems competently. The ideas flow both ways: Carole knows her son well. Furthermore, with Carole's full support, Alain is evaluated for speech and language issues. Everyone is pleased when he qualifies for services—we all believe he needs additional help now and will probably continue to benefit from extra support when he enters kindergarten.

It is a wonderful year for Alain. Not that he doesn't have his ups and downs: real progress, after all, doesn't mean constant progress. There are a number of stretches during which our team has to sit down together, figure out why Alain is beginning to slip once again, and add to or change what we are doing. But bumps in the road aside, Carole is tremendously proud of her son's gains. His teachers are delighted to see him begin to thrive too, and his good cheer infuses the classroom with sunshine now that he is no longer its terror in boy's clothing.

The team couldn't be happier when June arrives and Alain moves on. Not to see him go: all of us will miss him terribly. But to know that he is readier for kindergarten than we ever thought he could be. It is a pleasure to see that he has a crowd of buddies heading to elementary school with him. These kids no longer shy away as Alain draws near. Instead, they eagerly call out his name to see if he wants to join in at the train table or on the classroom's makeshift dance floor. There, he is the star of the show.

Connection Is Key

2

The children whose stories anchor this section have trouble connecting to others with pleasure, focus, and steadiness. For some, hard wiring lies at the heart of what is going on. For others, the basics of development have become challenging due to a hard start, some hard times, or the challenge of learning a second language in the midst of a busy classroom. Sometimes, a combination of these factors is at play, along with interactive patterns that have been making things worse rather than better. In each case, it's not just connection that is at risk; other important aspects of development end up being involved as well.

The stories about these children serve as a reminder of two points. The first is that connection is key; it is the foundation on which many other areas of developmental mastery rest. (That is why many of the strategies found here bear on the help we offer the kinds of children described in parts 3 and 4 of this book as well.) The second is that a youngster's success mastering skills linked with any one developmental trajectory can have profound implications for others.

For all of these youngsters, the relationship-enhancing idea of "seeding the day with connection," explored fully in chapter 9, is a central focus of intervention. The question is, though, how do we learn to offer warm connection in a form that a particular youngster can receive? To answer that question, each story includes information about how the "seeding" idea can be adapted in child-specific ways.

A note: All of the children featured in part 2 come from the same classroom as part 1's Alain. Although the stories you're about to read are true (identifying information aside), there is a slight fiction involved. In reality, I don't observe these kids on separate occasions, nor do the teachers and I talk about them in different meetings. All of us in the field are aware that we have to juggle the needs of multiple kids at the same time. Thus, as a practitioner, I would love to present the work our team did to understand and help the classroom's children in the mixed-together way it really unfolded. But that kind of everyday juggling becomes complicated on the page. Instead, for clarity's sake, I've focused on each child separately.

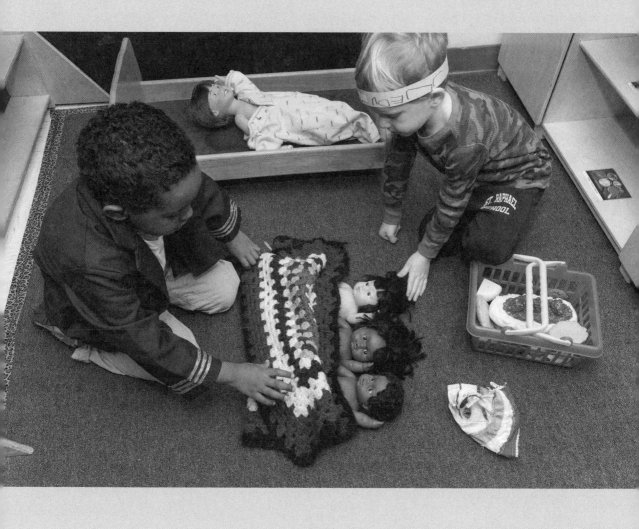

7 Spotlight on the Three Cs
Connection, Communication, and Cue Responsiveness

Hannah, Jenny, Kevin, Isabel, Jonathan, and Emilio. Six very different children struggling to cope in the midst of Claudia and Nancy's busy classroom. Each one has a place in the chapters to come; this chapter sets the stage for their stories by exploring ideas needed to understand the work their teachers do with all of them. These children all struggle with aspects of connection. A few are grappling with difficulties related to connection, communication, and what I call cue responsiveness all at once. That trio of challenges is quite common—the "three Cs" are powerfully linked to each other, developmentally speaking.

To begin, this chapter takes a look at each of the three Cs separately. Then it explores how they unfold in tandem during infancy, and how they show up in play. Those explorations are followed by an examination of play support for all kinds of children. Finally, the chapter offers some thoughts about how teachers can integrate the ideas presented up to this point in the book as they work to understand and help the most worrisome children in their classrooms.

Connection Is Key: A Brief Look at Attachment

Any exploration of the three Cs must start with the influential idea of attachment, a construct that originates in the world of theory but has become central to early childhood practice. In brief, attachment refers to the quality of connection a child experiences in her earliest relationships and on forward. It runs in two directions, from a child to her caregiver(s) and back again. Theorists emphasize (and few in our field would disagree) that a child's experience of attachment is incredibly important: it will shape how he ends up feeling about others, about the world at large, and, perhaps most importantly, about himself.

Fortunately for some kids, unfortunately for others, the quality of attachment can vary widely. A child's attachment to a particular caregiver can be pleasurable and steady. It can be deeply insecure. Or it can feel and look disengaged. Sometimes a youngster's attachment to his primary caregiver is kind of wobbly. In this case, it has an on-again, off-again quality that makes it hard for him to feel at ease in himself and comfortable in his world—he is too busy scanning his environment to see if, at any particular moment, safe connection will be available. (For a review of these ideas, see pages 91–145 in *The Developing Mind* by Daniel Siegel 2012.)

Knowing what theorists and researchers have suggested about attachment helps us understand intellectually what we sense intuitively: when a child has had the good fortune to experience warmth and steadiness in his earliest connections with caregivers, he'll have the foundation for many of the skills he'll need to thrive. If that hasn't happened, a healing focus on building safe and trustful connections will need to be a prime focus of intervention.

Understanding "Circles of Communication"

The wonderful theorist and practitioner Stanley Greenspan gave our field a powerful visual image for how children's capacity for communication is forged through relationships: circles of communication (1992, 7). This useful construct refers to the way humans send signals and energy between them in a dance of connection and meaning. When two people engage in circles of communication together, Greenspan suggests, one "opens" a circle, the other responds, and the initiator then "closes" the loop (1992, 334–35). One example of such exchanges can be seen as a baby and mother delightedly coo back and forth. Another takes place as a child chats with his beloved grandpa about a recent trip to the zoo. Yet one more unfolds as two children passionately debate whether they are going to build a castle or a grocery store. Circles of communication happen with words and without. Sometimes they are filled with tenderness, sometimes with anger.

This image of opening and closing circles can be tremendously useful: helping children engage successfully in such "loops" strengthens their experience of warm connection, their communicational skills, and their level of focus all at once. Such intervention is undoubtedly important in the case of youngsters like Alain and his classmate Jonathan, partners in the grunt- and crash-filled train play seen daily in Claudia and Nancy's classroom. These boys both rest on a low rung of the ladder of communication. Although we hope to see kids their age engage in many circles consecutively, they both struggle to open and close just one. In cases like theirs, our first goal is to get single circles of communication going more successfully. The second is to get more circles to occur in one "sitting." Our eventual goal? Helping such children climb their way up the ladder of communication, one rung at a time.

Cue Responsiveness: A Foundational Skill

The term *cue responsiveness* is not widely used in discussions about young children but represents something we in early childhood education know well. As teachers and specialists, we support kids as they learn to "stop, look, and listen" and are concerned when, over time, they can't. We talk about the importance of attention and sustained focus as well. The capacity for cue responsiveness lies at the foundation of all of these skills. The reason I give it a label of its own is that doing so allows us to more fully understand an area in which any number of kids show signs of difficulty.

Children who struggle with cue responsiveness are easy to spot. Some of them are our "up in the clouds" dreamers and our "can't get him to listen" wanderers. Some are the youngsters who may be able to repeat what we've just said yet can't seem to take it in and use it. "Natalie, go wash your hands," we tell a child like this. She nods. Then she wanders off to check out the science table. What lies behind the capacity for cue responsiveness that all these kids need to develop? This question is best answered by a look at how cue responsiveness can be seen at work in the midst of daily life.

When a child is cue responsive in his classroom, he hears his name and looks up, ready to find out what is to come. It might be a friend saying, "Let's build a zoo." It might be a teacher asking him to get ready to clean up at the end of free play or to pass the bread basket at lunch. A cue doesn't have to start with a child's name, however. And it doesn't have to include words. It might be a classroom's "time for cleanup" song. It might be a much-used "hands in the air" signal that tells kids to temporarily halt what they're doing and wait for a teacher's instructions. Alternatively, the cue might be a friend saying, "Stop! That hurts!" It could even be a teacher meeting a child's eyes during circle time, smiling, and putting her fingers to her lips. What might this last prompt convey? "Jonah, you're making it hard for others to listen. You're probably having trouble listening, too. Can you settle down and tune into this story? You might like it!"

Whatever the signal—verbal or nonverbal—a cue-responsive child *pops up* out of his inner world and *tunes in* to the world around him. He packages up his body, energy, and mind. Often (though in some cultures more than others), he also directs his eyes toward the individual who is requesting his attention. He gets ready to receive whatever information may be coming his way, and takes that information in. Finally, he acts based on that information. All of this usually happens quickly, so that the steps of "popping up and tuning in" aren't easily observed separately. All the same, there are steps involved. For kids who have trouble demonstrating cue-responsive behavior, "chunking down" those steps and teaching them one by one can be a big help. (See chapters 11, 12, and 13 to learn more about what that help looks like.)

Cue responsiveness helps kids become cooperative members of their classroom's communities and to be successful learners as well. It's also an important element behind being a good friend. "Tommy, I want that red truck!" a boy declares to his buddy. "You can have it when I'm done," Tommy replies, "Want the bulldozer for now?" Cue responsiveness is not the only skill reflected in this interchange. Tommy is also demonstrating flexibility, impulse control, and problem-solving skills, alongside communicational abilities and empathy. But without his ability to pop up and tune in to the interchange, none of these other skills would have a chance to shine through.

The Three Cs: Separate Yet Inextricably Linked

There is no doubt that considering connection, communication, and cue responsiveness separately helps illuminate what is involved for each. Yet, developmentally speaking, the three Cs are inextricably linked. To feel connected, a child must be tuned in. To be tuned in, it helps if he feels connected. Both are essential in the slow development of his communication skills. But that youngster's growing ability to communicate doesn't just rely on connection and cue responsiveness; it allows them to develop more fully as well. This interrelatedness is seen most easily when observing infants and toddlers growing and learning. That doesn't diminish its importance for the preschool-aged children this book targets. Stepping briefly into the world of babies, however, can shed some light on work with slightly older kids, as the following story illustrates.

The Three Cs in Infancy . . . and Beyond

About ten years ago, I was at a conference watching a film about some compelling infant research. In that film, a two-and-a-half-month-old baby was nestled in a baby seat. Nearby, a research assistant instructed the baby's mother to interact with her infant son the way she usually did. While his mother listened, that infant could be seen drooling, waving his arms around, and kicking his legs. His eyes wandered, seemingly unfocused.

Instructions complete, the baby's mother moved in front of him to a place about ten inches away from where he sat. She began smiling and cooing at him, her face animated, her voice gentle but excited in tone. The baby stopped drooling. His arms stopped waving. His eyes locked onto his mother's face. After a moment, he lit up with a huge smile. Then the film's audience had the joy of watching a pleasure-filled back-and-forth between mother and son. Those exchanges revealed what appeared to be a perfectly choreographed dance of tuned-in connection and nonverbal communication. But as I watched the film, I found myself pairing it with a very different (and less uplifting) "film" that began playing in my mind's eye. That imaginary film captured what I'd seen while observing a worrisome five-year-old just the day before.

Nicole, I'd noted as soon as I entered her preschool classroom, was a particularly distractible and active child. She rarely looked directly at anyone, even when asked. She had trouble following directions. And her classmates gave her a wide berth because playing with her almost always turned sour. Life at home was difficult, too. Nicole's single mother had reported to teachers that her firstborn, a son, had been a handful from the start. He was only a toddler when Nicole came along, and unfortunately she turned out to be just as fretful a baby as he had been. This mother had hoped family life would get easier as her children grew older, but it hadn't: Nicole's brother didn't listen well, and Nicole didn't either. Apparently, things had gotten to the point where Nicole's mother rarely got through a day without screaming multiple times.

As I sat in the conference, imagining the "film" of Nicole playing side by side with that of the mother and baby, I began wondering: What might I learn by comparing them? Because Nicole still couldn't do what the filmed baby was already showing signs of. At a mere two-and-a-half months he was more able to harness his attention, calm his body, and focus his eyes than a child over four years older. That moment of recognition led me to think further about how to help Nicole master a skill that many children begin demonstrating shortly after birth. It also gave me more compassion for parents whose children don't tune in naturally and easily. In addition, it spurred me to reflect on the challenges kids face when their parents are chronically overwhelmed and don't have the energy or inner resources needed to engage regularly in the kind of dance I had witnessed on film.

My "split screen" reflections have stayed with me and deepened my understanding of some basic ideas. They're worth keeping in mind anytime we encounter kids struggling with the three Cs:

- Sometimes difficulties with the combination of connection, communication, and cue responsiveness begin with a baby's challenging hard wiring. Sometimes, they start with a parent's having too much going on. Occasionally, there is a problem connected to "goodness of fit" in the parent-child relationship.

- Whatever the reasons, when the three Cs aren't developing well, they will need to be part of our goals for growth. Finding a way for older kids to experience ample doses of the kind of back-and-forth I saw on that film will be an important element of intervention.

- "Dosing" children in this way may require going down the developmental ladder to meet them on the rung they're having trouble climbing. When an older child has never mastered the basics of tuned-in connection and communication, it is unfair (and will be unsuccessful) to ask him to respond the way other kids his age can.

The Three Cs and Play

As is evident from my film story, the way infants interact with their caregivers tells us a great deal about how the three Cs are developing. Watching how children play as they grow older can do the same, especially if the three Cs aren't emerging in the way we hope they will. Because, as is true for Alain in part 1, children's challenges almost always play out in play. One youngster, for example, may have trouble creating or sequencing stories using language. Another may have difficulty sharing his story lines with others. Yet a third may be so challenged in the area of cue responsiveness that he rarely takes part in what his peers have in mind. And that's just a start.

In the same way that play gives us a clear sense of how a child is faring in regard to the three Cs, it can also shed light on other areas of development.

Furthermore, given its centrality in kids' lives, play is useful in allowing us not just to understand them but also to help them: it's an amazing medium for supporting growth. Using play in this way—a kind of intervention I call "play-based support"—takes both skill and creativity. Because this kind of support can be so important for kids struggling with the three Cs, and for so many other children as well, it is explored in depth here.

Play-Based Support: A Powerful Tool

Using play to support growth makes sense because it allows us to join children in what they spend much of their time doing. But that's not the only reason that play is a good place to intervene. Play, after all, is what kids love. It's what connects them to their peers. It offers children an opportunity to express their difficult feelings in stories rather than having to act those feelings out in life. In addition, it helps children learn to wait, to plan, and to think. Play is a vehicle for them to gain problem-solving skills, too. In short, play is connected to children's learning, friendships, and overall well-being (Heidemann and Hewitt 2010).

When we engage in play-based support, our efforts are based on the same kind of see→think→do progression we turn to regularly. We use child-specific portraits to figure out where a particular youngster stands developmentally and what he's struggling with emotionally. We use our three-part flips to ask and answer questions about what isn't going well, what we hope to see instead, and how we might support progress. Our goals in offering play support will range from deepened connection to successful communication and from greater cue responsiveness and focus to more frustration tolerance and flexibility. They may involve attention to increased assertiveness as well. In addition, for some youngsters, a number of goals may connect to emotional expression and emotional healing. Play support can help with all of these. And because play is by nature pleasurable, intervention can become pleasurable too. That's true not just for the kids whose growth we're targeting but for us adults as well.

Choosing a Role for Effective Play Support

What does play-based support look like? How do we get started when we want to use it? I've learned much of what I know about the answers to these questions from my colleague Loretta Wieczner, who is a master at this form of intervention. A preschool teacher and then program director,

Loretta now teaches about the power and possibilities of play. She emphasizes the importance of making some key choices before jumping in to offer play-based support. She also outlines three possible roles teachers can take when engaging in play-based support. Many of the following ideas are hers. Some of the wording is as well:

- The first role is that of *observer*. In this role, we stand or sit close by the action, showing genuine interest in what is going on. Our presence communicates that what kids are doing is valuable. It reminds them to control themselves, too. For some children, a set of adult eyes nearby is all that's needed to make progress. An additional plus is that while we're observing, we can learn a great deal about where particular youngsters are getting stuck in their play and their development.

- The second role involves *intervening from outside the play*. We still place ourselves on the periphery of the play episode itself. In this option, however, we make comments and suggestions to children as they play. In Loretta's words, "we breathe new life and depth into the play, and help kids extend their experiences." In this role, we can also watch for the moments when easily frustrated children are about to lose their cool, and offer help and support for emotional regulation and problem solving before that happens.

- The last role requires us to *intervene from within the play*. This one can be the most fun and the most powerful, too. Loretta describes what it involves as playing the part of the "wise child." That is to say, the adult plays like a child but one with almost perfect social skills. The "teacher as wise child" has great ideas and offers them happily. She listens to others' ideas as well. When a challenging youngster is getting stuck and play is in danger of turning to war, the wise child often has a fantastic idea for making things work once again. "I know," she may chime in excitedly. "How about if Emily cooks soup and Joe cooks pizza and we make a restaurant that Lizzie can come to when she's hungry? Want to do that?"

From "Wise Child" to Adult Coach and Back Again

The wise child has wonderful skills as a playmate, but she has other ammunition on hand as well. Most importantly, she's a bit of a split personality. That's because she has an adult play coach residing within her, ready to jump into a particular play scenario at a moment's notice. Making that shift involves some acting. Thus, while a teacher's wise child voice is often eager and easy to hear, the adult coach's voice may sound more like an exaggerated whisper. In addition, that coach often frames her ideas in the form of a "we," so that the targeted child doesn't feel he has done something wrong. Here is what that assistance might look like:

"Billy," Loretta whispers as she models this kind of play support during a classroom-based mentoring session, "I'm noticing Owen's face. I'm not sure he likes our idea! Maybe we should ask him if building a castle is okay with him . . . You think we should, too? Okay . . . Do you want me to or do you want to? You? Great! You could say, 'Owen, is a castle okay with you?'" After Billy repeats the question to his buddy, Loretta whisperingly offers some more help until the negotiation is complete. Then her voice gets louder and her tone cheerfully flexible as she once again jumps back into the child role. As the period of play support continues, she switches from wise child to adult coach ten or twenty times, seamlessly and comfortably.

Envisioning Possibilities

Choosing a role for play-based support is just one element behind the mental "prep work" involved in using this kind of intervention successfully. Envisioning where you hope to guide the play is another. Is your goal to focus on extending story lines for a child whose language is limited and whose play is choppy and repetitive? Then how might you join him as a play partner, build on his ideas, and offer some of your own when he gets stuck? Is it cue responsiveness and sustained focus that challenge a particular youngster? What then? How will you use your facial expressions and your ideas to rein him back in when you see his attention wandering? What play ideas might be so compelling that his mind stays honed in on what you're doing for longer than usual? All of these questions point to the idea that it helps to be clear about what we have in mind before getting started.

Keeping Numbers Low and Engagement High

There is another aspect to play-based support that requires some prep work—thinking about and involving the other members of your team. Imagine that you have a child in mind for this kind of intervention. You know you're going to narrow your focus for the five, ten, or even twenty minutes you're at work. That will require assistance from the other adult or adults in your room. Thus, if you are going to drop in for some targeted play support, you have to cue a coteacher to do two things. First, she'll need to watch what is going on elsewhere and be ready to help any children that need a hand. Second, she'll have to keep an eye on numbers. You'll want only a few kids to join you—maybe even just one other if you are at the beginning of this process. That can be a challenge: when you sit down to play, you will probably be a magnet for many kids.

It is going to be your job to decide how many children you want to start with, and your coteacher's responsibility to direct other youngsters to different activities. Otherwise, the work you hope to do will go by the wayside. The youngster whose growth you're targeting may be too overwhelmed by the amount of language he hears swirling around him. He may feel distracted by the level of activity he is encountering. Or he may get so frustrated by the demands of multiple play partners that he will explode rather than learn. This last point leads to one more question to consider before offering play support: you won't in general want too many kids to join you in your efforts, but which ones in particular might work best as "play partners" for the child you're hoping to help?

Choosing and Using Child Co-facilitators

It is probably clear by now that part of your job in offering play-based support is to serve as a kind of "human glue" between a worrisome youngster and her peers. And when you are such a "gluing agent," other children become co-facilitators. Usually, those other children aren't aware of the role they are playing. All they know is that they are getting some pleasurable attention from a teacher and having a good time with a classmate. All the same, not every child makes a good teaching partner. That's why it can be important to think about which kids might be well suited for the role. A good example of this, found in the next chapter, lies in the way four-year-old Annie slowly helps her classmate Hannah come out of her shell.

Understanding Deeply, Proceeding Efficiently

This chapter's foundational explorations set the stage for the stories that follow. As Claudia and Nancy get to work with Hannah, Jenny, Kevin, Isabel, Jonathan, and Emilio, they're well aware of the power of connection, the importance of communication, the centrality of cue responsiveness, and the usefulness of play as a medium for intervention. Hannah's story comes first, unfolding over two chapters. The other children's stories are shorter. I offer these briefer narratives for a reason. When you're in a classroom with multiple children who are struggling, you probably hope to go through the reflective process for each one as quickly as possible—not more quickly than you need in order to see clearly and act effectively, but as fast as you can. Luckily, once the ability to generate individualized portraits becomes second nature, there is often some shorthand for what's going well, what's not, and why. There are usually some brief ways to describe the questions you will need to answer as well. For example:

Jenny has some temperament-based caution. Patterning has made it worse, and she now appears to be locked inside her reserve. What patterning do we need to change? What version of "seeding the day" might allow her to feel more safely connected and more steadily communicative in the classroom? How can we bring her parents in so they are partners in any efforts to make things better?

Or . . .

Emilio is a second-language learner and on the distractible side, too. His flitting around the classroom stems from both. He might have some mild language processing issues as well. How can we go down the developmental ladder with him, beefing up connection, communication, and cue responsiveness all at once? How will our knowledge about language acquisition—and second-language learning—help us do this in little doses?

These snippets are too short to be fully useful, but you probably get the idea. My hope is that the material presented up to this point in the book will allow relatively quick descriptions to work for you. In fact, what I do in the following chapters mimics how we proceed when thinking about children who trouble us. We move forward quickly when we feel grounded and clear about what is going on. We make time for further observation and reflection as needed. We seek out fresh ideas when our old trusted ones aren't sufficient. And we develop our own personal shorthand for the kinds of strategies we'll use for a particular child. "Let's get some circles going," we might decide in a team meeting. "We need to seed the day," we might declare. Or, perhaps, "We have to climb farther down the ladder, attention-wise. We've been up too high for where he's at." Such shorthand is a big part of my conversations with Claudia and Nancy as we think about helping the most worrisome children in their classroom.

8 Getting to Work with Hannah
Helping a Child with Dark Moods and a Dark Past

I have just arrived for my weekly visit to Claudia and Nancy's program when Claudia catches me in the hallway. Can I come observe soon? She and Nancy are really worried about Hannah.

Several weeks later, I'm sitting in Claudia and Nancy's room for a quick briefing before the children arrive. Nancy describes how Hannah, just four, seeks out a lot of adult attention. She is militant about getting it, and rarely willing to share it with other kids once she does. Hannah can be provocative, too, even downright mean. Her meanness is a puzzle, Claudia notes. First of all, it often appears to emerge out of the blue rather than in response to what someone has said or done. In addition, it feels odd given her age—the dismissive tone she uses makes her sound more like an alienated, rebellious teenager than a young preschooler.

Claudia and Nancy are also concerned that Hannah, an intellectually gifted child, seems bored with the classroom's activities. She rarely gets involved in the bustle going on all around her. Instead, she spends most of her time alone at the art table making beautifully detailed drawings or doing puzzles that even older children can find challenging. They are wondering: could it be boredom that is leading Hannah to act in such provocative ways? Nancy points out that Hannah won't be going off to kindergarten until a year from next September. They have been thinking that a more academically focused program might be a better option for her final year of preschool. Can I watch to see if that idea makes sense to me too?

In the course of our conversation it comes up that Hannah had a rough start in life; she was removed from her home at nine months due to neglect. The foster parents who took her in decided to adopt her, the teachers tell me, an adoption that was finalized just a few months back. This mother and father adore the newest member of their large family. However, they're increasingly worried—Hannah's inflexibility and meanness is taking a toll on their other children and on them as well.

There is clearly more to learn about Hannah, but children and parents are beginning to gather at the classroom's door. Claudia glances at the clock. One minute before opening time. As she stands up, her manner changes from relaxed to engaged. *Time to get to it*, she seems to be thinking. As the kids begin tramping in, the noise level rising by the second, I am aware of just how lucky they are to have teachers who care as much as theirs do. Will I be able to lighten Claudia and Nancy's load by doing some deep seeing alongside them? Now it's my turn to get to it. I settle in for some observation time, keenly interested in what I may discover along the way.

GO AWAY! (Come Close?): Noting a Child's Style of Relating

It is ten minutes into the classroom's first free play period. Hannah is sitting at the art table, drawing a house surrounded by trees with a cat standing by the front door. Her face looks serious, her eyes intent only on her work. Other children are drawing there too, chatting with each other as they do. Not Hannah, who looks up only when she wants to change marker color. Hannah stays at the table for a good twenty minutes, drawing with precision and skill unusual for a child her age. At some point while she's there, despite my efforts to stand unobtrusively nearby, I have the sense that she knows she is one of the children I'm watching. Is it my imagination, or is there a kind of silent growl flowing in my direction?

Do newcomers to the classroom make Hannah uneasy, I wonder? That wouldn't be a surprise given her history. Maybe introducing myself to the children at the table is a better idea. I walk over, kneel down, and smile at the other youngsters. Then I turn a friendly gaze Hannah's way. Most of the kids respond with interest. Hannah, on the other hand, looks at me with a face so impassive and eyes so devoid of expression that she seems to be communicating either complete disinterest or massive distrust. "I don't know if you remember me, but I was here a few weeks ago," I say. I smile again, meeting the eyes of whichever children are continuing to look up. "Sometimes I come to watch children play and to help teachers learn! My name is Deborah."

I am used to introducing myself to kids in this way and try to convey a gentle, open presence. My hope is to communicate to a group's reserved or mistrustful members that there isn't any pressure to engage. I want them to know that I will be a benign visitor in their room, interested both in what happens there and in them should we end up interacting. The latter is important because at times I find it helpful to move from the stance of observer to that of more active participant. That more active role allows me to get a better feel for how a particular youngster relates, communicates, and plays. It also gives me the chance to try out strategies I think might be useful to teachers and to see how they go.

As the other children appear to relax in my presence, I learn their names and talk with them about their drawings. Hannah, however, erects a wall of silence. She might as well have a large "GO AWAY" sign nailed up where I can't miss seeing it. And yet . . . might she be interested in but wary about who I am and what's to come? Is she hoping I will knock on the wall and ask to be invited in? It's hard to tell.

What Must It Have Been Like? Considering a Child's Early History

This is a moment when the task of "generating maybes" becomes central. Hannah's strong reaction to my presence undoubtedly fits into a bigger picture, and these teachers need to understand more about what that picture entails. Because right now, they're just puzzled and frustrated. Perhaps I can help. I begin wondering about how this girl's behaviors may connect to her early experience of neglect.

What must it have been like to be an infant who got so little of what babies need, or one who got what she needed on and off but not steadily? Was she ever physically hurt in those first months? Screamed at? Left alone, crying and helpless? Whatever happened, how might issues connected to attachment affect how she feels and behaves now? Do such issues bear on how she is responding to me? Might they also relate to the neediness, aggression, and apparent boredom I learned about just a few minutes ago?

Claudia and Nancy have emphasized that Hannah's language and cognitive strengths are impressive, and her artistic gifts and capacity for focus are already peeking out though the morning is young. A lot is going well for her. But in the land of "maybes," I'm starting to think that her strengths may be masking a basic vulnerability that involves trust and pleasure in connection. Does she ever brighten up? Will I see a smile when she seeks out adult attention? If so, will she melt into connection with ease, or will she carry her stiffness with her even when she's trying more actively to engage?

I'm wondering about some other things too. It's true that Hannah, at first glance at least, appears bored. Her face doesn't light up with interest in what other children are doing. She gives barely a nod to what has been set out on the science discovery table and in the dramatic play area. And there is a lack of bounce in her step and an aloof quality to the way she moves around the room that suggests disengagement. However, other signs point to involvement. She likes to challenge herself with difficult puzzles. She spends significant amounts of time drawing and loves books, especially books that feature cats. Even when she appears to be more engaged, though, Hannah's face maintains a consistently flat expression. Witnessing that expression is truly disconcerting.

The way Hannah seeks attention from her teachers is striking, too. As the group assembles for circle, she nestles up next to Claudia, eventually climbing into her teacher's lap when she notices Kevin aiming for the same place. It is clear that Hannah wants and needs *something*. But her face shows no signs of pleasure when Claudia responds to her with warmth. Instead, it remains flat.

Dumb Babies and Stupid Teachers: Seeking Windows into a Child's Inner Experience

As the class settles into group time, Hannah gives Kevin a push, staking out Claudia's lap as hers alone. He plops down next to his teacher, leans on her shoulder, and pops his thumb in his mouth. "Dumb baby," Hannah declares. Her tone couldn't convey any more disdain if she were a trained actress. A few minutes later, Claudia prepares to run a group activity. She gently tells Hannah that it's time to sit by her side, not on her lap. A loud "You're stupid!" quickly follows.

Hannah proceeds to place herself in the middle of the circle, lying belly down on the floor. Nancy attempts to direct her back to a spot that is less distracting to the other children. But Hannah is in "flop and drop" mode. Making it clear that moving her will involve a tussle, she gives Nancy a fierce yet dismissive glare. In a way, it is the most engaged expression I have seen her make, even though it is one that conveys anger.

After circle ends, it's time for toileting and toothbrushing. During this transition, Hannah is both oppositional and demanding. She wants Nancy's hand on the way to the program's shared bathroom, and shoulders Isabel aside to get it. She drags her feet, making it hard for the rest of the group to make progress. Muttering her way down the hallway, she comments on how the toilets "always smell gross." Then, while brushing her teeth, she begins staring at her reflection in the bathroom's mirror with a kind of impassive interest.

Impassive interest. I jot the expression down on my notepad. What an odd pairing of words, I find myself thinking. Is she both interested and impassive? Can a child even be both at once? There is a lot to puzzle through here, not just about Hannah's expression but also about another question of note: what is it about staring at herself in the mirror that is so compelling to this child?

What Would Happen If? Generating "Maybes" about Intervention

The work of deep seeing is in full swing here as I observe, wonder, then observe some more. Even as I continue to watch the class, a corner of my mind is considering the way Hannah is mesmerized by her reflection in the mirror. I think about how infants and their caregivers gaze at each other during feeding times, and about the kind of cooing, babbling, and smile-filled exchanges they enjoy together. Theorists and researchers repeatedly note how important this kind of affectionate back-and-forth is for the development of a child's basic sense of security and sense of self. Given that Hannah probably didn't get enough of such exchanges early on, is she seeking a kind of connected back-and-forth between her actual self and her reflection?

What would happen if we joined her at the mirror from time to time, watching her watch herself, and smiling as she noticed us seeing her? Could that be one piece of what we do to begin to make up for what she didn't get early on? Would such exchanges support her in feeling more connected? The maybes now aren't just about why we're seeing what we're seeing. They are also about what we might do to help out. I tuck them away and refocus on my observations as the class heads to the playground.

As the children play outside, Hannah crouches down in the sandbox. She takes a pail and shows no interest in sharing it, despite the fact that there aren't quite enough to go around. Directing a forbidding stare in the direction of anyone who comes near, she lets other kids know that they are not welcome to join her. I approach Claudia and Nancy, explaining that I have some hunches about Hannah, about how and why she's both holding back and lashing out. Would it be okay for me to move in and try some things with her when we get inside? That might allow me to learn more about who she is. It might give me a chance to play around with some ideas for how to help her, too. The thing is, I tell them, I'm not sure how Hannah is going to receive what I do. My trying to interact with her may make things more difficult for them. After checking in with each other, the teachers give me the go-ahead to try whatever comes to mind. I'm welcome to ask one of them to jump in if I get stuck, they tell me; they know Hannah can get pretty tough.

Claudia and Nancy, with their ever-present warmth, have just given me the kind of permission I always hope for as a consultant: to be as lost as they sometimes feel. That permission will allow me to try out some "maybe informed" ideas rather than having to be an expert who has all the answers. Perhaps it will help me relax into a stance of curiosity and playful exploration, too. I will need that kind of lightness in the face of what I am sensing is some heavily guarded darkness on Hannah's part. That is, if my hunches are correct.

A Place of Need behind a Wall of Protection: Storying Hannah's Experience

The hunches I've generated about Hannah might best be placed in the kind of "storying" first described in chapter 5. In this case, one might tell the story of a child who came into a world not able to receive her with the warmth, care, responsivity, and steadiness that all babies need. A child who, in the face of severe neglect of some unnamed sort, experienced what theorists call "toxic stress" (National Scientific Council on the Developing Child 2005, 1). It is widely accepted that such stress can have an impact on how children relate to others, and on their brain development as well.

What if certain places in Hannah's brain, which would have been activated by the experience of secure attachment, never got the input they needed? Might she be a bit like the children seen years ago in René Spitz's heart-wrenching film footage of orphanages overseas, children who were cared for physically but not relationally? After all, some of those children ended up with a more extreme version of the emotional flatness that Hannah displays. Perhaps, early on, an increasingly deadened response to deprivation—something that now comes across as a kind of prickly guardedness—was the only possible response for Hannah.

The story goes on: However it was that infant Hannah responded to what must have been a truly difficult environment, she was eventually welcomed into a large, loving family. There, she found a home filled with the kind of warmth she needed then and needs to this day. She developed language, and passions like drawing and cats. She had a safe bed, a safe home, and plenty to eat. She adapted.

Now, though, there is a funny set of contradictions. Hannah knows there is attention and warmth to be found and she wants both, perhaps even desperately. However, because early on she didn't experience adequate caregiving, she hasn't learned to take in warmth and respond to it. Nor has she fully developed the neural pathways in her brain that emerge in tandem with the kind of engaged back-and-forth she missed out on. She seeks out what she yearns for over and over again. But she can't fill up the place of need that's deep inside her, behind a wall of protection. Aggression and attention-seeking noncompliance follow, as does a disengaged way of being that looks a lot like boredom but isn't.

We Can't Go Back in Time—What Can We Do?

This is just a story, a set of maybes. Even so, it leads me to wonder about how I might knock on the wall behind which I see a needy little girl and—in my imagination—a needy infant who is lying alone in a crib, crying and unheard. Will it be possible to "find" that little girl (and the little baby she once was) in the midst of a busy classroom? What's happened already can't be changed. And I certainly can't barrel my way into Hannah's soul and rock her for hours, a bottle of warm formula in hand. What *can* I do? What can Hannah's teachers do? Researchers, theorists, and experienced clinicians emphasize that children are able to heal from early trauma, though it can take a while (Osofsky 2004). Many of them also suggest that as children begin healing from trauma emotionally, their brains start to "rewire" neural pathways to work more successfully too. So there is plenty of hope to be found. Now it's time to experiment and see how to act on that hope. That is to say, it is time to play around with what relationship-focused intervention might look like.

Kitty Cats and Cooking: Using Everyday Moments to Build Safe Connection

The kids are inside, and Hannah is once again at the art table. There is a forty-five-minute open play period before lunch—plenty of time to try out some ideas. I head over to where Hannah is sitting and crouch down. "Hi Hannah! I've been watching you draw. There's a kitty cat in this drawing, just like in the other one you made. A brown and black one this time. The other one was orangey. I'm guessing you might really like cats!" No response. I'm not expecting one.

Part of my plan is to beam some warm connection Hannah's way without anticipating anything back. And while not moving in too quickly in a way that might be threatening to her, *not being deterred by her lack of responsiveness either.* "Well, I sure like cats," I say. "They're so soft and furry. Sometimes it feels so good to pat them!"

I have been musing about Hannah's interest in cats. While on the playground, I heard from Claudia that the family has several at home with whom she loves to snuggle. Apparently, her parents have mentioned that Hannah can get too intense with these animals but is getting better at being gentle. I find myself wondering what her face looks like when she is stroking their fur. Does it soften with pleasure in a way I haven't yet seen?

These musings lead me to think about whether there is a way we can pique Hannah's interest and involvement by introducing some cat-related curriculum into the classroom. My mind flashes on a little girl I worked with years ago, one with an even more extreme history than Hannah. At first, this child would talk with me only if I pretended to be an electrical appliance. She would be one too. It was an amazing day when she decided we should be kittens and purr at each other. When she finally started calling me "Deborah," I almost began to weep. The world of people was beginning to open up for her.

I look around. Who in the classroom might be my partner in helping Hannah begin to join that world more fully? Annie, one of the group's most flexible and friendly children, is in the dramatic play corner, where she is pretending to cook for a family of doll babies sitting in high chairs. Wondering whether there's a way to get something going between the two girls, I begin talking to Hannah once again.

"Oh Hannah, I see that Annie is at the stove. I wonder what she's making. Want to come with me to go see?" I smile invitingly. In return, I get a dismissive shake of the head, no eye contact to be found. "Well, I'm going to go over and find out!" I say. "And I'll come back and let you know." Is that a sneer in response this time? Reminding myself that my plan is to act as if we're having an engaging conversation, I offer an upbeat "I'll be back!" Then I head off to the other side of the room.

In a voice loud enough that I hope Hannah can hear, I begin telling Annie that I am curious about what she's cooking. And that Hannah might like to know too. Once I find out what's up in the kitchen, I remark, I'm going to head back to let Hannah know. Annie explains that she is making vegetable soup with noodles.

We talk about what specific vegetables she's cooking with and how her babies are getting really hungry while they wait—they love Annie's special soup. With a nod of enthusiasm, I once again loudly broadcast my plan. "Well, I'm going to go tell Hannah. Can I come back and find out how the soup is coming along? It's starting to smell so good. Yum!"

Returning to the drawing table, I tell Hannah what I've found out. She looks up briefly, her face as impassive as ever. I feel a hint of encouragement. *At least she looked up this time. Could she be letting me in just a little? Is there a spark of interest in what Annie is up to as well?* I smile at Hannah once again, talking as if I have a fully responsive conversational partner. About how the vegetable soup smells just delicious. About how the babies are waiting to be fed and are very hungry. And about how Annie is waiting for me to return and find out how the meal is coming along. Would she like to come? I get another, rather grim shake of the head.

"Why won't this annoying woman get the message?" I imagine Hannah thinking. "Can't she tell I'm not interested?" I smile in response to Hannah's nonverbal message of dismissal, seemingly unfazed. "Well, I'm going to go check things out, Hannah. I'll be back soon to tell you if the soup is almost ready. Bye!"

I may be acting unfazed. However, after my brief moment of encouragement, I no longer feel that way. Yes, Hannah looked up. Even so, we're not even close to experiencing the kind of mutual connection I sense she needs. *I wonder if this is going to get us anywhere. It must be hard to hang in there with this child, day after day. Well . . . onward and upward. It's worth a try anyway. But I'm starting to feel like this smile is pasted on my face.*

I go over to Claudia, who is standing close to where Annie is playing. "I'm not sure if this is going to work," I remark. "But do you mind keeping an eye on what I'm up to? I'm trying to see if I can help Hannah to open up in a different way. She's pretty locked up inside herself, do you know what I mean?" Claudia nods. "I may look like quite the clown," I say ruefully. "Because I'll be running back and forth between Annie and Hannah, and I doubt Hannah will let me know if she's actually getting interested in what's happening. There's a method to my madness, though. Or at least I think there is!"

I'm not sure if I am explaining all of this more for my sake, to give myself a pep talk, or for Claudia's. Whatever the balance, by poking fun at myself, I am trying to set the stage for a kind of classroom-based work that may feel a little awkward to these teachers at first. That is, if my efforts lead to hints of progress to come. Claudia gives another nod. She'll be happy to pay attention to what is happening even as she continues on with what she's doing elsewhere.

She Does→We Do→She Does: Identifying Patterns That Hold Back Progress

One of the issues with children who are having trouble connecting is that the things they do (or don't do) have an impact on the people around them. Not infrequently, those people get pulled into a way of interacting that can lead to more of the same. (This is a version of the she does→we do→she does patterning first described in chapter 1.) For example, a youngster like Hannah emanates a surly disinterest and responds to warmth with flatness. After a while, the people around her feel rebuffed. They get used to what that child does, and they respond accordingly. Children tend to look elsewhere for play partners and buddies. Caregiving adults usually stick around. But inevitably those adults start to feel sort of flat themselves. They may begin feeling annoyed and helpless too.

Claudia and Nancy have been articulate about this phenomenon, with an honesty that is admirable and a sadness that is easy to understand. They care deeply about Hannah's well-being. But they're increasingly acting *as if* they experience genuine warmth toward her *rather than actually feeling that way.* The same thing happens to me as the smile I continue to offer Hannah starts to feel pasted on my face. When I meet Hannah's mother later in the morning, I sense she is in a similar bind. It is all too easy to start backing off from a child like Hannah emotionally even if not literally. No one likes feeling both rejected and targeted day after day.

One of Claudia and Nancy's jobs, then, is to think about their end of the patterns that are holding Hannah back from making progress. And it's clear: they haven't yet figured how to respond to her "flatness" in a way that allows her to begin engaging more fully. It is this challenge that I begin playing around with as I continue to reach out to Hannah, despite feeling a bit like I'm in a clown show and a bit like I'm doing battle with an invisible foe. I believe that somewhere inside of her Hannah craves connection. I sense she can't allow herself to get it. And despite the uneasy feeling that I am barging in on her protected world, I am trying to ignite a spark of interest that I can fan into a small fire of pleasurable connection. Will I see any results before the morning is out? If I do, how might the teachers and I come up with an approach that will build on what I've learned?

Countering Mistrust with Gentle Insistence

It is almost time for cleanup, lunch, and then pickup. Having filled Hannah in on the progress of Annie's soup making, I head back to the dramatic play area one last time. Annie looks up. The soup is ready, she reports. Her babies like it a lot. Would I like to try some? I take a sip and tell her that now I know why her babies gobble it up—it's fantastic. "Does Hannah want to try it, too?" Annie inquires. "There's one more bowl here if she wants me to pour her some!"

I tell Annie that I'm not sure if Hannah is hungry for soup. Would it be okay if I bring a bowl over to where she's drawing and see if she'd like to taste it? Annie, with her usual good cheer, is more than willing to ladle out a large serving. And off I go, reminding myself that Hannah may well decline her classmate's offer of soup and friendship. That is just what happens. But Hannah does look up—at me, at the soup, and then over at Annie—before turning back to her drawing. This time, she isn't frowning. That feels like a shift, even if a tiny one.

After the cleanup signal is given, Hannah stalls her way through tidying up the art area, needing a number of reminders from Claudia that she has a job to do. In response, she glowers at her teacher with an expression I have now seen numerous times through the morning. Then, dour-faced and solemn, she walks to the lunch table.

There is an empty chair next to the one Hannah chooses. As Annie heads over, Hannah looks at her, taps the seat forcefully several times, and looks at her again. The message couldn't be clearer. "Sit here! Sit here next to *me*!" Annie appears pleased by the invitation as she settles in next to her classmate. She puts her hand on Hannah's forearm and begins chatting animatedly about the soup she just made.

Turning to face Annie, Hannah nods. And even though her flat expression is ever present, a glimmer of interest makes itself felt all the same. By the end of lunch, the girls are talking back and forth. Hannah's contributions have a kind of monotone quality, but she doesn't clam up until the meal is over. Then she wanders off by herself as she waits for her mother to arrive.

I find myself feeling curious, hopeful, and more pleased than might be warranted given the very small amount of progress I have just seen. Those feelings increase after I check in with Nancy and hear that Hannah's inviting *any* classmate to sit next to her at lunch—and even more, her chatting through a meal—is highly unusual.

Building on Small Signs of Progress

There is just a hint of an opening. But such openings are exactly what we look for in early childhood practice. They offer pathways to growth and are what we build on as we continue to explore how to best help a particular child. In Hannah's case, these small signs of progress can serve as fuel for discussion and action planning during the team's post-lunch meeting. In the meantime, though, I'm wondering if I can find any more opportunities to support the connection Hannah has made with Annie, and to check out further possibilities for intervention. There is not much time left . . . Annie's father is on his way through the door.

As Annie puts on her coat, I go over to where her father is standing. After introducing myself, I mention that Annie and Hannah enjoyed being together this morning. Does Annie have time to go say a quick good-bye? Permission given, Annie heads over to the library corner, where Hannah is leafing through a book about cats. I follow close behind.

Annie looks at her new friend with eagerness. Her voice is eager too. "Good-bye, Hannah. See you tomorrow!" Hannah glances up. Her face is as impassive as ever, and she says not a word. There doesn't seem to be anything prickly about her expression, though. Instead, it almost looks blank.

"Hannah," I say as I crouch down to her level. "Annie had fun with you today! And she's excited that she'll see you tomorrow . . . You could say, 'Bye, Annie. See you tomorrow!'" I model what her good-bye might look and sound like by making my facial expression full of happy anticipation and my voice full of feeling.

Hannah stares at me and then at Annie. There is a long pause. And then, as if the sun just came out from behind a thick cloud, a huge grin emerges. She looks at Annie with real warmth. "Bye, Annie. See you tomorrow!" Her words convey real warmth too. Annie grins back and then skips away to her dad. Hannah's face goes flat once more as she settles back in with her book.

It is a truly amazing moment to witness. It feels as though some long-buried yearning has come bursting out and a place in Hannah's brain—barely used—has lit up like a one-hundred-watt bulb, with neurons firing just as they do for most children and adults. Then, suddenly, it's as if that bulb goes out again, and this lonely, traumatized little girl returns to the protected darkness in which she lives most of the time.

Claudia, who has been nearby watching, glances my way. "I'm not sure what just happened," she says. "But we've never seen her smile like that. I didn't know she could. It will be good to talk." Soon all the children are gone, and Claudia, Nancy, and I do a first pass at cleaning up. Then we sit down to discuss Hannah.

9 Getting to Work with Hannah, Continued
"Seeding the Day with Connection" and Other Strategies

After we get our notebooks out in preparation for our team meeting about Hannah, Claudia starts us off. "That was interesting," she says. "Hannah did have a different kind of morning, in some ways at least. But do you see why she's worrying us so much?" I do. We talk about how what I saw tallied closely with what she and Nancy described before the morning began. Hannah's seeming boredom. Her isolation. Her neediness and aggression, so closely tied to each other. The ways in which these teachers never quite know what's coming, nor what to do about it. This awful feeling that they're not really managing to reach Hannah even though they're giving her a lot of attention.

A Basic Dilemma: Reaching Children Who Need Connection but Fear It

Hannah's story shows how a youngster's struggle to connect can impact not only her deepest sense of self but also her feelings about her world. It raises an important question: How do we support kids who are needy yet hard to reach—children who have trouble responding to our efforts to help them feel trusting and fully engaged? This chapter explores the answer to that question in depth, by looking at the range of strategies we can use to strengthen feelings of safety and pleasure in connection. One of the most important is what I call "seeding the day with connection," a way of helping kids feel that we see them, cherish them, and will work to "find" them where they live—even if they reside in an angry or withdrawn universe all their own.

Hannah's way of fending off connection is one of many possibilities we see when youngsters are struggling with the basics of relationships. For that reason, a few other children appear in this chapter as well. Through their stories, I explore some options we can consider as we work to "seed the day" in different ways for different kids. The chapter serves another function as well. It makes clear that the various strategies it describes can be applied to many children—not just to those, like Hannah, who missed out on so much of what they needed early on.

Helping Hannah: A Child-Specific Approach with Universal Applications

Claudia, Nancy, and I talk further about how uneasy they feel when Hannah tries to hurt a classmate yet looks emotionally deadened. They haven't seen quite this combination before, they tell me. Can we talk about why she looks and acts this way? We begin discussing what issues might be fueling what they see, with her early experience of neglect looming large. Then we start sketching out a brief summary of what is going on.

Even that short summary takes us a while to put together. Hannah, we agree, isn't an easy girl to understand or describe. But eventually we have a picture to work from. Developmentally speaking, we agree, Hannah's capacities for communicating her ideas and focusing her attention are strong. Her abilities to connect, manage intense feelings, and be flexible are not. Emotionally, we believe she is carrying a load of mistrust and anger, along with a yearning for closeness that she doesn't know how to act upon. Her relationships with adults tend to be strained, and the patterns underlying those relationships aren't working in the service of growth. And her play? Her life at home? Unsurprisingly, she plays well on her own but rarely with others. Life at home is loving but hard.

Our portrait of Hannah is more fully fleshed out than the words I have just used to capture its basics. In its entirety, it sets the stage for thinking about where we hope to head—and what we can do to get there. Our goal, of course, is to help Hannah in all the areas just outlined. Our assumption is that problems with connection lie at the heart of much that isn't going well.

Will strengthening Hannah's experience of safe and warm connection help her begin to feel more content, relaxed, and open, we wonder? Will it allow her to manage her impulses better, be more empathic, and have a flexible response when she needs to share attention with her siblings or classmates? Will it make life at home more pleasurable? The answers to these questions remain to be seen. But it is connection we decide to target, first and foremost.

We begin thinking about approaches that can take advantage of things Hannah already loves to do (like drawing) and passions she has (like cats). We also want the team's efforts to rely on the power and pleasures of play as a motivator, and on the goodwill of other children in the classroom. Some of those children, we believe, would enjoy Hannah's company if only she'd make it available to them. Annie, it's already clear, is one of them.

Seeding the Day with Connection: One Strategy, Many Forms

The plan Claudia, Nancy, and I eventually design has a number of elements. Seeding the day with connection is the first. But describing this strategy as the plan's first element doesn't do it justice: seeding the day is an ever-present intention that runs through all the other strategies this chapter explores as well. In truth, it is so powerful—and important—that it runs through intervention for almost all kids. That makes sense. Safe and pleasurable connection rests at the bottom of the seven building blocks of development, holding up the other six. It lies at the heart of children's well-being too.

Seeding the day is not only an important but a wonderfully adaptable strategy. Given its central place in the work we do with so many kids, I want to explore more about what it involves by looking at a few of its variations. The child whose story anchors the first variation had a history similar to Hannah's: he was born into a family situation that was far from ideal. The results in his case, however, looked quite different than in hers.

"Love Bombing": Offering Connection Steadily and Straightforwardly

A few years back, I began describing the seeding strategy to a program director. We were discussing how her staff could help a four-year-old boy who carried around what felt like a backpack full of anger. Max's aggression could be frightening, and his teachers were working hard to keep their classroom safe. Things were under control (though barely), but they didn't seem to be improving. I shared the idea that underneath Max's rage might be a huge well of need—knowing his difficult history, I sensed that he was starving for warmth and didn't know how to ask for or get it successfully. Could we make sure he got steady doses of that connection all through his days in school, I asked? "Oh, I get it," the director said. "We need to love bomb this boy!" It was a great image, especially since his behavior sometimes left her staff feeling like they were living in a war zone.

Max responded eagerly to extra hugs, special errands with a favorite teacher, and friendly conversation about things that interested him. Big doses of eye contact, waves from across the room (what I call "innocent flirting"), and connection-saturated play support were part of the love-bombing approach, too. But it wasn't just that this child basked in the increased attention he received through the day. The team also found that as his experience of pleasurable and steady connection ramped up, his aggressive behavior began to die down.

This response is not unusual. Connection and care are powerful antidotes to anger and aggression. It's important to note, though, that seeding the day is often a necessary but not sufficient approach to moving things forward. Rather, it paves the way for adults to offer the skill-building assistance a child needs in the areas that cause him difficulty. For example, after a few weeks of "love bombing," Max became far more able to take the help teachers offered when he began acting out. Staff continued to shadow him for quite some time. They had to. However, their shadowing became more about offering support for problem solving and successful peer interactions during play than about keeping other children from getting hurt.

Max's responsiveness to what his teachers did serves as a reminder that difficulties with connection lie under the surface of many worrisome behaviors, not just the kind Hannah displays. However, not every youngster will respond to seeding that comes in the form of love bombing. Given her intense guardedness, it certainly doesn't feel like the right option for Hannah.

"Gentle Beaming": Offering Connection in the Face of Guardedness

Imagine for a moment that seeding the day with connection is like being in the early stage of a romance. *"I really like you and want you to know it,"* one person thinks to him or herself. *"What can I do to show you how I feel?"* Max, the boy I've just described, would accept a beautiful bouquet of roses with a huge smile and a hug. Hannah, on the other hand, would take one look at the bouquet, turn up her nose, and say, "I don't like red roses. Why didn't you bring yellow ones?" When presented with yellow ones a few days later, however, she wouldn't find those to her liking either.

The question is: if not love bombing for this particular girl, then what? In the previous chapter, I talked about trying to "beam" warm connection Hannah's way without expecting her to respond to it in kind. That might be the closest I can come to describing how we offer connection that children like Hannah can begin to receive. Beaming the energy of connection toward such a child is like directing a gentle, steady stream of light at places of guardedness, hurt, anger, or unmet need. Sometimes that light involves humor and playfulness. Sometimes it conveys interest in what the child is drawn to—cats, cooking, whatever the moment suggests. The light may take a while to penetrate the particular darkness in which that child is living. That's why, in the case of a youngster like this, we have to tell ourselves not to give up when we don't get much (if anything) back for a while.

This idea of projecting safety, warmth, and interest toward connection-challenged kids—without expecting a response—is one my teaching colleagues and I return to often. It is certainly a useful way to approach children like Hannah whose earliest experiences include terrible deprivation. It works well with kids who are locked up inside some intense shyness or reserve as well. It can also play an important role when a child has come to her adoptive family months or years after birth. Some youngsters in this last category have lived in orphanages or other group care situations since they were born. They haven't necessarily experienced neglect. But they may not have gotten an ideal version of attachment-focused early care either. These children often benefit from seeding the day to relax fully into their relationships. A brief look at one child like this helps demonstrate a third form that the seeding strategy can take.

"Slipping in Warmth": Offering Connection to Soften Stiffness

A few years ago, the teachers of a prekindergarten class asked if I would come in to observe a child who had been adopted from China at fourteen months. Now an almost five-year-old, Maya was able to do most things for herself. She could manage her snow pants, gloves, and boots without a hitch. She had taught herself to read. She would put on her painting smock without assistance and keep her paintbrushes from dripping on the floor. Then—all on her own—she'd carefully bring her completed artwork to the classroom's drying rack and lay it out flat.

Maya had friendly relationships with her classmates but rarely approached her teachers for help or conversation. She was fiercely independent with her single mother as well. At home, however, things didn't play out quite as calmly as they did in the classroom. There, her independence led to some difficult arguments when Maya's mother wanted one thing and she wanted another. Maya's teachers felt uneasy. This girl was not a behavior problem in the classic sense. However, something didn't "sit" comfortably. "It feels as though she's missing out on being a little girl," was how one of them put it. "We've had lots of kids who are reserved, it's not that. But Maya feels stiff, not shy. And even though she doesn't seem unhappy, we hardly ever see her smile."

After observing this child, I shared the staff's uneasiness. I had a worrisome thought: If Maya couldn't begin feeling closer to adults now, she might be in danger of looking to early sexual experiences or teenage drug use for her sense of vitality and connection later on. When I mentioned this fleeting thought to her teachers, they knew just what I meant. With this shared concern as a backdrop, the teaching team and I spent some time mulling over this child's early history and all that she had adapted to with such resilience and independence. Then they got to work, sending the energy of warm connection this girl's way—gently, steadily, and playfully. The frame we came up with this time? They would need to *slip in moments of warmth and humor under the armor of independence this girl wore all day long.*

For a few weeks, the teachers saw no signs that what they were doing was getting through. Then, one day, Maya accepted her first hug. Her body couldn't have been more rigid nor her face more serious as she took it in, but it felt like progress all the same. A few weeks after that, we began to notice a hint of a smile when staff would find her eyes from across the room or seek her out to tell a silly joke. It was a noteworthy day when Maya approached her favorite teacher and requested a hug of her own accord. Months later, we began to see her melt into a pleasurable experience of being cared for and loved. With our support and guidance, Maya's mother was trying a similar approach at home. She reported that, slowly, Maya was warming up and their arguments were calming down. The power of steady, safe, and pleasurable connection was at work once again.

Trusting Yourself, Trusting Your Colleagues

Clearly, seeding the day with connection can take many forms. That is not just because the children you encounter are all so different. Teachers are all different, too. Part of the art of teaching is learning approaches to intervention and then making them your own. The idea of love bombing, for example, may not suit you. If it doesn't, then there is surely another possibility that will work better *for you*. No matter what approach you choose, however, you'll need to remember that the process of reaching a connection-challenged child can be frustratingly slow. Along the way, you may have to keep reminding yourself that some kids are harder to like than others, and that it is those children who need our warmth the most. On occasion, you may need to turn to colleagues for a little warmth of your own. They will probably have some to offer. It is the rare teacher who hasn't been in the same boat. It's a boat Claudia and Nancy know well in regard to Hannah.

Turning on the "Light Bulb of Engagement"

Hannah has been wearing Claudia and Nancy down. But our conversation has helped them regroup—as conversation and reflection often do. One reason for this shift is that as we've been talking, Claudia and Nancy have begun picturing the baby Hannah once was, in need of rocking, cooing, and caring she didn't get. That picture, Claudia tells me, allows her to feel more compassion for Hannah than she has experienced of late. It clarifies the reasons behind her prickly ways, too. As a result, the idea of beaming steady connection Hannah's way makes increasing sense. But Claudia has a question. How can they do that effectively, given how guarded Hannah can be?

Claudia wants to talk about something else, too. She'd like to understand what happened when Hannah suddenly smiled at Annie at the end of the day. Hannah's good-bye was as affectionate and excited as that of any happy four-year-old. Was there something I did that helped that happen, she wants to know? If so, could she and Nancy learn to do the same kind of thing as teachers? Nancy turns to Claudia with confusion: she missed out on the unusual sight of Hannah's face radiant with pleasure and warmth. Claudia, with a kind of puzzled enthusiasm, fills Nancy in on what she witnessed.

What Claudia conveys to Nancy is that Hannah's smile was wonderfully *animated*, giving it a look very different from its usual flatness. Some thinking that comes from the worlds of theory and research may shed light on the reasons for this change. That thinking suggests that kids like Hannah have a place in their brains that is underused, one that's linked to the experience of attachment and connection. When kids have gotten the steady, warm connections they've needed early on (and have not been exposed to excessive stress), that same location in the brain works well, allowing them to feel fully alert and interested in what is going on around them (National Scientific Council on the Developing Child 2005). This way of thinking suggests that when teachers and parents reach such kids successfully—as I did when I helped Hannah register and respond to Annie's friendly good-bye—that place in the brain gets activated. Opportunities for growing and learning get activated, too.

Some years back, thinking about these ideas left me with a visual image that has since helped me and my teaching colleagues work with many children like Hannah. What I pictured was a brain-based *"light bulb of engagement"*—one that all kids have and that connects to their engagement with the world of people, ideas, and activities. When this light bulb is switched on, children are fully present. When it isn't, they are often lost inside of themselves in one way or another.

The image of a light bulb in the brain allows us to think about a number of issues in fresh ways. Connection is clearly one. But this image is also useful when considering kids who struggle to attend or communicate. Metaphorically speaking, we see light from that light bulb of engagement shining through the faces of children who are attending fully. It is dimmer on youngsters who are distracted. We see it glowing when kids understand and enjoy a book someone is reading to them. If they can't follow what's going on in a conversation between their friends, however, the bulb may seem switched off entirely. You may see the bulb's light beaming away when a child is playing with a friend in your classroom's doll corner, tenderly feeding her babies some cereal. That makes sense. Dramatic play with peers involves connection, focused attention, and successful communication all woven together. As a result, when kids participate in dramatic play successfully, the light bulb of engagement shines brightly.

Claudia and Nancy immediately take to the light bulb image. In Hannah's case, they agree, that bulb seems switched off much of the time. They're more than willing to shoot for moments when they help turn it on, even if briefly. Then, as more of those occur, they will work to boost the amount of time it stays lit up. How long the bulb shines before flickering out once again will be a gauge as to how things are going. Their pressing question is how can they do this?

We come up with a list. Claudia and Nancy will start keeping Hannah company and showing warm interest when she is doing something she enjoys, like drawing. They'll become a bit cat-obsessed like she is, bringing in books about cats, excitedly sharing magazine pictures of cats, telling stories about cats, and more. They'll also tell goofy jokes, reminding themselves that Hannah's response may be to stare at them impassively. What else? Perhaps they'll do some innocent flirting from across the room as they catch her eyes, then smile and wave. They will also try offering an occasional hug, or some rocking if she's willing, and let her know how good it feels to hold her close.

There is one more idea we toss around, although we aren't quite sure what it will look like. I share my interest in watching Hannah stare at herself in the bathroom's mirror. She seemed to be intrigued by her reflection, I note. Would these teachers be willing to do some work with mirrors and reflections—both with her and perhaps other kids, too? Might they try smiling at her in the bathroom mirror as she looks both at her reflection and theirs? It could be that something about such interchanges will be healing for this child. I remind us all about the power of attachment and the basic back and forth Hannah didn't get early on. It's so hard for her to let in the experience of connection, we agree. Maybe this kind of mirror play will help. The teachers commit to giving the idea a try.

Opening the Door to Peers and Play

Hannah is not only disconnected from adults. She is also disconnected from other children. Given that the team is now thinking that it's not boredom but emotional guardedness that is fueling her isolation, another goal looms large. That goal involves Hannah beginning to open up and enjoy the pleasures of friendship and play. Here is where the work Claudia and Nancy do can start building on itself. If they can be successful in forging a deeper connection with this girl, they'll be able to use their bond with her to help her engage in pleasurable relationships with other kids.

As Claudia, Nancy, and I continue our conversation, I offer the image of their becoming a kind of human glue between Hannah and her classmates. That is what I was experimenting with earlier, I tell them, when I kept crossing the room between Hannah at the drawing table and Annie at the stove. First I worked to connect with Hannah. Then I started experimenting to see if I could use her initial engagement with me to spark her interest in other kids. I instinctively chose Annie as my child co-facilitator, I explain, because she seemed so cheerful, flexible, and open. Is this something they'd be interested in trying? They would.

Adding an Additional Tool: Compassionate Emphasis

Claudia and Nancy fully understand the reasoning behind providing Hannah some "gluing" support for friendship and play. They are less clear about how they can offer that support effectively. One of the strategies that can be introduced in situations like this is what I call "compassionate emphasis." Understanding what this kind of emphasis involves and why it is such a helpful addition to any teacher's toolbox requires returning one more time to the moment Claudia is so curious about: the point when Hannah lights up with pleasure in saying good-bye to Annie. I want to deconstruct that moment even further.

It is highly unlikely that Hannah would have said anything to Annie—much less a good-bye full of enthusiasm—if I hadn't gone over to her, crouched down, and noticed that Annie had really enjoyed playing with her. In addition, I gave Hannah specific words she could say, and used both *an exaggerated tone of voice and a magnified facial expression* to model what an engaged good-bye might look and feel like. I like offering this kind of help because it frequently seems to move things forward. When I do so, I'm relying on a well-worn idea that helps with scaffolding, no matter what area of mastery we are targeting. The idea is this: when we offer scaffolding assistance to children, it isn't just our words that they need. What we do with our faces, say with our eyes, and convey through our tones of voice have a large impact on how we get through as well.

A British theorist, Peter Fonagy, has a lot to say about this idea. Fonagy believes that children learn to feel comfortable and calm inside of themselves through the ways their caregivers interact with them and help them *feel seen through someone else's eyes* (Fonagy et al. 2002). And he suggests that one way adults do this naturally is by using slightly exaggerated facial expressions and tones of voice. Those expressions and tones say, in essence, "I see what you're feeling. I see you!" Fonagy calls this quality "markedness" (2002, 9).

A father I once explained this idea to wryly called it "active listening on steroids." As mentioned earlier, I describe this quality as a "compassionate emphasis" that involves eyes, faces, and tones of voice. Whatever they decide to call it, Claudia and Nancy commit to making use of this kind of emphasis as they respond to Hannah and model the ways she can begin interacting with others. Teachers of many other children who are fragile, distractible, or explosive may find it helpful too. I have sometimes been astonished at just how powerful it can be when used well.

Building a "Curricular Bridge": Using Classroom Themes to Invite Healing and Growth

Hannah doesn't just need help in being able to take in the warmth and care her family and teachers offer her regularly. And although it is tremendously important, her being able to turn on the light bulb of engagement when socializing and playing won't be sufficient to foster the progress we hope to see either. Hannah also needs ways to heal from the terrible experiences she had early on. A creative use of curriculum can help.

Claudia and Nancy have already agreed to become Hannah's cat-obsessed partners. That won't be hard: Nancy has a kitten at home and can start bringing in pictures and telling cat stories. There is more to build on, though, in regard to cats. Our musings about Hannah have left us thinking that there is something about the softness and independence of these animals that speaks to her. Just as I did when I observed Hannah earlier in the day, we wonder together whether nuzzling the fur of her cats at home is deeply soothing to her in a way she needs and craves.

This leads to an idea. Can we bring some animal-focused curriculum into the room, curriculum that will help Hannah work on feelings about abandonment and loneliness, closeness and care? What if we set up a cat and dog hospital in the dramatic play corner for a few weeks? Or a pet store? What about one and then the other? If we follow through on this idea, can we bring in some relevant children's stories, too? Might we also offer some puppet-inspired (or teacher-generated) conversation about the themes we're targeting? Furthermore, if this approach proves successful and Hannah is drawn to play in new ways, can Claudia and Nancy sit with her and support her growth? Aiming for the biggest bang for the buck, can they also use such curriculum to help her connect with her peers?

The possibilities we are envisioning here relate to a fascinating and useful concept, that of "building a curricular bridge." This concept takes up several chapters in a wonderful book, *Unsmiling Faces: How Preschools Can Heal* (Koplow 1996, 123–41). There, author and preschool director Lesley Koplow and her colleagues offer numerous examples of how teachers can design curriculum that invites children to work through their emotional confusions through theme-related play and conversation. The topics they suggest range widely. There is a unit on "my special animal" that helps kids learn to manage transitions, one on "big and little" that encourages children to explore feelings about growing up (yet wishing to be small), and yet another on "boats and bridges" that supports kids in working through feelings about separations. There are many more as well.

The concept behind these specific examples is powerful: inventive and child-friendly curriculum can build a bridge between children's emotional lives and their experiences as thinkers and doers. Healing and increased emotional well-being often follow. Chapter 15 offers an example of teachers developing a curricular bridge targeting Brian, a boy who struggles with intense anger and who has become terribly frightened by the idea of zombies. Children like Brian and Hannah carry a big emotional load. They can often make use of yet another kind of help: assistance in learning to "embed" their feelings in play rather than act them out in life (Scarlett 1998, 59). That idea, too, is explored more fully in chapter 15.

Putting It All Together: A Plan for Hannah

As the teachers and I wrap up our meeting, we put the ideas we just explored into a brief action plan. Here is the list we come up with:

- They'll seed the day with connection—broadcasting warmth, interest, and curiosity without expecting a response, especially at first.
- They'll work to help the light bulb of engagement "switch on," and respond warmly when it does.
- They'll try acting as human glue in numerous ways—seeking out child co-facilitators, going from those co-facilitators to Hannah and back again—and, overall, looking for frequent opportunities to support increased connection and satisfaction in Hannah's relationships with peers.
- As Hannah becomes increasingly open to ongoing play with friends—something we hope will happen soon—they'll offer play-based support as well. Some of that support may include their taking the role of the wise child (see chapter 7), through which they'll offer Hannah the assistance she'll need to get comfortable connecting with others through play.
- They'll remember the power of compassionate emphasis and use it to model responses that Hannah can have to her peers. They'll also use that emphasis when relating just to her.
- They'll find opportunities for creating curricular bridges, especially—at least at first—using cat and animal-focused possibilities for involvement and healing.
- Above all, they'll remind themselves that progress will be slow, with an on-again, off-again quality that is to be expected. It may take quite a while for Hannah to begin experiencing the pleasures of openness and optimism. Even then, it's likely that her aggression and prickly ways will make their appearance from time to time.

Hope Comes First, Intervention Follows on Its Heels

We all agree that our plan is well considered and sensible. And knowing these teachers, I have no doubt that they will work hard to carry it out. But as our team meeting nears its end, Nancy suddenly appears unsettled. Before she's ready to embrace this plan, she blurts out, she wants to know something. With the kind of "damage" Hannah experienced early on—and that is Nancy's word, not mine—can she really be reached? Isn't it intensive therapy she needs? Are we trying to do something in the classroom that actually won't make a dent in Hannah's level of hurt and frustration?

Nancy has been an eager participant in our conversation. However, as she considers the task ahead, her discouragement makes sense. She and Claudia come to their work with a lot of skill, but Hannah's way of both shutting people out and acting out has made her particularly hard to help. The action plan we just laid out may make sense on paper. But is the effort it will entail going to pay off, she wonders? Claudia nods in response to Nancy's concern. She has been wondering the same thing herself.

It's clear that before they fully embrace the plan we have painstakingly designed, these teachers will need a dose of the hope I feel. Part of that hope comes from the small shifts I observed through my morning in the classroom. Part comes from the progress I have seen many children like Hannah make over my years of practice. And part comes from the collective wisdom of practitioners that have come before me, paving the way for us all. Children are resilient beings, those practitioners insist. With steady and compassionate help they can rebound from truly difficult circumstances.

Nancy, Claudia, and I remind ourselves that Hannah is, in fact, in therapy, and that her mother and father are committed to keeping her there for a while. That's good, we agree. Therapy with a skilled clinician undoubtedly helps children in her circumstances. Without it, it is sometimes hard to make progress at all. That said, I tell these two, I passionately believe that teachers' and parents' efforts are almost always more important than therapy. And what I saw through the morning leaves me profoundly optimistic. Can they inhale a bit of that hope until they have some of their own?

Claudia is more ready than Nancy to do so. She gives her worried colleague a pat and a smile. She will hold the hope for them both if she needs to, at least for a week or two. I promise to come back soon to see how things are going.

A Bumpy Road to Growth

As Claudia, Nancy, and I predicted it might be when we finished putting together our action plan, Hannah's year in the classroom involves both growth and continuing struggle. I see signs of the former, and happily so, in a visit to the classroom several weeks after my initial observation.

I enter Claudia and Nancy's room and am immediately struck by a few things. When I approach Hannah the first time and remind her of who I am, she nods. After I comment on a drawing she is making, she even replies. Her voice is flat, and her eyes when they meet mine are too. But she is "with me" a bit more than last time. Even more impressive is what I see at the art table. Jenny—silent as usual—comes over to where Hannah is drawing. She sits right next to Hannah and begins to draw herself. Hannah glances her way. "You're making a cat," Hannah notes. Jenny nods. For the next few minutes, the girls draw side by side, with Hannah occasionally commenting on what each of them is doing. Her face even shows a little animation, or so I'd like to believe.

I check in with the teachers. They have been doing plenty of back-and-forth gluing, they tell me, and now Hannah appears to be more interested in what is transpiring around her. Occasionally, they will succeed in helping her to become more actively involved, and she is even drifting toward the dramatic play area to watch the goings-on. Annie is the one she most likes to sidle up next to, and the girls have been talking at lunch. Hannah seems to like drawing next to Jenny, too. The fact that Jenny isn't talking yet is almost a plus, because it makes interacting with her particularly unpressured. Especially since Jenny has started smiling at Hannah and appears to enjoy her company.

Hannah continues to insist on a lot of attention, they note. And she still tries to shove Kevin out of their laps, often calling him a baby as she does. But other than that, her aggression and meanness seem to be lessening. They have tried the innocent flirting thing across the room, too. Sometimes, they get a hint of a smile back. It feels like the light bulb is turning on more often, though it isn't staying on for long just yet.

"Must We Start Back from Scratch?": Keeping the Long View

I keep checking in through the year. Not surprisingly, there are times when Claudia and Nancy have just begun to feel as though Hannah is really starting to open up when her guardedness and aggression reappear with a vengeance. That's hard. You probably relate to what these teachers feel at points like this. Imagine seeing things begin to deteriorate after you have noted a challenging child making real progress. You may know that what you're seeing is expectable. But what you *know* and how you *feel* can be different. Must you start from scratch once again, you exhaustedly wonder? That's the kind of discouraging question Claudia and Nancy ask themselves regularly through their year with Hannah.

Sometimes my job is to offer hope in the face of these teachers' discouragement. No, not from scratch, I remind them. Growth will likely start up again far more easily than it did the first time. Children don't lose the gains they have made when they slip back—those gains are real. And if we chart their progress over time, we usually notice that the top rung they make it to when things are going well is becoming ever higher. But moving forward in the face of significant challenges isn't easy, and it's usually not linear either. When a child heads down a ladder she has been climbing, we must head there too, remembering what originally helped her in starting the journey up.

It helps that Claudia and Nancy have each other. When one gets frustrated about how things are going with Hannah, the other often rallies. When they're both flagging, I do what I can to offer encouragement and help with brainstorming. I also support Claudia as she coaches Hannah's mother and father to do at home what we are trying at school. Claudia stays in touch with Hannah's therapist as well, so that there is communication about how things are going and what to do next.

The pet hospital curriculum is a huge hit with many of the room's children, and helps Hannah join more fully in the classroom's activities. She becomes the room's expert on cats and kittens, and the whole group eventually explores felines of all kinds. The week about lions has great appeal for Hannah. After all, they are powerful yet appealing animals who both care for their young and prey on others—a mix that offers more opportunities for her to embed her feelings in play and to explore them through curriculum.

At the end of the year, Claudia and Nancy are clear: Hannah should stay with them until she heads to kindergarten. Though no longer bored, she's not fully engaged either. But they know, without a doubt, that she needs her increasingly warm relationships with them to grow and thrive. Annie will be back, too. In June, it doesn't take an adult to scaffold her and Hannah's good-bye. The girls hold each other's hands as they walk out of the building, and their parents promise to keep them in touch over the summer. Hannah, we hope, is on the road toward deep connection and care.

10 Getting to Work with Jenny
Helping an Intensely Shy Child

Claudia and Nancy have asked if I'll take a look at Jenny. They're getting worried: it's already November, yet this four-year-old seems as frozen with caution as she was on the first day of school. The thing is, they tell me, it's hard to know why Jenny is having such trouble feeling comfortable in the classroom. Her history is so different from Hannah's. Life with her family has been stable and loving from the start.

Jenny's parents, Susan and Marilyn, are concerned, too. They have told Claudia and Nancy that their daughter looks very different when she is at home with them and her three siblings. That's not a surprise to these teachers. The minute Jenny sees one of her mothers arrive at pickup time, she begins to brighten up. By the time she heads out of the building, she is usually chattering away.

In the classroom, however, Jenny barely says a word. It isn't second-language learning that is causing her to hold back—Jenny's only language is English. Furthermore, it is doubtful that challenges in language processing are causing these difficulties. Claudia once overheard Jenny talking with Marilyn when she didn't know anyone else was around. Her vocabulary was impressive, and her way of making herself understood was too.

Jenny watches a lot, Nancy remarks. She is probably taking in far more than she lets on. And these teachers have noticed that when there is group singing, Jenny mouths the songs' words to herself. But that's about it. Jenny is a child who, like Hannah, spends a lot of time on her own.

Jenny's parents have told Claudia and Nancy that what is going on isn't new; their daughter has always seemed shyer than most kids. New things and new people seem to topple her sense of confidence, though she has plenty of that at home. She hates having sitters, even those she knows well. She won't talk to any of them for at least half an hour after they arrive—sometimes not even then.

Jenny loves school, her parents have emphasized, although it might not seem that way. Over dinner, she talks about everything that happened there and everything she did. But just seconds before she walks into the classroom, she turns into an iceberg. Nothing her mothers have tried has made things any easier. They're open to some help. Do Claudia and Nancy have ideas about what to do differently? Or is this just how it is going to be for a while?

Understanding Jenny: A Cautious Temperament Joined with Problematic Patterning

After observing Jenny in the classroom and then hearing more about her from Claudia and Nancy, I come up with a "best guess" picture of what's going on. With a focus on both temperament and interactive patterning, it suggests the following. First, there is probably a temperament-based reason behind what Jenny's teachers and parents are worried about. Research suggests that about 10 to 20 percent of kids react to novel experiences with caution (Kagan and Snidman 2004), and Jenny is most likely one of them. Second, Jenny's temperament seems to have led to some patterning that doesn't help her warm up. The other children in her preschool group, for example, respond to her as a sort of ghost in the classroom. She offers so little interactive energy that they no longer approach her to play. They don't speak with her when she is nearby either. They probably feel it's not worth it—they know she won't answer.

The problematic patterning I am positing doesn't involve just Jenny's classmates. Claudia and Nancy appear to be engaging in it as well. Sometimes they ask Jenny questions she never answers. Then they answer for her, with their best guess as to what she might think, need, or want. At other times, they reluctantly but resignedly leave Jenny to her withdrawn state. Each of these situations is likely contributing to the way Jenny seems to be increasingly imprisoned in her reserve.

My thoughts about Jenny include reasons for this unfortunate outcome. When the teachers ask her questions she can't get herself to answer, they unwittingly amplify her feelings of intense discomfort. But if they leave her to her own devices, she remains stuck in her state of quiet isolation. The problem is that like so many teachers dealing with a child as cautious as Jenny, Claudia and Nancy sense that what they're doing isn't helping but are stymied about what to do instead.

Based on information I've gotten from these teachers, it appears that Jenny's parents feel much the same way and are also involved in patterns that aren't helpful to their daughter. These mothers have told Claudia and Nancy that Jenny hides behind them, not only when she enters the classroom but at parties, community picnics, and family gatherings too. Apparently, they sometimes tell people she is shy and speak for her. Sometimes, however, they nudge her forward and push her to at least say hello. She never does.

The picture I have of what is going on for Jenny is just about complete. In summary, whether out with her family or in school with her teachers and classmates, I envision this girl as like a musician who freezes up at performance time. Her inborn temperament makes the experience of being "in the spotlight" truly overwhelming for her. Her hiding behind her parents and her silence in the classroom are both efforts to make that spotlight go away.

Seeding the Day? She Won't Let Us!

Claudia, Nancy, and I talk about my picture of what is going on for Jenny. It makes a lot of sense to them, they tell me. We begin putting our heads together about how to help her, and agree that seeding the day with safe connection will be important. If Claudia and Nancy are successful in their efforts to do that, we hope Jenny will begin coming out of her shell. But the teachers are wondering something: what will it take for them to be successful? Due to the power of her temperament-based caution, Jenny clams up whenever they approach. She'll nod or shake her head if they ask her a yes or no question, but that is all they can get from her. Sometimes even such questions appear to make her uncomfortable.

The plan we come up with is indeed based on the idea of seeding the day. But it will include an emphasis on offering safe connection *without expecting a response*. That way, the work Claudia and Nancy do will begin to address the patterning that hasn't been helpful. (Our discussion, in fact, has led us to wonder if the teachers have unintentionally been making Jenny's experience of caution even more extreme.) Jenny needs safe connection, but she can't yet respond with words, we realize. Thus, Claudia and Nancy will start approaching her and animatedly chatting about anything of interest. They'll bring in silly stories from home or humorous things they saw on television. They'll talk with Jenny's parents about what she has been up to and chat at her (not with her) about what they have heard. They will do some "innocent flirting" from across the room, too.

Through all of these efforts, Claudia and Nancy won't expect Jenny to demonstrate interest in what they're saying with words nor even with nonverbal signs of engagement. They do know she has a great sense of humor, though, because sometimes they catch her holding in a laugh when a classmate has done something especially funny. So, in addition to some silliness, joke telling may be an interesting option. They decide to bring in some joke books. They'll make a daily habit of offering one or two jokes to Jenny and any friends who are nearby, and catch Jenny's eyes during the punch lines.

Turning Connection On but the Spotlight Off

Much of this work parallels what the teachers are doing for Hannah, but there is one important difference. In Hannah's case, Claudia and Nancy don't expect a response. In Jenny's, *they won't ask for one.* Here is what this shift entails. Remember that with Hannah, seeding the day sometimes involves asking a question that she isn't required to answer or that she can answer in the negative. ("I wonder what Annie is making at the stove. Want to come with me to go see?") With Jenny, however, these teachers will frame their words so that, except when necessary, there is almost never a question addressed to Jenny at all.

For example, Claudia might tell a goofy story. At its end, she'll refrain from saying something like, "Don't you think that's silly?" Instead she might remark, "Jenny! That was so silly when my sister's yogurt splashed on her puppy's nose! That puppy looked like a circus dog!" Then Claudia will smile at her quietest student. In another instance, Nancy might go over to the art table where Jenny and Hannah are drawing. "Jenny," she'll say, "I see that Hannah is making a picture of a brown cat. I bet he's so soft. Hannah loves cats. I wonder if you do. Hannah probably wonders too!" Then she'll turn to Hannah and begin chatting about the different kinds of cats Hannah likes to draw best.

Note that in this last example, Nancy is *wondering but not asking. Then she quickly shifts her attention to a different child.* That is part of the seeding strategy, too. The message she's trying to send: "I see you. I am interested in you. But you don't have to let me in until you're ready. I'll keep inviting you to come closer. One day, you'll relax. Your words will feel okay about coming out. Until then, we can still connect!"

There is a reason for this shift from not expecting to not asking. Consider the patterning that has been in place. Every time someone poses a question Jenny doesn't answer, she experiences the uncomfortable "I'm in the spotlight" feeling. That leads to more rather than less frozenness. If teachers can beam warm connection her way without asking for a response, she may begin to relax. And if they do that over many days and weeks, Jenny can get used to the idea that the dreaded spotlight feeling won't come up too often. At that point, her guard may start to come down, and she'll be more able to fully engage without words. That nonverbal engagement may eventually make it easier for her to feel comfortable talking.

Responding Casually to Signs of Progress

The hope (and likelihood) here is that Jenny will slowly begin to speak up. If and when that happens, it is going to be important for her teachers to *show almost no reaction other than friendly but mild interest.* In addition, *they'll need to take their focus off of her as soon as possible.* This sounds easy, but it isn't. When children like Jenny finally begin to speak, we notice. We are delighted and make that clear. We respond with extra warmth or even a happy, "I knew you had some words in there!" That is understandable. We have been waiting for a long time. However, a marked reaction is usually a mistake. When a reserved youngster begins to speak out loud, it is usually a sign that his caution is just beginning to ease up. If we put too much focus on his words, that caution may once again increase. Thus it is better to turn to another child quickly and interact with them. If we can insert something about the cautious child into our dialogue, all the better.

Here is what this idea might look like if it were possible to fast-forward to a moment further along in the process of working with Jenny. (And, in fact, although this is a fictional exchange, I see something quite similar when I visit the classroom later in the year.) Imagine, now, exactly the same words as those you read earlier. Nancy, Jenny, and Hannah are back at the art table.

"Jenny," Nancy remarks, "I can see that Hannah is making a picture of a brown cat. I bet he's so soft and furry. Hannah loves cats! I wonder if you do too. Hannah probably wonders too . . ."

Now Nancy turns to Hannah and says: "Jenny is looking at your picture, Hannah. Do you think she likes cats too?"

"Maybe," Hannah replies.

"I do," Jenny whispers.

This is a crucial moment, one after which Nancy must take the spotlight off of Jenny. Thus, this teacher quickly addresses Hannah once again. "Oh Hannah, Jenny does like cats! Maybe sometime you can show her your favorite cat book. The one with the tiger cat in it!"

Supporting Play and Conversation with Peers

Jenny's action plan mirrors Hannah's in another way, in its efforts to promote first steps toward successful and pleasurable interactions with peers. In this imagined interchange at the art table, Nancy isn't just taking the spotlight off of Jenny while inviting adult-child connection. She has two other goals in mind as well.

The first is *to begin redrawing the classroom's circle of play and involvement so that Jenny is on the inside, not the outside.* The idea here is that some unfortunate interactive patterns have left Jenny's peers experiencing her as a kind of ghost in their midst. Their picture will need to change in order for them to include her. With a little help, they'll probably be willing to make this mental shift. Preschoolers have wonderfully short memories and often happily include a particularly cautious youngster once he has made himself available for some fun.

Nancy's second goal is *to offer adult support for child-to-child connections.* How does Nancy attempt to achieve both goals in the hypothetical art table example? Part of her effort involves weaving Jenny's name into the conversation regularly as she talks with Hannah. (She weaves Hannah's name in as she talks to Jenny, too.) In addition, she uses her growing connection with both girls to help them notice and get interested in each other.

This double-focused version of gluing is enormously useful. It certainly can be applied to conversations at the art, science, or lunch tables, places that offer many opportunities for adult-supported peer connection. Such gluing can be used, in a slightly different form, to support successful peer play. It works in the housekeeping corner and can be adapted to support block, train, or dollhouse play, too. In fact, anywhere kids like to go, a mix of gluing and play support can be initiated and is tremendously helpful to kids like Jenny.

The "Wise Child" as Gluing Agent

It's about a month after the teachers start implementing their action plan for Jenny, and I'm in for one of my observational visits. Jenny still talks rarely, the teachers tell me, though they have witnessed a few moments of success. Even with her continued reserve, however, I note that she is visibly more relaxed. She laughs and smiles regularly, too, and seems increasingly willing to play next to other children.

Other than drawing next to Hannah, Jenny's favorite spot appears to be the classroom's dramatic play area. The area is filled with doll-sized high chairs, dolls, cooking supplies, dress-up clothes, doctor kits, fire and policeman outfits, and a cash register. The cash register gets woven into the corner's house play quite regularly, in a way that only makes sense if you know preschoolers.

Jenny is tending to that register. Annie, as usual, is tending to her babies. Claudia, I can see, is hovering nearby. My guess is that she's wondering what she might get going, ready to jump in as play coach or "wise child," whatever the moment might inspire. I am right. She cues Nancy to keep an eye on the rest of the room so she can hone in on the action. Nancy also knows to gently redirect other children once one or two more have arrived in the dramatic play area to join the fun. Too many kids and Jenny will shut down. She may shut down anyway.

One of Annie's babies doesn't want her baby food—it appears that she has a stomachache. Claudia's attention is piqued, she tells me later: doctor play is often interesting to children. Might Jenny catch a ride on that theme?

Claudia jumps in. "Oh Annie, does your baby have a tummy ache?" Annie, the ultimate child co-facilitator, goes along. Yes, the baby does, she tells her teacher. "I wonder if she needs to go to the doctor?" Claudia asks with concern. Annie isn't sure. Claudia turns to Jenny. "Jenny!" she exclaims. "Annie's baby is sick! She might need a doctor! I wonder where the doctor's office should be?"

Elizabeth, one of the classroom's four-year-olds, has just wandered over. "Over here!" she replies to her teacher's question. Elizabeth grabs the doctor kit and heads to a free table nearby. "I'm the doctor," she declares. "Bring that baby here!" Elizabeth is always game to play but is on the domineering side. Using her as another co-facilitator may require some artistry on Claudia's part.

"Jenny, Elizabeth is going to be the doctor," Claudia announces. She pauses, then looks at Elizabeth encouragingly. "You're a busy doctor! What should we call you?" Elizabeth wants to be "Dr. Liz." "So many babies to help, Dr. Liz!" Claudia says. "So many children who need you when they're sick!" Claudia sounds admiring but thoughtful. "Maybe it would be good to have some nurses to help you in your office!" Dr. Liz nods. In response, Claudia adds, "Maybe Jenny and I can help!"

Dr. Liz nods again. "Annie!" Claudia's voice sounds concerned in a way that tells the kids she's now "inside" the play. "There's a doctor's office right here. Do you think you should bring your baby over? Is her tummy getting worse?" Annie begins wrapping her baby in a blanket. She doesn't seem to notice that her other babies will be left alone. Preschoolers shift story lines rather easily.

Claudia turns to look at her shyest classroom member. "Jenny . . . I think Annie might be on her way to the doctor with her baby! Maybe we should go over and help out. Because the thermometers need to be washed and the medicine isn't ready. And Dr. Liz is so busy!"

Elizabeth puts on a harried expression as she bustles about her office. Jenny sidles up to Claudia, seemingly interested in her potential role. Claudia hands her a thermometer and a bowl with some pretend soap. "Dr. Liz, Jenny and I will get the thermometers clean," Claudia calls out. "Is there anything else you need us to do?" Elizabeth reminds Claudia that she's going to need some medicine too. "Jenny, we need medicine! Where can we find some? Maybe we should look around . . . I'm not sure where it is. And that baby is sick!"

Jenny starts looking. "Annie, Dr. Liz. Listen," Claudia's voice once again tells kids she's solidly inside the play scenario. "Jenny and I will find the medicine." She turns to address Annie's doll baby. "Don't be sad, baby, you'll feel better soon," Claudia says comfortingly. "We'll help you. Your mommy is worried about you!"

Annie—the quintessential worried mother—mimes a concerned face and rocks her baby. Dr. Liz reaches for the doll, and Annie hands her over carefully. *Don't drop her*, she seems to be saying. The doctor, serious and confident, lays the doll down on a table. "What's the matter, baby?" she asks.

"Waaa, waaahhhhh." Annie is now playing both mommy and baby. Claudia looks at Jenny. "That baby seems pretty sick, Jenny. Do you have the thermometer ready for Dr. Liz? Is it all clean? Dr. Liz will need it soon." Jenny seems increasingly roped into the play theme as Claudia goes on. "I hope that baby doesn't have a temperature that's too high," she says worriedly. "But we better have our medicine ready just in case."

Jenny nods and hands Elizabeth a small plastic container she's found. "Here," she says quietly. "Medicine." She looks at Elizabeth gravely. Will the baby have a high fever, she seems to be wondering? Will she be okay? Claudia jumps in quickly. "Oh good, Doctor Liz! Nurse Jenny is right here. Let her know if there's anything else you need!"

Jenny has said some eagerly awaited words during classroom play. Yet the baby is so sick and the play so compelling that no one but Claudia has noticed. Jenny may not even have noticed herself. That's what Claudia has been aiming for. But how does she get there? First, she weaves Jenny's name into an unfolding play narrative, thereby drawing the classroom's circle of play so this child is inside, not outside, of it. Then she joins Jenny as a "we" player rather than asking her to be an "I" player before she is ready. In addition, she offers Jenny an interesting role as a sidekick who can talk—or not. And she welcomes her involvement (and eventually her words) as if both are a given rather than a surprise. Furthermore, Claudia does all of this in a particularly artful way as she inhabits a role halfway between play coach and wise child.

"I'm Hiding . . . Can You See Me?": A Curricular Bridge in Action

A month later, in another visit to Claudia and Nancy's classroom, I notice that there are many pairs of sunglasses lying around. Apparently, the class recently celebrated "Beach Day" as part of some curriculum on the seasons. The sunglasses had been such a hit that the teachers have left them out. A number of the group's children are enjoying putting them on and off. On a whim, I grab a pair, place them on my nose, and head to the dramatic play area, where Jenny is playing by herself at her beloved cash register. Outside the circle of play once again, I notice. I stand by the register and, with a mix of silliness and high drama, ask Jenny if I might buy some gum. Once she has rung up my pretend purchase, I start chomping on it. Loudly.

Jenny begins giggling. "Oooh lah lah," I declare. "I do love my gum!" I prance around a bit. "And I love my glasses, too. I bet you can't see me, Jenny!" Jenny nods her head up and down with an intensity and eagerness that are palpable. If she were speaking, I'm pretty sure she'd be saying, "I can too!"

"No, you *can't* see me!" I respond. "Because they're dark glasses. I'm hiding, Jenny!" The grin that accompanies my definitive statement lets Jenny know that I'm not completely serious. She lets out a belly laugh. Then I hand her a pair of sunglasses. "I'm being silly Jenny . . . I'm pretending! You can too if you want to," I say. "I like to pretend no one can see me when I wear these!"

I am just in a goofy mood. It has been a long week, and it's good to see Jenny making progress. I'm not too worried about pushing her away, because I am perfectly willing to prance off to another child if she finds my silliness too intrusive. But perhaps because I'm having fun, she doesn't. Out of this playful moment comes some conversation with Claudia and Nancy. Can we build a curricular bridge about hiding and being seen? And about having control over both?

The teachers find the idea compelling and enjoyable. With their help, the children start exploring the idea of hiding behind glasses, costumes, and masks. They learn about animals whose skin color changes when they need to blend into their surroundings. They read about how turtles use their shells, too. Then they play with turtle puppets, having those puppets pull inside their shells when they want a break. Jenny is an eager participant in this curriculum. It's not that this theme has a magical impact on her ability to come out of hiding herself. But it helps. Working through some of her feelings via this curriculum, embedding those feelings in play, and having many opportunities to engage without words until she feels safe to use them, Jenny ends up having a year full of growth.

Parents and Teachers, Hand in Hand

Part of Jenny's growth is supported by some changes in the way her family responds to her. With encouragement and guidance from Claudia and Nancy, Susan and Marilyn make a commitment not to ask their daughter to say hello when she first enters a new situation. There will be plenty of time for that when she is a little older, they realize. Instead, they talk comfortably with her by their side, allowing her a chance to feel that the spotlight won't turn on, at least for a while. At the same time, they work on talking less *for* Jenny when she is locked up with caution. They've come to understand that when they speak for her in this way, they don't give her the chance to get comfortable enough to speak for herself.

Claudia and Nancy also encourage the two mothers to introduce Jenny's babysitters and relatives to a different way of spending time with her, and those adults agree to try interacting steadily with Jenny without asking unnecessary questions. Susan and Marilyn start previewing where they are going with Jenny as well. As part of that previewing, they help her think of things she can do once she arrives at their intended destination, things that will help her feel okay until that "scared feeling" starts to get smaller. They remind her that the feeling will get smaller if she gives herself a chance, and tell her it's okay to take her time.

As a result of their ongoing conversations with Jenny's teachers, Susan and Marilyn institute one more change. Whenever there is time, whoever does the drop-off starts coming into the classroom at the beginning of the morning and sits at a table with her daughter, trying to act like a wise child/play coach herself. It takes both mothers a while to learn what those roles look like, but Jenny loves the mornings when they get it right.

Jenny is still shy at the end of the year. She may always struggle to feel comfortable quickly in new situations—we don't know. But instead of that temperament-based quality dominating so much of her experience when she is away from home, she is beginning to have options. She is learning to take her time, catch her breath and, when she's ready, to reach out. And in the way preschoolers so often do, her peers have responded to her increasing openness with openness of their own. No longer the group's "ghost," she has a valued place as a quiet but kind member of the classroom.

11 When Home Has Been Hard
Helping Children Climb (or Re-climb) Developmental Ladders

Three-year-old Kevin is sucking his thumb. Glassy-eyed, he slumps in Claudia's lap like a sleepy toddler. When she puts him down, he begins to wander. He stops at the block corner, gazing vaguely at the elaborate zoo his classmates Alex and Maria are making. Then he sits beside them. Slowly and haphazardly, he begins placing one block on top of another. I watch Kevin's expression with interest. Is he exhausted? Tuned out? Unhappy? It's difficult to even venture a guess.

The tower is now four blocks high. Suddenly, with no apparent feeling of "There, I did it!" and no need to knock his creation down with a satisfying bang, Kevin gets up. Then he begins to wander yet again. Kevin's eyes light on Nancy. Now, he appears more purposeful. He heads her way and leans against her leg. "Hi, Kevin." Nancy's voice has a high-pitched warmth that I associate with the mothers of babies. "Did you want something?" He turns toward her and raises his arms in the air. Nancy scoops him up and holds him close. His dazed look shifts to one of contentment as he rests his head on her shoulder.

Different Approaches, Common Ground

This chapter tells the stories of two children. The first is Kevin. The second is an almost five-year-old named Isabel. Both Kevin and Isabel struggle in ways that leave them looking less engaged than other youngsters their age. Kevin has experienced not only a hard start but some hard times, too. He appears profoundly delayed, and Claudia and Nancy's job will be to figure out how to help him climb a number of developmental ladders. Isabel's situation is quite different. Responding to a particularly stressful period in her family's life, she has fallen down some ladders she had previously ascended. The teachers' job in her case will be to help her find her way back up.

How these teachers get to work with Kevin and Isabel involves some striking contrasts, and for good reason. They are very different children struggling in very different ways. But the strategies Claudia and Nancy turn to for both have much in common: they all rely on the power of connection to spur developmental mastery or emotional healing. Many of these strategies will be familiar by now—seeding the day, compassionate emphasis, and play-based support, for example. A few are introduced for the first time here. Overall, the chapter highlights an important aspect of effective intervention: mixing and matching approaches based on a particular child's unique situation can make all the difference in our ability to promote growth and healing.

Delayed or Disengaged? Getting to Work with Kevin

Claudia and Nancy have asked me to observe Kevin and, as usual, give me a heads up before I take a look. A child who often has his thumb in his mouth, Kevin seeks out their laps constantly. Even when he's more active, they tell me, it's hard to get him to move through the day successfully. He bumps into other children when it's time to line up for the classroom's midmorning bathroom trip. He wanders away from the line as the group heads down the program's long hallway. If given a teacher's hand so that he'll be more successful—which, Nancy emphasizes, they do regularly—he slumps to the floor. The teachers do manage to get Kevin to the bathroom eventually, of course, but it's a draining process. Not only that, once he's there, things don't go any more smoothly: he tends to just stand by the toilet without pulling down his pants.

Claudia makes clear that these are just a few examples of what goes on all day long. The truth is, Kevin is strikingly unable to manage the overall expectations they have for the children in their classroom. As a result, she and Nancy often end up carrying him from here to there as if he were much younger. They do a lot of things for him too, she tells me. He can't put on his coat by himself, wash his hands by himself, or pour his milk without spilling it every time. Claudia and Nancy have tried working with Kevin on these skills. It's not that he seems oppositional about learning them, she emphasizes. It's more as if he can't focus on the basics of what they ask him to do.

Now the teachers begin filling me in on Kevin's troubling history, relating that he has already been removed from his single mother's care twice. Right now he is back with her once again, and things at home seem to be going better for the time being. But sometimes these teachers wonder whether she will be able to care for him adequately over the long haul. They worry about Kevin every day, they tell me, and can't imagine what his future holds. "He seems delayed in so many ways," Claudia remarks sadly. "And I don't think it's because he was born with challenges."

Observing Kevin: Worrisome Challenges, Considerable Strengths

As I settle in for some observation time, I see why the teachers are so concerned about Kevin. At the same time, it becomes apparent that he's not always in the dazed state that is setting off alarm bells. He is very drawn to puzzles. He's skilled in putting them together, too, suggesting that his visual-spatial competence is strong. And as he works on a puzzle, Kevin's face seems more alive with engagement. Kevin enjoys the time he spends playing on the classroom's computer as well. There, his back gets straighter, his eyes seem more focused, and his skill level shines through. At one point, three-year-old Alex watches him play one of those games. Alex has some questions, which Kevin answers willingly. I'm relieved. It turns out his language development is far more advanced than I had feared.

When I ask Claudia about the language issue, she confirms what I have noticed. Kevin has a large vocabulary, and on the occasions when he is tuned in and interested, he uses it well. His communicational abilities, she tells me, actually seem more advanced than many other kids his age. It's just that he doesn't talk all that often. Claudia remarks that she and Nancy believe Kevin is intellectually gifted. It is not only his skill at puzzles and computer games that have led them to this conclusion. There have also been a few times when they have been reading a book that tweaks his interest and, suddenly, he'll have a lot to say. At those moments, it becomes clear that he has been learning and thinking even at times when he appears to be lost in a daze. All of this, though, leaves Claudia confused. Why is a child who is occasionally so "with it" usually so out of it, she wonders?

A Child Thirsty for Connection: Storying Kevin's Experience

When Claudia, Nancy, and I sit down together, we come up with a story that helps make sense of Claudia's confusion. Kevin has had a particularly hard start. His now twenty-two-year-old mother has tried as best she can to take care of him. But when he was just under a year, he was removed from her home due to neglect. The best she could do, it seems, wasn't enough to fill his needs. Kevin, like Hannah, very likely missed out on some of the basics of connection.

From what the teachers have learned, the foster home where Kevin then lived was a loving one. His foster parents became very attached to him—and he to them. Perhaps it was during his time with those parents that his language development started to kick in. Perhaps it was also with them that he learned to seek out laps and hugs. Whatever the specifics, Kevin was eventually returned to his mother's care. Then he was removed a second time, once again due to neglect. Did the gains he had made in his foster home get overshadowed by another bout of less than ideal caregiving? That seems possible. Certainly, Kevin has had to change home environments far more often than is good for any child, especially one who hasn't had his needs met adequately from very early on.

Now this child is back home once again, and his mother is working hard to offer him the love and stability he needs. However, Claudia and Nancy have watched her with her son. She can be on the severe side with him—strict in a way that doesn't always appear to have warmth underneath. Furthermore, when Nancy did a home visit, she was concerned: there was barely a toy or children's book to be seen. She quickly helped Kevin's mother make contact with a program that donates clothing and toys to families that can't afford them. The teachers hope that Kevin now has more to do at home, but they're not sure.

How might all this information be linked together in a narrative that explains the puzzle that is Kevin? Perhaps, as Claudia believes, Kevin came into the world constitutionally equipped to thrive. His strong language and visual-spatial skills, which developed even through significantly hard times, make that seem likely. But he has had an on-again, off-again experience of safe and pleasurable connection. Maybe, as a result, he is thirsty for extra connection now. Could that be why he seeks out laps and hugs to an extreme? There is another maybe, too. Could the reason he sucks his thumb so often be that he lacked adults to help him feel calm and regulated early on? Might he have used thumb sucking as an always-available strategy to soothe himself through many difficult moments? If so, it may be a deeply ingrained way he has found to feel secure.

This hypothetical story includes one additional piece. Children who don't get enough of the basics when they are very young aren't always able to explore their environments with eagerness and focus. It's not just that they don't learn to engage with people—they don't learn to engage with their worlds fully either. Thus, one way of understanding Kevin's disconcerting vagueness is that his brain's light bulb of engagement isn't turned on all that often. Without it being lit up, it is hard for him to tune in and learn. That might be why Claudia and Nancy have had such trouble teaching him basic self-help skills.

Claudia and Nancy are intrigued. This picture makes sense. But then why does Kevin perk up when he works on a puzzle or plays a computer game? Computer games, we remind ourselves, are colorful and lively. They provide a kind of stimulating entertainment that some kids find hard to create for themselves. (It is for this reason that Claudia and Nancy's program only allows children access to computers for brief periods each day, and also why there is a list of resources about the important topic of young children's exposure to "screen time" in appendix C.) Perhaps, we end up thinking, computer games invite Kevin into a certain kind of engagement—one that is both passive and active at the same time. Such an invitation might "trump" his default mode of inattention and disconnectedness. And what about puzzles? We're not sure. Perhaps they call out to this child's visual-spatial gifts and trump his default mode as well.

From Storying to Goal Setting

The three of us mull over the storying we've done for Kevin. If it gets at something real, and we believe it probably does, what should happen next? We list our concerns as a way of getting started:

- Kevin's way of relating feels sort of "floppy" and tuned out even though it's sweet.
- It is hard for him to package up his attention and stay focused.
- He has difficulty with transitions and self-help skills. It's as if he isn't fully aware of where he is, what he should be doing, and how to do it. Even though his language is strong, he can't seem to follow directions. Again, it feels as though he's not tuned in enough to attend to what is being asked, much less to follow through.
- His play repertoire and play skills are quite limited.
- He rarely connects with other children, either in conversation or play. When he plays alongside them, he doesn't seem to notice or catch a ride on what they're doing.

We move on. How can we "flip" these concerns in order to come up with an agenda for mastery? In another quick list, we set out some basic goals:

- We'd like to see Kevin connect with more steadiness, depth, and tuned-in pleasure. First with us, and then with other kids as well.
- We want him to learn to package up his body, his attention, and his mind so he can become more organized in the way he connects and plays.
- We hope he'll start talking and sharing his ideas more often, and begin listening to others' input more often too.

- We'd like him to develop the ability to notice where he should be, to take stock of what is coming next, and to be aware of expectations for behavior.

- Finally, we hope he'll learn to focus at group time, to wait his turn, and to follow directions.

This list of overall goals is a hefty one, but they are linked to one another. Given the storying we have just done, it feels as though the key to all of them lies in helping Kevin feel more connected. Part of that, we agree, will involve working to turn on his light bulb of engagement.

Tying Shoes and Washing Hands: Finding Everyday Opportunities for Engagement

As the three of us turn to the question of an action plan, we think about the patterning that has evolved since Kevin arrived in the program. Kevin's classmate Hannah has sneeringly commented that Kevin is a baby. And although her condescending tone speaks more to her needs than Kevin's situation, she is on to something. The teachers do relate to Kevin as a much younger child. He seems to need them to.

Part of what Claudia and Nancy end up doing, as noted earlier, is to move Kevin through the day. They *do for him* because they can't figure out how to *do with him*—or even to help him *do for himself*. They get him to the bathroom, somehow or other. They dress him, brush his teeth for him, and more. Is there a way to slip connection-saturated intervention into the moments when they're giving him a hand? I believe there is. I also believe that such efforts will eventually help Kevin become his own "engine" rather than these teachers having to take that role.

Hannah calls Kevin a baby. Well, what do engaged parents do when they're interacting with their babies and young toddlers? What are their voices and faces like as they change their children's clothes, tie their shoes, or wash their hands? Sometimes, they initiate a playful interchange filled with pleasure. Sometimes they speak in a warm, high-pitched, and slightly exaggerated way, often called "motherese." Sometimes they turn what they're doing into a game. Picturing a few examples of what such interactions look like can shed some light on what Claudia and Nancy can eventually try with Kevin.

A mother kneels down in front of her eleven-month-old son Leo as she gets ready to put on his sneakers. She gazes at his face as she takes Leo's feet, one in each hand. Then she gently taps them together, in a steady rhythm. "Leo, Leo, how are you? Leo, Leo, time for shoes!" she chants. Then she and her son smile at each other as she talks with him, pulls his socks up, and ties his sneakers.

A father stands above a changing table. His fifteen-month-old's diaper is now clean, but her shirt is stained. Off the shirt goes. In the process? A smile-filled game of peek-a-boo as he takes a few extra moments to pull her dirty shirt up over her eyes. "Where's Emma?" he asks with a shade of concern. As he pulls his daughter's shirt back down with a "There she is!" his voice conveys both surprise and happiness. It's clear Emma wants more.

I sometimes refer to exchanges like these as "dances of engagement." They go on throughout children's early lives, nested in the everyday moments they experience with their caregivers. Such exchanges can easily be replicated in the classroom for kids like Kevin, who benefit from them enormously. And the wonderful thing is that they're easy to slip into things teachers have to do already: whenever there is something a child needs done for her—or something she wants help with—there are possibilities for "dancing into" some warm connection.

Mixing and Matching: Combining Strategies with Artistry

Claudia and Nancy think about times they could relate to Kevin in this way. Certainly during shoe tying: Kevin's shoes seem to come untied almost as often as he becomes unfocused. Moments when he needs to wash his hands may offer some interesting possibilities as well. In addition, they'll try doing some of the "I see you in the mirror" work they are already finding useful with Hannah. And they'll take advantage of a technique called "playful obstruction" (Greenspan and Wieder 1998, 124). That is when a child wants something and adults playfully hold back from offering it until they have engaged her attention and interest more fully than usual. As they do so, they make clear that what they're doing is a game, not a taunt. Here is what that might look like in Kevin's case:

Kevin wants a particularly challenging puzzle that is currently in the classroom's locked closet. He knows he is allowed to ask for it, though it's not often left out. He drifts over to Nancy and asks for her help. "Oh, you want a red crayon?" she says with a goofy smile. "The crayons are on the art table!" "No, the puzzle," Kevin replies. As usual, his face looks somewhat dazed. "Oh. I'm sorry. It's playdough you want?" Nancy makes sure her facial expression demonstrates that she is eager to help.

"I WANT THE PUZZLE!" Kevin's voice is loud, but he doesn't seem angry. He appears to understand that there is a playful quality to the interchange. He looks straight at Nancy, as if to emphasize that he needs her to listen more carefully. And he is fully engaged now—the light bulb has turned on. "Oh! It's the *puzzle* you want. Of course! You *love* puzzles, don't you Kevin? I'll get it for you. Come with me." She beams a big smile his way before they head to the closet door.

Note that at the end of this interchange Nancy is pairing playful obstruction ("Oh . . . it's playdough you want?) and compassionate emphasis ("You *love* puzzles, don't you?"). With the big smile she gives Kevin before they head to the closet, she is seeding the day as well. All in order to infuse a set of interchanges with as much engagement as she can.

Connecting First, Directing Next

Claudia and Nancy have a question. Can we come up with some ideas to help Kevin deal with transitions more easily? Right now he's so spacey that they feel as if they're constantly herding him down the hallway to the bathroom or out to the playground. Getting him to circle is easier; they just offer him their lap. But that doesn't feel like a good long-term solution.

It makes sense to them, they tell me, that Kevin's light bulb of engagement is usually switched off during transitions. (After all, it's off in general.) They also understand that if this imaginary bulb were switched on at such times, Kevin would have a better chance of attending to what he's supposed to be doing or where he's supposed to be going. But they don't know how to help him go from one state to another, especially during the normal chaos of transition times. They certainly wish they did. They don't want to be herding him down the hall in six months—not for his sake and not for theirs either.

As we talk further, we come up with the idea of fostering connection-saturated moments *before* a transition is going to take place. Once these teachers engage Kevin's attention and interest at such moments—assuming they are able to—they'll be able to help Kevin preview what's coming. We decide that printing out and laminating some small visuals picturing transition-time steps will help. They'll use them in combination with a "planning board" that lays out what is about to happen and what Kevin will need to do at that time. With Velcro on the back of the visuals and on the front of the board, it will be easy to vary what

Kevin sees. But connection will need to come first. We remind ourselves of the principle that staff in Claudia and Nancy's program return to over and over again: "Connect before you correct . . . or redirect."

These ideas make sense to all of us, and we flesh them out in detail. That way Claudia and Nancy can get comfortable with the new approach to transitions they're going to put in place:

- First the teachers will seek out Kevin and engage in a few circles of communication. They'll use their interest in what he is doing combined with some compassionate emphasis or motherese to invite his attention.

- Once Kevin is engaged, they'll continue to beam connection his way as they preview what is about to take place and what will be expected when it occurs. They'll point to the elements on a transition-specific visual planning board, unless they find that such a board doesn't appear to help.

- Then they'll have Kevin point to the planning board's elements himself. They'll support him as he reviews what is about to happen, where he needs to go, and what he is supposed to do. And they'll be sure to receive this "rehearsal" with warmth.

- Next, they'll engage in a little more friendly conversation, giving Kevin time to get himself ready to move along.

- Finally, there will be a prompt of some sort. It will include words, warmth, and a return to the planning board. "Okay," Claudia might say as she points to the board's picture of children in line. "Time to line up. Here we go, Kevin! I see Alex is there already!"

The plan for Kevin is complete, at least for now. Claudia and Nancy start implementing it immediately. With a focus on connection-saturated interchanges alongside previewing and planning for times that are especially hard for Kevin, they use the storying we have done together to keep themselves buoyant and motivated. They're committed to reaching this lovable, dazed boy more fully if they can.

Up and Down the Ladder

It would be comforting if every story of intervention had a perfectly happy ending. Kevin's journey doesn't. The wonderful part of that journey involves tremendous progress. The instincts our team has—to go down the ladder and to help this youngster turn on the light bulb of engagement— end up being right on target. The teachers' efforts don't lead to immediate changes, but over time Kevin is beautifully responsive to the shoe tying, mirror gazing, and playfully obstructive strategies they employ. They are relieved and surprised to find that they need to spend less rather than more time with him. Furthermore, the time they do spend has a more intentional quality to it than it used to.

Kevin begins to "wake up." His eyes focus more often, and his play begins to have some purpose and extension to it. He slowly becomes more interested in talking with both kids and adults. As he starts playing with peers more often, Claudia and Nancy find it necessary to add play support to their action plan. Step-by-step, they begin to see a boy who can make friends, share ideas, and much more. He still goes through moments when his greatest need is to find a lap and suck his thumb. Now, however, those feel more like periods of refueling than a reflection of his default mode.

One day in mid-February, I arrive to an amazing sight. Kevin is in the block corner with Alex and Alain, chatting and building like a very competent three-year-old. Claudia comes over with a smile. "It has been a fantastic stretch for him," she tells me. "And his mom seems to be doing really well with him too. I think that's part of why he's making so much progress. I talked with her case manager the other day, and both she and the family's therapist are very pleased."

Several months later, however, things don't look nearly as rosy. Kevin's thumb is once again in his mouth more often than not. He appears dazed, almost shell-shocked. And his play skills are far less in evidence. Claudia is beside herself. Apparently, things at home have slipped dramatically, and the state agency that deals with such things is considering a final removal. How will Kevin cope with yet another change, she wonders? Will he be able to keep coming to the center if he leaves his home? We agree to keep in close contact with his case manager. We feel strongly that if at all possible, Kevin should stay enrolled in our program. Claudia and Nancy run a mixed-age group, and he can be placed with them again next year. They may be his most stable caregivers for the time being.

I remind the teachers that when children fall down a developmental ladder they have started climbing, the gains they have made don't disappear. Thus, as tragic as this situation feels, their job is to go down the ladder of engagement and identify the rung to which Kevin has regressed. If they provide the same strategies they used to help him make progress before, there is a good chance they will be able to rekindle a sense of connection, safety, and engagement in school.

Over time, their joining Kevin on that ladder helps him once again. However, the buoyancy we saw in this boy months earlier hasn't fully returned at the end of the school year. He does have friends. He is speaking and attending far more successfully than he was in September. But hard times have taken a hard toll. At moments like this, it helps teachers to remember that research on resilience suggests that their warm connections with kids who are at risk can make a huge difference in the long haul. Claudia and Nancy remind themselves of this often. But, in regard to Kevin, they end the year with a mix of care and sadness. They hope he'll be back.

When Sunshine Turns to Sadness: Getting to Work with Isabel

At about the same time that they first approach me about Kevin, Claudia and Nancy bring up their concerns about Isabel. These teachers have found it hard to connect with Isabel, though they keep trying. She used to be such a relaxed and sunny child, they agree. She certainly isn't these days. They are fairly sure they know why. Things in this child's family have suddenly become very stressful—and not just for her parents. They'd like me to take a look at Isabel and then sit down with them for a chat. They're hoping we can come up with some ideas about what will help her feel better, at least while she's in school.

Before I observe Isabel, I get some initial information about what has been going on. About two months ago, Isabel's father lost his job. Just a week or so later, her much-loved abuela (her mother's mother) had a stroke. Isabel's father, desperate to support the family, has cobbled together some part-time jobs that mean he's rarely around. Splitting her time between home and the rehabilitation facility where Abuela is recuperating, Isabel's mother is away a lot as well. Luckily, Isabel and her older brother have a big extended family. They now spend about half their time in the home of a loving aunt and uncle. These adults, however, have an infant, two preschool-aged children, and a first-grader of their own. Thus, their niece and nephew must adapt to family life that is filled with friendly clamor and a certain amount of chaos.

Claudia and Nancy recently found time to catch a few moments with Isabel's mother. Her son has been rather trying through this period of crisis, she told them, and makes a fuss when he doesn't get what he needs.

Isabel, on the other hand, has responded quite differently. She holds her baby cousin while her aunt prepares dinner. She draws rainbow-filled cards for her grandmother. And on the occasions when she gets to be home, she willingly pitches in to help set and clear the dinner table. Five-year-old Isabel, this mother relates, has been a rock for everyone. In school, however, Isabel's melancholy and confusion couldn't be more evident. I see this immediately as she walks into the classroom at opening time.

Isabel stops by her cubby and solemnly hangs up her jacket. Stepping into the room with an impassive expression, she offers a somber hello in response to Nancy's warm greeting. Then she heads to the library corner and settles in on a comfortable pillow. Claudia comes by to offer her own friendly welcome. Isabel glances up, but this time there are no words in return. Moments later, Annie bounds over and invites her friend to play house. Isabel looks at Annie sadly and shakes her head.

I know from Claudia and Nancy that Isabel's classmates used to turn to her eagerly for play ideas. They relied on her for the good cheer that helped everyone carry out those ideas without a fight, too. But apparently, like she has just done, she currently declines most requests to play. What is going on, I wonder? Things at home are indeed difficult, but the classroom is full of warmth and care. And I can see that her teachers and friends reach out to Isabel regularly—she seems very well liked by both. Why can't she take a break from her stressful family situation and get some pleasure in a place where things are easier?

A Valued Role Leads to Quiet Suffering: Storying Isabel's Experience

When I sit down with Claudia and Nancy during team time, I get some additional background. They had an extensive conversation with Isabel's mother before Isabel joined their classroom, they tell me. At that time, she described her daughter as wonderfully easygoing and sociable by nature. As an infant, Isabel adapted easily to changes in schedule, to large groups, and to new foods. As a toddler, she sought out opportunities to lend a hand—even if a tiny-sized one. Isabel's older brother is quite different, the teachers were told. He is very intense and has always needed a lot of attention to manage his way through his days.

Adding this information to what we already know, we begin asking ourselves some questions. Their answers lead to our coming up with a story that could account for Isabel's distress. Have this child's parents relied on her to be the steady one given that her older brother can be so demanding? That would make sense. She has been a cheerful delight of a girl from the get-go. But what happens when a child like Isabel hits a stretch of hard times? She hasn't learned to ask for help—she has rarely required it. She hasn't learned to seek out connection either, because it has always emerged naturally.

Perhaps all Isabel knows how to do, the story goes on, is to keep on fulfilling the role for which she has been valued. But what is happening now is probably overwhelming to her, and being the sunny, helpful one may be leaving her feeling increasingly overwhelmed. Suddenly, rather than appearing to be a resilient and confident youngster, Isabel might end up looking disconnected and sad. Not in her family, where she valiantly continues to play the role she is known for as best she can. But at school, where things aren't as stressful, a girl like Isabel might just end up walking solemnly into her classroom and searching out a soft pillow on which to rest, lonely and uncertain.

Claudia, Nancy, and I consider the story we've envisioned. If there is truth to it, and Isabel's temperament and role in her family have left her with an inability to seek out help and connection when she needs them, what can be done? Might there be a different way to reach out to her? She certainly could use some extra support. Maybe she needs some assistance in making sense of what has happened recently too. We start brainstorming—playing around with ideas to see what we might come up with.

A Simple Plan for a Sensitive Situation

The plan we eventually design to help Isabel has three main parts. The first involves seeding the day with connection, which the teachers will offer through a mixture of the love bombing and gentle beaming described in chapter 9. And, as they have done before with both Hannah and Jenny, *they won't expect Isabel to relax and enjoy herself in response to their efforts, at least not at first*:

- They'll do lots of innocent flirting from across the room—seeking out Isabel's eyes and smiling or waving at her.
- They'll approach her with warmth and tell stories of things they've seen or have been thinking about.
- They'll sit next to her as she rests in the library corner, offering quiet company and maybe an arm around her shoulders rather than an expectation of conversation.

- They'll goof around with her. She used to have a terrific sense of humor and we assume it is still there, even if it's buried under some sadness.

The second piece of our action plan involves teacher-supported peer connections and teacher-supported play. Thus, Claudia and Nancy will start doing the "gluing thing." They'll eagerly notice play happening elsewhere, check it out, and return to Isabel with updates about what they've seen. As they do this, they'll add some compassionate emphasis. Their tones of voice and facial expressions will convey to Isabel that somewhere inside of her there is probably a desire to start having fun again. When she shows signs that possibilities for play and friendship are striking her fancy, they will offer her some lend-an-ally support as she begins to get re-involved.

The final element of the action plan involves Isabel's probable confusion and sadness about what is going on at home. This girl's grandmother has been a huge part of her life. Now it's not only troubling that Abuela is unavailable for comfort and care but also that, post-stroke, she's scary to look at. At the same time, Isabel's mother isn't around much, and her dad isn't either.

Claudia and Nancy agree to set up a "caring place" in lieu of their usual dollhouse. They'll set out doctor and nurse figures, accompanied by those of kids, parents, and grandparents. Then, they'll keep Isabel and other children company as they explore the option of creating a pretend nursing home in the caring place. These teachers will also see if they can help Isabel work through some of her feelings through play by having a mother or father going back and forth from a home to the caring place to take care of both children and elders. In addition, they'll use puppets, children's literature, and group conversation to create a curricular bridge about things changing yet staying the same. Families can have hard times, but there is still love to be found. Children sometimes have to sleep in different beds, but there are still people to tuck them in. Parents can get grumpy and tired, but they can still make jokes. And so on.

Even the Family "Rock" Has Needs

To Claudia and Nancy's relief, our action plan works well. Within a few weeks, the upbeat child they remember from not so long ago begins to reappear on the scene. Isabel is once again playing with friends. She has a bounce in her step and energy to spare, at least some of the time. And when she has had a particularly hard stretch at home, she heads to the caring place. Her friend Annie often joins Isabel there as she plays out stories filled with illness and love, loneliness and care. Claudia and Nancy find times to sit with her there too.

At some point, when Isabel's mother has time to come in, Claudia and Nancy sit down with her. They offer a family-friendly version of the storying we did and the action plan we have set in motion. They emphasize that, indeed, Isabel is an easygoing, thoughtful, and wonderfully caring girl. But, they gently suggest, even children like this have needs. Is there a way for the family to carve out some time here and there for her to get the comfort—and the explanations about what's going on—that will help her feel seen and cared for? There will be, her mother responds. What the teachers have explained makes sense to her. She just hadn't thought about Isabel in this way before.

The process of reaching out to Isabel and her family has important implications not just for her present but also for her future. Claudia and Nancy learn to make sure that this child's needs don't get lost in the midst of their busy classroom. Even more important, her parents learn the same with regard to their family. We hope that Isabel has discovered something too. Help and comfort are there to be had if she needs them. She can still be the family's rock. But the family can be hers, too.

12 When Language Is Limited
Helping Two Boys Who Struggle to Communicate

Jonathan and Emilio are friends. As best they can be, that is, given how hard it is for each of them to communicate with the other. These boys first appeared in chapter 2. Jonathan is the child who spends much of his playtime at the train table, where he can be seen running trains back and forth along the track with "choo-choos" and "woo-hoos" accompanying their repetitive journeys. Emilio likes trains, too, though he doesn't play with them for long. Actually, Emilio doesn't play with anything for long. Nancy once called this boy an "odd little butterfly," and it is an apt description; he appears to flit through the classroom, alighting here and there for mere moments of interest before taking off again.

Two Children, Two Variations on a Theme

Claudia and Nancy have concerns about both Emilio and Jonathan and would like me to come in and observe them. That way, I'll have a picture of how they're doing before we brainstorm about ways to offer each one some additional support. I schedule a morning's visit to their classroom, with a team meeting to follow the same day. A few days beforehand, Claudia gives me some initial background about the boys and fills me in on some of what she and Nancy are thinking and wondering about. She has a lot to share.

Claudia and Nancy are quite sure that Jonathan has some hard-wired challenges connected to language processing. They're just beginning to wonder whether the same may hold true for Emilio. That's because Jonathan, who is almost four, has grown up in an English-speaking household. Emilio, on the other hand, is a second-language learner.

Emilio's parents are from Mexico, and Spanish is the only language spoken at home. This is his first year in a child care program—he just turned three. Up until this point, Claudia and Nancy have felt comfortable giving Emilio extra time to settle in. He has a lot to get used to: a new language, a group setting full of children, unfamiliar routines, different foods. Now, however, it is early January and these teachers are getting concerned.

It's not how rarely Emilio uses any English that has Claudia and Nancy worried. They have had many kids arrive in their classroom speaking only their family's native language, and they know that the rate at which children learn a second one can vary widely. But Emilio's progress in using even a few words of English feels like it's on the slow end of what's typical, and it turns out that he's not speaking much Spanish at home either: his mother recently mentioned that he isn't talking the way his older brothers did at this age.

So Claudia and Nancy are beginning to have questions. Should Emilio be evaluated for possible language-processing issues? What about his striking lack of focus and frequent silliness—are they connected to how little Emilio understands of what is going on around him? Or do they stem from a different source? Claudia sometimes describes Emilio as a "love." Yet neither teacher feels they have forged much of a bond with him—it's too hard to pin him down for an interchange that feels truly connected. Would it be best to give him yet more time to settle in, they wonder? Or is there something they should be doing differently?

In regard to Jonathan, Claudia and Nancy aren't just starting to be worried; they *are* worried. These teachers have been so concerned about Jonathan's struggles to communicate that some months back, in partnership with his family, they requested a speech and language evaluation from the local school system. He didn't qualify for services, an outcome that makes no sense to either teacher. It's not just that Jonathan is hard to understand for an almost four-year-old. It's also that the words he knows to use—and the words he seems to understand—are so limited. The repertoire of things he likes to talk about is strikingly limited, too, as is his repertoire of play themes.

The teachers have other concerns about Jonathan as well. It is so hard for him to communicate what he's thinking that he tends to let other children dominate when he is trying to play with them. Some of them barely give him time to utter a word or two before they take over. He is remarkably patient about this much of the time. But sometimes—and such times are increasing—he gets very frustrated. Then he is apt to screech or hit. The teachers are worried about what is in store. Will Jonathan end up being seen by his classmates as a difficult playmate? Will they become afraid of him? That isn't happening yet. On the other hand, some of the children are beginning to treat him like an annoying younger sibling. Claudia has words for the message she thinks Jonathan gets at times like this: "You're not welcome. You can't keep up."

Specialists Can Help . . . but We Must Too

Because the basics of communication develop in children's first years, early childhood educators are usually well aware of an important point: many youngsters who are struggling to socialize and play, to control their frustration, or to learn successfully have underlying vulnerabilities connected to language processing. Offering such children the scaffolding they need to communicate more effectively can help them make progress in these other areas too.

When I say this, it doesn't mean that kids who struggle with language processing shouldn't get additional help from speech and language specialists. When it is available, that help can be enormously useful. But sometimes, as in Jonathan's and Emilio's cases, speech and language specialists aren't on the scene at all (at least not yet). Even when they are involved, such specialists often provide services for only an hour or two a week. And that level of intervention is just not sufficient on its own. Luckily, there are many possibilities for intervention that can be offered throughout a child's days in his classroom. Through the stories of Emilio and Jonathan, this chapter explores some of what they involve.

Getting to Work with Emilio

My morning observation has begun. The first thing I notice about Emilio tallies with what Claudia has already mentioned: he wanders *a lot*. As he does, he appears friendly and content. He stops at the sand table and plays briefly. He smiles at every child there. And he sings to himself or chatters away with words that don't sound like either English or Spanish. But he never appears to settle in.

The more I watch Emilio, the more I note that he seems neither cue responsive nor steadily attentive. Could his temperament be making language acquisition harder, whether or not he has language processing issues? Is he by nature a distractible child who has trouble filtering out some stimuli so he can screen in others?

The kinds of questions I have about Emilio aren't always easy to answer without engaging directly with a child. For that reason, I begin doing what teachers of kids like this do every day when they want more information: interact with him to see what I can learn. In addition to hoping that I can come to understand Emilio better, I'm also curious to see if there are strategies I can test out that might give the team some ideas about what more they can do to help him. (Note that as I describe my interchanges with Emilio, the words I emphasize are italicized, and those I say especially loudly are italicized and set in bold print.)

Drums and Delight: Nonverbal Routes to the Three Cs

Emilio has drifted to the classroom's basket of rhythm instruments. He pulls out a triangle and a small drum. Will I be able to grab his interest before he floats away? Given what I have seen through the morning, I probably don't have much time in which to try. I pick up the triangle and take its stick from the basket. "Emilio, listen!" I give the triangle a light hit. Its bell-like sound captures his attention. "That's a *pretty* sound, Emilio!" I say. "Do *you* want?"

I hand Emilio the stick as I hold the triangle. "Emilio! *You* try!" I look at him eagerly. My voice is full of enthusiasm, as if there were nothing else he could possibly want to do. He gives the triangle a hit of his own. "Oh, Emilio . . . it's *pretty*!" He giggles. I'm not convinced he understands a word I am saying other than his name and perhaps the word "you." But I have him with me, at least for now.

I gesture that I'd like the stick back, and holding the triangle in my right hand while pointing to the stick with my left, direct my eyes from Emilio's face to my hand as well. Emilio willingly gives me the stick, and I ding the triangle again. "Pretty, Emilio! It went ***ding***!" The silliness teachers have mentioned is in view as Emilio giggles with a kind of fiendish delight. I giggle back. "***Ding ding***!" I say as I hit the triangle twice more. "Here, Emilio." As I offer Emilio the stick—and the triangle too this time—my gesture is exaggerated. My facial expression is as well. If someone were watching me, it might look as if I were performing a mimed version of giving, not offering something in an everyday way. "*You* do! Make it ***ding***, Emilio!"

He does. Each time that the stick connects with metal, I chant some happy dings. Emilio seems pleased. Then, suddenly, I sense he is about to take off. Can I stretch this moment of engaged attentiveness a little more? I'm not sure, but I want to try. "Emilio! Drum now! ***Bang bang***!" I grab the drum and give it a loud whack. Then—even though I'm seated—I move as if I'm dancing. "***Bang bang***!" I dance some more. He giggles as he watches me. "*You* do Emilio! Bang the drum. *See?*"

I bang the drum again, then hand it to Emilio. Still standing up as though he might leave but seemingly less eager to do so, he gives the drum a loud whack. "*Dance* Emilio. *Bang* and *dance*!" I show him what I mean by moving my body while using my legs as a drum. He mimics what I've just done, and I smile as I mirror his moves. His eyes glued to my face, Emilio smiles back.

Shortly after this last exchange, Emilio has had enough and takes off once again. But I am satisfied. He has stayed put for longer than usual. And I have the sense that what just unfolded offers some important clues as to how our team can open up pathways to growth for this likable butterfly of a boy. He has connected more fully with me. He has showed signs of increased cue responsiveness, too. And he has communicated in the way he knows how—with smiles, gestures, and imitation. He'll need to do more of all three, I find myself thinking, in order to begin his climb up the ladder of communication.

The team meeting I soon have with Claudia and Nancy is full of conversation about how to help Emilio climb that ladder. To set the stage for that discussion, I want to look at the work I just did with him—what I tried and why I tried it. That will shed light on the reasons behind the team's action plan for Emilio and also on the plan we come up with for Jonathan. In fact, nested in my classroom-based experiment with Emilio are some basic strategies that can be used with many children who struggle to communicate.

Buttressing, Repeating, and Expanding Language

What was I up to with Emilio? What thinking lies behind the strategies I was trying out? And how did those strategies allow Emilio to show little signs of progress? A start to answering these questions lies in considering what just happened from Emilio's perspective. Here are three different descriptions of what unfolded as Emilio and I dinged and danced together.

Emilio isn't yet using much language. He loves to cruise around and see what is happening in the room. On this day, as he cruised, he found some rhythm instruments. They don't speak, but they make intriguing noises. I joined him where he happened to be and made noises with him. That felt good.

Emilio started having fun. Having fun led him to stick around. Sticking around resulted in his laughing and playing with me in a back-and-forth way.

Using rhythm instruments, Emilio and I got into a rhythm together.

There is truth in each description. Without the benefit of enjoyable materials that don't require speech to be used, it is unlikely that Emilio would have been as interested as he was. Without my finding him where he had temporarily alighted, he would probably have flitted away in typical fashion. Without the element of fun, he wouldn't necessarily have begun engaging in the simple back-and-forth we got going. Finally, there is no doubt that we found a rhythm in that back-and-forth, even if it was—mostly anyway—scaffolded by me.

These three descriptions shed light on why Emilio stayed engaged in what we were doing and what that engagement allowed him to experience. A further set of descriptions, building on those above, provide another layer of understanding about what transpired between Emilio and me. They rely on some of the early childhood field's thinking about both development and intervention:

- The gesture- and enthusiasm-filled work I did with Emilio *helped him move into a state of attentive engagement*—his "light bulb of engagement" switched on.

- That set the stage for him to *participate in some circles of communication*. On his end, those circles didn't include words. On mine, they did.

- Repeating single words and simple phrases, I tried to help Emilio *make a connection between a word and the action it described*. (*Bang*, *ding*, and *dance* are some examples.)

- In addition, I used *nonverbal emphasis* to support Emilio's interest, attention, and learning. That emphasis included speaking more loudly at some moments and more passionately at others. It involved highly animated facial expressions and exaggerated gestures, too.

- Finally, when Emilio did something that expressed pleasure, *I would "mirror" it back*. When he giggled, I giggled. When he danced, I imitated his motions.

In her wonderful book *One Child, Two Languages* (2008), Patton Tabors talks about strategies adults can use to help second-language learners develop competency in their new language. Those strategies don't apply only to "typical" second-language learners. They're also relevant to children like Emilio who are learning a second language with a dose of distractibility thrown in to make things even harder. They are useful to the "Jonathans" in our classrooms, too—kids who speak only one language but whose processing challenges make learning that language a struggle. Here are five of the book's core strategies, with headings in Tabors's language (91–94) and the descriptions in mine:

- *Buttressing:* When we "buttress" communication to increase comprehension and learning, we don't just use words; we add gestures and actions too. Sometimes, we direct our eyes to whatever we're talking about as well.

- *Repetition and emphasis:* By emphasizing the most important words in a sentence—and repeating them more than once each time they're used—we help children begin to recognize the sound and meaning of what they're hearing. Sometimes it also helps to place the most important words we're conveying near the end of the sentence they are in—that makes them easier to focus on and to remember.

- *Talking about the here and now:* By talking about things that are going on in the immediate present, we give kids an extra handle on understanding what we're saying. Eventually this "here and now" focus gives kids a route into responding with words of their own because they can describe what is actually happening in the moment.

- *Expanding and extending:* Once children gain initial skills in expressing themselves, we focus on helping them elaborate on their thinking—bit by bit. But we try to remember to start with what they already know and what they can already say, encouraging them to build on their ideas from there.

- *Upping the ante:* Used too often, this strategy can shut children down. But sometimes, as kids are ready for a gentle push, we put a little "muscle" into our expectation that they use at least a few words before we give them what we know they want or need.

I use the first three techniques liberally with Emilio. I don't, however, even touch the last two. It's not that I am thinking carefully about these five options as I work with him—I'm just playing around with possibilities for intervention to see what might unfold. But I instinctively sense that Emilio isn't ready to extend what we are doing. Nor do I want him to feel pushed to begin speaking himself. Both can come later. (Jonathan, on the other hand, will be a great candidate for the work of expanding and extending—as becomes clear in his story.)

Drums and Delight, Continued: An Action Plan for Emilio

When I sit down with Claudia and Nancy for our post-observation team meeting, we quickly come up with a shared picture of what is going on with Emilio. We discuss how spacey he often appears and how much time he spends cruising the classroom lost in a contented but disconnected world all his own. We note that as he cruises, he seeks out situations that don't require much (if any) verbalizing, and that he's not showing the early communicational competence we'd like to see in either of the two languages he has been exposed to. Then, as we begin thinking about the "whys" behind what is going on, we agree that there is probably some mix of second-language learning and distractibility at play. What we don't yet know is whether Emilio also has some challenges in language and information processing that are making the whole situation harder for him.

We move on to goal setting. We agree that we'd like Emilio to have longer stretches of engaged and focused attention. We hope that he will start developing skill in using simple language to describe his world, his ideas, his feelings, and his needs. Finally, we'd like to see Emilio begin noticing more of what other kids are doing and to start imitating their play—even to share simple play ideas of his own. Eventually, we'll want his play to starting "going" somewhere too, to have more organization and intention behind it—though such progress, we agree, shouldn't be on our agenda just yet.

As we begin envisioning approaches to helping Emilio meet these goals, I share a little bit about the work I just did with him and the ideas on which that work was based. I also talk about how I used a version of "motherese" to enhance what I was doing. (As first introduced in chapter 11, *motherese* refers to how adults speak with infants and very young children using voices at a higher register and with more variable pitches than those they use with older kids. Adults using motherese also employ short sentences and simple phrases, emphasizing the important words in each.)

As our focus on action planning continues, we talk about the three Cs and how central they will be to the assistance Claudia and Nancy will offer this boy. We remind ourselves of the idea of developmental ladders and "rung-by-rung" approaches to scaffolding learning, too. Because just as I did in my morning's experiment of dinging, dancing, and drumming, these teachers will need to start offering their support from where Emilio is, developmentally speaking. Eventually, we land on a detailed action plan.

The action plan for Emilio includes the following elements:

Classroom-Based Support
Claudia and Nancy will support connection, nonverbal communication, and cue responsiveness as they . . .

- engage in lots of warm connecting, nonverbal mirroring, singing and humming, and playful back-and-forth exchanges without words when they're with Emilio.
- do some innocent flirting from across the room—waving to and smiling at Emilio when they catch his eyes.
- exaggerate facial expressions and gestures when they're with Emilio in order to grab and keep his attention.

They'll foster emergent language skills and verbally-based circles of communication as they . . .

- use simple language to describe what Emilio is doing while he's doing it.
- employ simple, short phrases, and emphasize the word or words they want Emilio to pick up on.
- think of enjoyable games/playful exchanges in which they can begin to give words to what Emilio does and what they do back.
- try asking Emilio to give them a word or two before they do what he wants, and respond with enthusiasm when he is able to do so.

And they'll support the capacity for both solo play and play with others as they . . .

- see what Emilio finds interesting and join him in his play—mirroring it, naming it, and slowly adding content and complexity to what he is trying to do.
- begin doing some "gluing" between Emilio and other children by noticing and naming what he is doing and what they are doing.
- give Emilio words and phrases that he can repeat to other children he is playing near (or even with) so he can participate in some give-and-take with them.

Later on, when Emilio appears ready, Claudia and Nancy will . . .

- add more lend-an-ally play support to the mix of what they offer.
- use that play support to help Emilio begin extending some of the ideas he plays out, and to include more elaborate language as he plays.
- facilitate successful engagement with peers through play by sticking by Emilio's side as he learns to develop and share his ideas with his classmates.

Family Involvement

Nancy (who speaks Spanish) will . . .

- talk with Emilio's mother or, if scheduling works, his mother and father.
- share what she and Claudia are doing in school and determine what they feel comfortable trying at home.
- model some of our ideas in the meeting and/or invite Emilio's parents into the classroom to watch and work alongside the team.
- talk with Emilio's family about the eventual possibility of a speech and language evaluation.

Once the plan is complete, Claudia, Nancy, and I check in with each other. We're comfortable with it, we agree; it has the elements needed to target the growth we're hoping to see. We agree, too, that we should probably wait before suggesting to Emilio's family that they request a speech and language evaluation. If they were to do that now, the school system would probably tag Emilio as a second-language learner rather than a child in need of services. That said, if things aren't much farther along in three or four months, pursuing an evaluation may be a good next step. The reason to bring that possibility up now is that we'd like the family to have a sense that a future conversation about this issue may be coming. Will that conversation actually need to take place? We don't know yet. It's time for us to jump into a new way of supporting Emilio and see what unfolds.

Getting to Work with Jonathan

As I begin to observe Emilio, Jonathan is on my radar too. It quickly becomes apparent that he is a very sociable child. When at the train table, he often glances around to see what others are doing. Jonathan's classmate Alain appears to be his favorite co-engineer. Neither child speaks much. When they do, they use one- or two-word phrases that are rarely linked together to extend their ideas. Thus,

Jonathan has a willing partner in choo-choo and crash-filled play that doesn't develop very far.

When other children arrive to play, however, it's a different story. As the teachers have noted, Jonathan has a hard time keeping up. He tries, but the language and play ideas swirling around him appear to leave him confused. Often, he eventually seeks a corner of the train table where he can play on his own. There, he seems relatively content. It's when children begin taking his trains that he starts screeching or hitting.

Group time can be difficult too. Jonathan seems happiest when there are opportunities to sing or participate in movement games. When books are being read, especially those with higher-level content, he appears to tune out. Then there are the moments when children are invited to share their ideas and stories. Jonathan is strikingly hard to understand if he attempts to answer a question or talk about a featured topic. Often, he doesn't even try.

As I watch, it's very clear that when Jonathan isn't frustrated or tuned out, he is a delight—cheerful, cooperative, and easy to please. Like the teachers, though, I am surprised that the assessment process hasn't led to speech and language services. I'm glad Jonathan will miss the cutoff for kindergarten next fall—there is no doubt that an additional year of preschool will be useful to him. And I find myself hoping that we can encourage his family to request a repeat assessment. It may be that since he was only three and a half when the last one was done, he was on the lower end of what is considered age appropriate. There is a chance that the outcome will differ if he is tested again after he has turned four.

We'll Help You Keep Up: Scaffolding Communicational Skill

As we talk about Jonathan, our team's goals for him become clear. We want to see him become more confident and capable as a communicator and to begin demonstrating more richness of language, more fully developed play ideas, and an increased ability to extend both play and conversation. In addition, as Jonathan gains communicational skill, we hope to see more give-and-take in his play with peers. And we hope for more engagement with those peers, more focus in his learning, and more success with both.

Communication-Saturated Connection

The strategies Claudia and Nancy decide to try with Jonathan fall into two main categories. The first is linked to the idea of seeding the day with connection. This time, however, seeding has a slightly different twist. It involves not just moments of connection but also moments of *communication-saturated connection.* In doing this version of seeding, the teachers will sometimes speak in motherese—though not in a way that makes Jonathan feel he is being treated like a baby. They'll also offer small-sized "bites" of language, using the strategies of buttressing and repetition to increase his understanding of what they are saying. And they'll begin targeting expansion. In other words, they will add nuggets of content to their conversations once they sense Jonathan can follow the starter content they have offered. Throughout these efforts they'll try to work on these goals in a "here and now" way, mostly through moments of engagement they witness him having right there in the classroom.

The second prong of Jonathan's action plan involves teacher-supported play. Time permitting, Claudia and Nancy will join this child for a mix of play coaching and wise child play. As they sit with him, or with him and a friend or two, they'll offer the words and ideas he needs to keep up. They'll provide some human glue between him and his friends as well because, at the moment, the ideas he can convey aren't interesting to most of the room's other children. And through the context of their "you and me together" alliance, these teachers will supply some ideas Jonathan *and his classmates* might like when he has run out of ideas himself. Then they'll see if he can catch a ride on those ideas and add depth to them, one step at a time.

Previewing the Content of Group Time

There is one more piece to this work, a strategy that is useful for many children who struggle to understand what is going on at group time. Whenever possible, Claudia and Nancy will take Jonathan aside before a preplanned circle time takes place. And they'll *preview the content of what is to come.* Giving him a heads-up about any questions that he may be asked, they'll offer him the chance to think about what his answers might be. They will show him the book they'll be reading beforehand, too, and highlight some of its most important content. All of this, they hope, will allow Jonathan to feel more a part of what transpires once the children have gathered together. They hope he'll be more able to learn from what he hears as well.

Family Help and Specialized Help: The More the Better

Claudia and Nancy seem relieved. They had wondered, given that Jonathan didn't qualify for outside services, whether he was going to need a lot of one-on-one attention in order to make progress. But this plan feels like something they can comfortably fold into what they already do in their classroom. They'll talk to Jonathan's family, too. What they have in mind for Jonathan's time in school feels easily transferable to life at home.

As a part of their family outreach, they will model what buttressing, expanding, and motherese look like, even if they don't use those labels. Perhaps, they say during our meeting, they'll even invite Jonathan's mother and grandmother—who are his main caregivers—to come in and watch what they are doing, and to get some friendly coaching right in the classroom. They'll also emphasize that they hope the family will request a repeat evaluation after Jonathan turns four. Perhaps the school system will agree to pick him up for extra help later in the year. They want this family to know that outside services could be a huge help to Jonathan if they are offered.

Onward and Upward

There is a lot of work to be done with both boys. But Claudia and Nancy feel grounded and clear, and in their usual, dedicated fashion they take our problem solving to heart. The support they offer is invaluable even though the progress they're aiming for, especially Jonathan's, happens slowly. That is often the case for children who struggle with communication skills.

Jonathan begins talking and playing more as the year unfolds, but he continues to need extra help. Offering him play support turns out to be hugely important. He loves having adult company and, bit by bit, learns to add complexity to what he says and plays. By the end of the year he is doing much better, though without an adult nearby his play often starts to get repetitive. That is the teachers' cue to move back in with additional assistance.

Jonathan's buddy Alain develops increased language and play skills more quickly than Jonathan does. And eventually Alain finds other favored playmates. That is hard on Jonathan—Alain has been his best friend and most comfortable play partner. Luckily, partway through the year, three-year-old Yan joins the group. This girl's family just arrived in the United States from China, and her communication skills in English are well below Jonathan's. Jonathan takes Yan under his wing—a win-win situation. For a while, he's the teacher and she's the learner. It is a pleasure to witness.

In February, the school system does reassess Jonathan. In late March, they decide he qualifies for twice-weekly speech and language services, which will start in the fall. At that point, Claudia and Nancy hope, the mix of the help he gets at home and in school—and the assistance he'll receive from the school system—may give him the boost he needs before heading to kindergarten. These teachers are guessing, though, that Jonathan's IEP (individualized education plan) will follow him to elementary school. Knowing he's a wonderfully kind and sociable boy, they believe he will do well as a friend and learner. But it's their hunch that he will need ongoing help with academics.

Emilio's progress unfolds far more dramatically. The motherese- and gesture-filled seeding strategies grab his attention beautifully. He begins focusing better, using words more, and—slowly—starts to play with friends. By February, he looks more like the other second-language learners in the classroom and less like a child with language-processing challenges. He is making progress in using Spanish at home, too. Claudia believes that our picture was correct: learning a new language was a piece of the problem but distractibility was as well. Once she and Nancy figured out how to target both, a faster pace to mastery was possible. And by the end of the year? Jonathan and Emilio are still friends. Emilio, however, has made his cheerful way into the thick of things. A multicolored butterfly with multifaceted language, he flits from group to group, welcome by all. And he stays awhile, almost everywhere he goes.

Farewell to a Classroom

Alain, Hannah, and Jenny. Kevin, Isabel, Jonathan, and Emilio. And, of course, Claudia and Nancy. Seven children, two teachers, and a school year full of bumps and growth, worry and celebration. There are happy and not-so-happy endings, stories of hope and stories of continuing challenge. In short, it is a real classroom with the real ups and downs that early childhood work always involves. Bumps and all, there is good reason to feel encouraged. Some of these kids are flourishing by the end of the year. The others have made notable progress—even those whose lives may not be easy in the years to come. And they have been well cared for by their teachers—teachers who have worked hard to understand and support each one with all the wisdom and skill they can muster. There is nothing more any of us can ask of ourselves.

Addressing Problems
in Self-Regulation

3

The children whose stories are featured in the following chapters all have trouble with the skills of self-regulation. It is difficult for them to calm their bodies, focus their minds, manage their emotions, and control their impulses. Children who struggle in such ways are often hard to have in our classrooms. They poke other kids. They ramp up just when we need them to settle down. They make transitions tricky, they make other kids unhappy, and they regularly topple the peace of the day. At some point, despite our efforts to remain patient, they get to us. We become annoyed, frustrated, or even quietly enraged. Increasing difficulties often ensue. The same can be true at home. Whatever the roots of a youngster's difficulties, the things he does there can make life very trying for the family members who take care of him. They can make life trying for him, too, leading to a home situation that is filled with tension for all. That tension makes its way into our classrooms each day the child walks in.

Part 3 begins with three chapters that highlight a range of difficulties connected to self-regulation. Chapter 13 first explores the nature of this all-important skill and then focuses on children whose bodies are often on the move and whose minds don't slow down enough to take in *and use* the information they need to be cooperative members of their classrooms. Chapters 14 and 15 feature children who, in different ways, get frustrated easily, lash out quickly, and solve problems poorly. Chapter 15 touches on another set of children as well—those whose anxieties regularly highjack their peace of mind.

Given how important the home-school link can be, part 3 concludes with an exploration of how teachers can help families learn new approaches to supporting their hard-to-manage kids. In particular, chapter 16 looks at how we can talk with parents and other family caregivers about setting and following through on reasonable expectations. Offering such mentoring is an important part of our job. These adults look to us to take good care of their kids, but they also turn to us for guidance. Knowing how to offer that guidance when things at home are not in good control is a gift we offer them—and their children.

13 Getting to Work with Gabrielle
Helping Out When Energy Is High and Focus Is Low

It's a Tuesday in mid-March. Julia, the lead teacher of a prekindergarten class, is wondering how a second day of unanticipated change will go for her group. Over the weekend, a frozen pipe in her school's building burst, and there was some flooding in a number of its classrooms. Julia's was one. Luckily, the flooding was discovered on Saturday afternoon. On Sunday, some key staff members came in to set up temporary classrooms for the week to come. The result is that Julia's group of eighteen children is sharing the program's "big room" with another displaced class.

Yesterday went well. That was made easier because Gabrielle—Julia's most active, impulsive, and easily distractible child—wasn't there. Today she will be. Gabby has made real progress since September. But transitions aren't her strong suit; change isn't either, and she still needs a lot of structure and prompting to succeed. How, Julia wonders, will this challenging youngster adapt to such a huge shift in her day at school? Will she be able to handle the increased noise and bustle without coming unglued?

Understanding the "Wiggly Ones"

Gabby's name may sound familiar. Featured in chapter 1, she is the whirlwind of a girl whom Julia worriedly brought up during a teacher drop-in group. At that point in the fall, Gabby's listening skills were marginal, her attention span was short, and her energy level was extremely high. She had been so domineering and impulsive with her classmates, Julia noted, that they no longer welcomed her as a playmate. Furthermore, it wasn't just school that was difficult—home was too. In fact, things had gotten so extreme in the family that Gabby's mother, Beth, was resorting to locking her daughter in her room when she was at a loss about what else to do.

Children like Gabby are often described as high-energy kids. I sometimes call them "the wiggly ones." Earlier this year, one of my supervisees shared the latter phrase with a teacher she was mentoring. That teacher, a lover of Winnie the Pooh, said, "Oh, you mean Tiggers! I know about them. One of my sons is a Tigger!" Whatever we call them, kids in this category are easy to pick out in their classrooms. They are the children whose bodies need to move a lot, who suck their shirts, poke their friends, and have a hard time stopping unwanted behaviors when asked. They are also the youngsters who may be relatively calm and focused during free play but who speed up the moment they hear the words "five minutes till cleanup." With a single gesture and a giggle, such kids can gleefully pull their buddies into a remarkably chaotic transition. (Gabby is particularly skilled at just that.) Sometimes, despite their teachers' best efforts, these children never manage to settle down once they get to group time. Packaging their minds and bodies back up afterward—so they can once more engage successfully in activities—can be hard for them as well.

These descriptions point to some of the developmental skills teachers need to target as they work to help their wiggliest classroom members. This chapter uses Gabby's story, along with a short narrative about another child, to illuminate the nature of that work. To explore classroom-wide approaches that are often a needed part of the mix, it also describes my efforts to help a young teacher facing a whole group of "Gabbys." The chapter begins with an exploration of some concepts useful in understanding the challenges high-energy kids face: self-regulation and executive function.

Self-Regulation: A Central Task with Component Parts

The term *self-regulation* is used so often in our field—and in such different ways—that it can be hard to know just what it means. I like to think of it as involving things kids learn to manage over time: their energy, attention, feelings, and impulses. In other words, children who are learning to self-regulate can begin to calm themselves when their energy gets high, focus themselves when their attention gets fuzzy, and soothe themselves when their feelings get big and distressing. Kids who are learning to self-regulate become able to stop themselves when their impulses are in danger of taking over, too. This last aspect of self-regulation is particularly important when paired with the capacity for regulating strong feelings. Because when feelings and impulses are under control, kids are more able to engage in successful problem solving as things start getting difficult. And that ability, in turn, plays a big role in being a well-liked friend and successful learner.

In recent years, the early childhood field has focused on yet another aspect of self-regulation: sensory integration. Many in the field now believe that some high-energy kids don't have an easy time regulating their sensory systems. Some children with this vulnerability eventually get a diagnosis of "sensory integration dysfunction"—meaning that their troubles regulating sensation are extreme enough that they are having a significant impact on development.

Whether a child's situation merits a diagnosis or not, sensory issues tend to show up in two different ways. Either a youngster needs more sensory input to feel calm, or the input she already gets makes her uncomfortable or overwhelmed. (Sometimes, we see a mix of the two.) In the first case, children can end up seeking the sensations they crave in ways that are very hard on others—banging into other kids, kicking and biting, punching and pinching, and much more. In the second, they may avoid sensations that they find uncomfortable, getting stuck when it's time to do things like put on their socks (too tight), their shirts (too scratchy), or some sunscreen (too "yucky"). They can get quickly overwhelmed when there is a lot of noise or commotion surrounding them, too.

Executive Function: A Brain-Based "Boss" (and That Boss's Staff)

As is true for Gabby, impulsivity is a problem for many wiggly kids. And while the capacity to manage impulses can be seen to fall in the just-explored category of self-regulation, it also connects to a group of brain-based capacities known as *executive function*. This term, also widely used in the field, speaks to the way in which kids and adults use their minds to monitor their bodies, emotions, and actions.

In thinking about the nature of executive function, it can help to imagine a place in every one of our brains where there is a long, rectangular table. A number of people are sitting around that table as if they were business executives holding a meeting. Each person at the table represents an aspect of brain functioning. There is the individual who helps us think about how much time is available to finish something before we have to switch gears. There is the one who monitors how well we are accomplishing a task. There is also someone who predicts the future while we're in the present. (That person knows that sometimes when we feel like doing something, it will be important to consider the potential consequences of our actions and do something else instead.) There is an individual in charge of planning, too. At the head of the table is the chairman of the board, the person who makes sure all the others sitting in on the meeting are keeping track of their jobs and doing them well (Zelazo 2014).

A classroom's wiggly ones often have executive functioning that's on the weaker side. As a result, it's hard for these kids to plan and predict. It is also difficult for them to monitor how well they're completing a task and to control what they're about to do. Sometimes, in fact, it feels to teachers as if these kids live in the eternal present. They aren't sure of where they are going, what they want to have happen when they get there, and what will result if they make a choice that—to the people around them—would seem unwise. When high-energy children do make unwise choices, it's not necessarily with harmful intent. Gabby, in fact, has always said she is sorry about what she has done. And she's meant it. But Gabby is a prime example of a child who lives in the eternal present. One moment she is deeply apologetic about having hurt someone's feelings or body. The next moment she has done the same thing again.

Supporting Focus with a "Focus on Five"

In a way, it isn't fair to offer generalities stating that high-energy children are like this or can't do that: we know that all kids are uniquely themselves. But by considering these children as a recognizable group, we can lay out overall goals for their development. The hopes we have for many of these kids tally with those that Julia's team has had through the year for Gabby. We hope they will learn to slow down their bodies and focus their minds. We want them to learn to mentally exit the present, consider the future, and act on what they envision. We hope they will develop the skills of sharing and waiting—two elements of being a good friend and compassionate family member. So many of these kids want to be both. It's just that their energy, distractibility, and impulsivity get in the way of their caring.

It isn't hard for teachers to picture such goals for growth when they have a wiggly one in their midst. What can be challenging is figuring out how to offer effective approaches to intervention in order to meet them. The kids being discussed here, by definition, move through their days with huge amounts of energy, inattention, and impulsivity. It's quite a challenge to capture and keep their interest for long enough to offer them the support they need to make progress. As a result, having a picture of the areas we attend to in order to foster that progress can be particularly helpful. I like to call what we do "supporting focus by a focus on five." Thus, as part of our efforts to help the wiggly ones, we:

- pay attention to *proactive teaching practice*—that is, how rooms are designed, activities offered, routines supported, and behavioral expectations set and enforced.

- offer step-by-step approaches to *skill development.*

- strengthen feelings of warm, safe, and tuned-in *connectedness.*

- work on changing problematic *interactive patterns* that have gotten in the way of growth.

- partner with families to offer *guidance and support* for what is going on at home.

Each of these areas is explored in this chapter, with a more extensive focus on the first two since the others are covered more fully elsewhere. The initial area, though relevant to our work with all children, is perhaps most important for those who have trouble with issues of self-regulation. Looking at it closely involves a return to Julia's program and the way in which staff set up the "big room" for temporary use by two classrooms together.

Room Design, Routines, Rules, and More

The big room is a large carpeted space that usually serves as indoor backup for playground time when kids can't go outside. Now, however, it has been cleverly arranged with activity areas and circle-time spots. Staff have brought in some bookcases and low-level room dividers to define those spaces and rolled masking tape onto the rug to make clear where each one starts and ends. Small rectangular signs show kids how many children are welcome in each activity area. In addition, the room's usual openness is broken up quite intentionally. Nowhere would a child look around and think, "Hey, good traffic pattern here. Time to run!"

The teachers have thought about additional ways to make the temporary relocation work as smoothly as possible. There is a quiet corner with comfortable pillows and books, set up for children who may need a break from the fray. Blocks are laid out in well-ordered groups. The boxes of cars and trucks, two distinct dramatic play areas, and several art and science tables are set out invitingly as well. Other spots, each with a featured activity, have been designed with equal care. In short, each area offers its materials in a way that helps kids notice and get interested in what is there. That, staff hope, will encourage a feeling of order and a level of focus in the room that it might otherwise lack.

The teaching teams sharing the big room have structured their time carefully as well, and they have made large visual schedules showing kids that each day will look and feel the same. Both groups went over those daily plans with their teachers when they arrived after their weekend break. Now the visual schedules are taped up on two of the big room's opposing walls. In addition, each class generated a list of "what's the same and what's different" rules for the week. Those lists are posted near the room's main door.

Julia and her colleagues have dealt with their unexpected displacement by doing the equivalent of pushing a reset button. In other words, they have approached their temporary quarters by replicating what they did at the beginning of the year. They've re-emphasized the child-friendly routines they first introduced in September, illustrated by appealingly designed visual schedules, which can be referred to as needed through this week in the big room. They've come up with a room design that supports focus. With the same intent, they've set out activities in inviting and well-organized ways. And just as they did near the start of the school year, they've encouraged the kids in both rooms to come up with community rules in order to foster group and individual "buy-in." Those rules can be referred to as needed—they are simply stated and easily visible on the big room's wall.

These proactive elements of teaching practice are a huge part of the work teachers do to set a tone for classroom life that supports emotional well-being and developmental mastery. You can find resources that address some of them (such as room design and routines) in appendix C, including freely downloadable materials put out by the Center on the Social and Emotional Foundations for Early Learning (CSEFEL). The CSEFEL approach, now widely embraced in the early childhood field, emphasizes these elements as part of a focus on "promotion"—what we do to ensure that all kids get the basic supports they need to thrive.

An emphasis on "promotion focused" approaches connects to a central idea, that there are things we should be doing for all kids that are particularly helpful to those who are the most challenging. In that vein, it is useful to remember an important point, one that bears on the experience of kids like Gabby: *well-regulated classrooms foster well-regulated kids.* When children walk into an environment that speaks of calm and order, they feel more calm and orderly within themselves. When a classroom feels on the chaotic side, they often experience chaos within themselves. The latter isn't so challenging for children who have easy access to internal calm— kids who self-regulate with ease. But for those who don't, our wiggly ones included, a less-than-orderly tone in a classroom can have disastrous ramifications. What do we see in such situations? A kind of group contagion in which one unregulated child begins to set off others. Before we know it, even our calmest kids can look riled up.

Pushing the Reset Button: A Child-Friendly Approach

Some years ago, I walked into a classroom that emanated just this kind of unsettled and chaotic feeling. Its young teacher, Lizzie, had many strengths, one of which was a wonderfully compassionate way of supporting children who were melting down during moments of emotional overload. Unfortunately, because Lizzie's approach to classroom management issues was an underdeveloped aspect of her teaching practice, she had any number of children melting down all day long. And the more she focused on those temporarily unhappy or frustrated kids, the more unruly her class became as a whole. By the time I was called in, things were in dire shape.

I was in a quandary. I wanted to help Lizzie push a particular version of a reset button—one that resets to a state the kids hadn't experienced earlier in the year. To do that, though, Lizzie would need to assemble the children at circle time and go over some ideas. At this point, however, many of her students refused to come to circle at all. When I arrived home the night after my first observation, I was not only alarmed about the classroom but anxious about my role. What could I possibly do to help turn things around? Feeling uncertain and in need of a friendly ear, I called my trusted colleague Loretta for some advice.

Loretta reminded me that when kids aren't behaving the way we hope they will, we have to think out how to teach them the skills they're lacking in a step-by-step way. I knew that made sense. But, I asked her, how could Lizzie and I get this group assembled so we could do this kind of proactive teaching? Even if we managed that, how could we hold the children's attention *when they were so unregulated as a whole group*?

Loretta's answer, as it often is, was to inquire whether a puppet might help. "How about a character like Duffy?" she asked. Duffy is Loretta's alter ego, an adorably fluffy and rather large dog puppet with a slow-paced manner and a Midwestern twang. When Loretta ran a classroom, Duffy used to teach her kids how to cross their legs, sit still, "button their lips," and keep their "paws to themselves" at group time. He did this at the beginning of each school year by telling children stories about when he was a puppy in school and had trouble learning to stop, look, and listen.

I asked Loretta if I could copy the idea of Duffy. And with her blessing, I went out the next morning and purchased a large dog puppet of my own. His name would be Gustopher, I decided. He'd be called Gusto for short because the word *gusto* means "with energy." Kids might like that idea, I thought to myself. And they might be interested to learn that when Gusto's teacher used to get frustrated with him, she'd use his whole name with a bit of verbal intensity thrown in. I imagined the story Gusto could tell Lizzie's class about how he used to get in trouble. "*Gustopher!*" his teacher would say during group time. "*I can't talk and kids can't listen if you're putting your paws on them and barking at them!*" But how might I help Lizzie gather her kids so that he could tell his teaching-packed story?

I hatched a plan. The next time I was in, I brought Gusto nestled inside a small wicker basket with a doll-sized blanket covering him as he slept. Then, I woke him up and began going around the classroom with him on my hand. In an amusingly gruff and appealing voice, I had Gusto introduce himself to each child. He asked them their names and what they liked to do—or perhaps what their favorite color was. (Often that was a color he liked too.) Then he mentioned that after he met the other children, he was going to take a nap under his blanket. He'd be back for group time though and had some fun stories to tell. Would they be there? He was clearly delighted as each child responded in the affirmative.

Gusto went down for his nap at the middle of free-play time. As that period came to its conclusion, Lizzie and I made the rounds. We were going to have a visitor at group time, did the children remember? Of course they did, they'd reply excitedly. Would they come quickly and get ready for our guest's visit? Yes, they'd do that, we heard back. And they did, every single one.

Once the group assembled, it was time to rouse Gusto from his nap. Doing that took some work—work that involved kids listening for a cue and then chiming his name all together. Their initial efforts weren't successful because they had to call his name not too softly but not too loudly either. By the third try, however, they nailed it. Gusto roused himself. By the time he did, the children were already more cue responsive and regulated as a group than they had been in quite some time, if ever. That, of course, was the point of the whole "let's wake him up" process.

Gusto (like Loretta's Duffy before him) began his work of storytelling. And in his appealingly gruff voice, he told the children about how he used to have trouble listening and waiting his turn and how he learned to sit quietly and to raise his paw when he wanted to say something. Then he asked a question: Would the kids like to practice those things with him like he had to a few years ago? They would? Fantastic. "Oh my," Gusto would say as they practiced. They were "much better" than he was when he was little. Lizzie, he wanted to know, could he come back tomorrow and see if the children were doing their jobs? He could? Well, woof, woof, that would be *good*. It would be *great* and *glorious*, too. Any "G" word would do, like *Gusto*! With a dose of high drama, Gusto suddenly got tired. Time for another nap, he told the children with a large yawn. After good-bye kisses to kids who would like them (one at a time, of course, with a small emphasis on waiting skills), he settled into his basket. Then his blanket was lovingly placed over his fuzzy body by a few particularly wiggly kids he'd singled out for the honor.

Gusto's work with Lizzie's children illuminates a few important points. Whenever possible, we offer promotion and prevention-focused strategies that are child friendly and classroom-wide. Finding ways to embed those strategies into playful contexts is always a plus. Breaking the skills we're shooting for into small steps is a necessity.

Finding a "Voice of Authority": Meaning Business without Being Mean

Chapter 16 explores how we can help parents develop a "voice of authority" when children have more power at home than is healthy for them. Teachers need to have such a firm and clear voice in their toolbox too—one that conveys an "I mean business" feeling without being harsh. Some teachers come by such a voice naturally. Others need to work on it.

Lizzie was in the latter category. She and I spent some time together talking about how, when she needed to convey that she was in charge, she could find a voice that would work better for her. The soft, nurturing one she was using nonstop now wasn't comforting to children when they needed a sense that they could and should be stopped from engaging in unwelcome behavior. *A more assertive voice would not only help her stop them, it also would help them stop themselves,* I suggested. Lizzie worked hard on finding a voice of authority that suited her, and we did some role playing until she landed on a tone that she felt conveyed a comfortable "in charge" feeling without being strident. She also started thinking about when to focus in on one child who was feeling overwhelmed and when to attend to her whole class. Over time, her ability to make such choices improved a great deal. Her children's skills at controlling themselves did too. She—and they—were on their way to a far better year.

Spotlight on Routines: Transitions as a Teaching Tool

The story I just related is about teaching the skills that lie behind success at group time. We can think about doing the same in the way we approach daily routines. Transition times are a prime example. Educators often see them as a way children get from here to there and, for some youngsters, that's true. But for our most unregulated kids, *transitions can be used as a teaching tool.* Consider the following points as they apply to transition times:

- If a classroom's high-energy/easily distractible kids can learn to stay on task in the midst of noise and commotion, they are developing better executive function.
- If they can keep their energy level steady (rather than having it get increasingly high), they are learning to regulate their "body states."
- If they can keep their hands to themselves and cooperate in cleaning up, they are mastering skills connected to frustration tolerance, impulse control, and flexibility.

Thus, if we chunk down our goals for transition times into little bits, teach those bits one step at a time, and reinforce success, we offer kids daily opportunities to learn the skills of self-regulation. If we don't, we end up issuing countless (and fruitless) reminders and dealing with transitions that are tough for everyone. One way to teach transition time skills is to use a puppet like Gusto as a "coteacher." For other ideas, see the resources on proactive teaching practice in appendix C.

Step-by-Step Approaches to Skill Building

Gusto broke down the skills of sitting attentively at group time. Button your lips, he taught the children. Keep your paws to yourself. Don't bark when it's not your turn to bark. This step-by-step approach to skill building is the second element of this chapter's "focus on five." When I spend a few hours observing in Julia's temporary classroom on the second school day after the March flood, this same kind of skill-building assistance is much in evidence.

Gabby has just arrived after her Monday absence and is making her way down the hall. Julia welcomes her warmly and asks if she's heard about the big change. Gabby has. Julia invites her to sit on a large pillow that has been placed just outside the big room's door. There, they go over the day's schedule, and Julia shares the list of rules kids came up with for the week. She tells Gabby about the quiet corner teachers have set up for children who need some time away from all the noise. Then they enter the room. Hand in hand, they take a tour to inspect what is out. Gabby decides to start at one of the art tables. She has always loved to draw.

For the first hour or so, Julia and I both are impressed with how Gabby copes. Now it's 9:45 and Gabby's energy is beginning to ramp up. Julia knows there is not much time to waste. Shortly, Gabby will be almost unreachable.

Gabby has left the dramatic play area and is cruising along somewhere between a jog and a run. "Gabby, stop and look!" Julia's face is bright. If she is feeling alarmed, she's doing a good job of hiding it. Gabby comes to a full halt, puts her hands by her sides, and glances up. It is clear that she knows what to do when she hears the "stop and look" prompt. That is not a surprise. The class has been using it—and Gabby, in particular, has been practicing her response to it—since mid-October. "Hey, great looking Gabby!" Julia exclaims. She gives Gabby's arms a gentle squeeze. "Can you keep those arms nice and quiet? It's still 'stop and look' time." Gabby is visibly trying to slow down and attend, although her eyes seem unfocused and her legs are jiggling.

"I'm about to tell you something. Do you know what it is?" Julia's voice radiates calm and interest. She smiles encouragingly at Gabby. "My engine is going too fast?" Gabby replies. "Yup! That *is* what I was going to say!" Julia gives her a smile, moving her hands to Gabby's shoulders with more gentle pressure. "And what do you think you could do?" she asks. "Slow it down?" Gabby knows the answer that is expected. However, it's not clear that she will be able to do what her words imply. "Yes again!" Julia comments. "Let's do it together, Gabby."

Julia puts her hands up in the air, and Gabby does too. They take a big breath. Then they bring their hands down to below their waists, breathing out slowly as they do. "Should we do it one more time?" Julia asks. Gabby seems to think so. Up their arms go, then down again with another slow breath. "Hey, fantastic, Gabby!" Julia's face radiates pride. Gabby is still looking a bit spacey, but she seems pleased all the same.

"Gabby, it's a big room with so many things to do. Do you want a break in the quiet space? We could read for a little while." Gabby isn't even remotely interested and looks as though she's ready to fly off once again. "Okay then, no reading for now," Julia says. "Let's head over to the wall and look around. You can figure out what you're going to choose next."

Julia places her arm on Gabby's back as they head to a relatively quiet spot at the side of the big room. Then they begin attending to what is happening where. Gabby decides she wants to play in one of the room's two block areas. "What do you think you'll do there?" Julia inquires. Gabby isn't sure—maybe build a stable for some horses. She *loves* horses. Julia wonders aloud if they should find some string to cut up for hay, and Gabby is interested. They locate a ball of string along with two pairs of scissors. As they cut some hay before heading to the block area, Gabby settles down a little more.

On their way to the blocks, Julia asks Gabby if she might like a friend to join her. Gabby seems unsure—or maybe just unfocused. But Gabby's buddy Abigail happens to be nearby, and Julia heads her way with an inviting smile and a question: Would Abigail would like to join Gabby? She would—she loves horses too. Julia sits with the girls as they get started, helping out as they begin placing blocks in a large rectangle. She makes sure the bin with horses is close at hand, too.

"Gabby, stop and look!" Julia gives her prompt one more time. Gabby looks up again. "This is a really wonderful stable you and Abigail are making! How many horses do you think you'll put in?" Once again, Gabby isn't sure. "Lots," is her vague answer. Abigail chimes in. "Probably ten," she adds.

"Okay then! Lots of horses—maybe even *ten*!" Julia's voice is filled with energy and emphasis, as if she wants to trump Gabby's distractibility with a dose of charisma. "Gabby, Abigail," she goes on, "I'll be back to check out the stable in a little while. I want to find out if the horses eat all their hay!" Gabby nods as she and Abby begin feeding their herd. And Julia heads off to check on some other children.

Tuning In, Slowing Down, Thinking Ahead: Promoting and Practicing Mastery

There is a lot of growth to be seen in this unfolding vignette. Step-by-step teaching has a great deal to do with why. Gabrielle knows just what to do when she hears the stop-and-look cue. She stops moving. She puts her hands by her sides. She "zips her lips." And she focuses her eyes on the person talking. *Four steps, each one previously practiced* during group games, group instruction time, and then at individual moments throughout many months in the classroom. This approach to skill building—which is practice based, step-by-step, and child friendly—threads through many other aspects of what Julia offers Gabby as well.

"I'm about to tell you something. Do you know what it is?" Julia inquires after her student has stopped her body and focused her eyes. Gabby does. "My engine is going too fast?" she responds. When we experience a child joining us in this way, there is reason for encouragement. That child—like Gabby—is slowly learning to self-monitor. And self-monitoring, we know, is an important element of self-regulation. Once again, the idea of child-friendly versions of targeted skills is important here. Julia has helped Gabby learn a new competency by using the easy-to-understand language of "engine speed" (Williams and Shellenberger 1996, 2–1).

It isn't only self-monitoring that Julia is working to foster. That comes first. Then comes another *specific action sequence* Gabby has learned to use to help her regulate her energy. Together teacher and student raise their hands in the air. Together they lower them as they breathe out slowly. And Gabrielle begins to slow down. *Begins* is the operative word here. As her response shows, she is in a stage of what we call "emergent learning" connected to a competency that her hard wiring makes particularly difficult to master.

You can see Julia's way of fostering emergent learning in yet another set of interactions—those during which she targets previewing and planning. "Let's go head over here to the wall and look around," she says. (*You need to stop and think before you start moving again.*) "You can figure out what you're going to choose next." (*Look forward in time, just a little. Then you can go somewhere rather than anywhere.*) "Oh, the block area? What do you think you'll do there?" (*Can you make a plan, not just have a destination? Might your next steps unfold with purpose?*)

This focus on planning undoubtedly targets pieces of executive function. But another goal is embedded in it as well: avoiding the after-the-fact chastising and correcting that our Tiggers so often experience. "Let's consider this in advance so you don't have trouble afterward," Julia seems to be saying to Gabby. "Let me help you think first and act next."

Offering Sensory-Focused Input and Sensory-Sensitive Breaks

It's probably apparent that Julia, in addition to everything else she is doing, slips some sensory input into her work of helping Gabby slow down. When she says, "Great looking, Gabby!" she gives her student's arms a gentle squeeze. As they talk about the question of engine speed, she provides additional pressure to Gabby's shoulders. In fact, although sensory-focused support isn't at the center of Julia's work on this particular morning, it has been a big piece of what she and her team have offered this girl throughout the year. That support is often needed by high-energy kids whose behavior suggests that their sensory systems aren't well regulated.

There are many creative possibilities for sensory-focused work, and appendix C lists some excellent resources for further study. One of the options those resources explore is how to provide kids with what our field has come to call a "sensory diet." In such cases, we offer regular opportunities for kids to get the sensory stimulation they crave: special chairs and pillows that give their backs (and bottoms) extra support and input, "fidget" toys they can squeeze during group time, weighted blankets and vests, movement breaks halfway through free-play periods, and opportunities for lifting and carrying heavy things. (In regard to this last option, at times when she's particularly wound up, Gabby is sometimes given the task of carrying a heavy box down the hall to the program's director.)

Whatever the specifics, offering kids a sensory diet means that they'll be less likely to resort to unwelcome behaviors to get the sensory input they truly need. For kids who find sensory input of all sorts on the overwhelming side, we pay attention to how much stimulation a child is receiving so that she doesn't become overloaded. (The quiet area Julia and her colleagues set up in the big room offers a concrete example of how they have tried to take kids like this into account during a time of unexpected stress.)

Multimodal Approaches: Using More Than Just Words

There are yet other strategies that can be used to help high-energy kids with some of the skills Julia is working on with Gabby. These strategies, which we label as "multimodal," use more than just words to help kids learn the skills they lack. Julia, for example, uses only a verbal stop-and-look cue to get Gabby's attention, and that works for this child. But some children can't easily take note of such a purely auditory cue, at least at first. With a child in the latter category, we may choose to teach and then regularly proceed through a set of steps to foster cue responsiveness. In such cases, we do the following:

1. Go over to where the child is.
2. Tap her shoulder three times.
3. Call her name.

The child's job is to respond by looking up and saying,

4. "What, [teacher's name]?" (Or at home, "What, Mom?" or "What, Dad?")

If the youngster in question doesn't look up, ask her "what" question, and demonstrate she's ready to listen, we try once more. First, we warmly remind her of her job. Then, once again, we give three gentle taps and call her name. This time, if we still don't get the response we are looking for, we know further practice runs are in order—perhaps with a friendly puppet to cheer the child on.

Three gentle taps may seem like a small thing. But for some kids, the kinesthetic reminder helps grab their attention, especially if they practice this progression either in a group setting or in a playful way with a parent or teacher. For the first week or so after children have learned the protocol, we follow their "What, [our name]?" only with positives. That way, they learn to "pop up and tune in" through pleasure-filled reinforcement. Later we use the "connect before you correct" rule to pair this strategy with any course corrections that are needed.

A second multimodal strategy involves helping kids plan ahead using a *visual choice board*. In this case, the child is presented with a simple board that has two (or sometimes three) spots where she can place visual pictures of what she'd like to do first and then next. Such boards help kids consider where they're going and what they want to do there, rather than cruise around waiting for something to grab their eye. Over time, a child's using them serves to strengthen the planning element of executive function. Planning boards can be paired with a timer that helps kids stay put at their chosen activity for more than just a moment. (If you don't already offer such boards to your most impulsive, distractible children, you can learn more about them on the CSEFEL website, which is listed in appendix C.)

Yet a third multimodal strategy involves using visually appealing "I need a break" cards for group times. We give a child like Gabby one or two such cards before a group experience begins. Our expectation is that she'll come to group calmly and sit in her place attentively. But when she is starting to feel very squirmy (note the self-monitoring function that's being reinforced here), she can quietly show us her break card. Then she takes a two- to five-minute time away in one particular spot. (Roaming the room isn't an option, but having some especially appealing activities in that designated spot is.) When her break is over, she calmly returns.

Working on Waiting

Many of our wiggly ones have trouble waiting. And, indeed, waiting is yet another competency that has been on the radar for Gabby. If this child can learn to wait more successfully, Julia's team believes, kids may feel less frustrated with her, classroom life will be calmer, and she'll gain some pieces of mastery central to success in kindergarten. The team has something else in mind as well, because they are quite sure Gabby is having similar difficulties when she is with her family. If they can find a way to teach Gabby to wait in school, they agree, Julia can have a conversation with her mother, Beth, and support a parallel approach when Gabby is at home.

The team has broken the skill of waiting into a set of easy-to-learn steps. (These steps target some of the same self-regulatory skills as the "stop and look" work Julia does with Gabby in the big room.) Thus Gabby is learning that waiting isn't a vague thing people are constantly telling you to do and that you don't seem to manage very well. Instead, it involves four specific actions:

- First, putting your hands by your sides (rather than repeatedly tapping your teacher's shoulder while she is talking with someone else).
- Second, "zipping your lips" (rather than calling her name multiple times).
- Third, keeping your body calm (rather than jumping up and down with frustration).
- Finally, listening for the phrase, "I'm ready for you now!" before letting your needs be known.

Each chunk has been learned with the help of a sweet but rather jumpy monkey puppet who used to have the same difficulty waiting that Gabby does. In addition, there is a chart the class made that lays out the four steps of waiting. (As could be expected in a typical preschool classroom, Gabby isn't the only child who has this problem.) Now, each time Gabby starts ramping up when she wants their attention, her teachers take a break from what they are doing. They turn to her with warmth.

"Gabby, I'm talking to Mary now. You'll need to wait. Do you remember the steps? Should we look at them on our chart? Okay, here we go . . . Hands by your sides. Great! Zipped lips. Terrific! Calm Body. Excellent! Now, let's see if you can listen for my 'I'm ready for you now!'"

Thus, waiting becomes yet another developmental-behavioral skill to be practiced repeatedly. To Gabby's great credit, she is beginning to learn how to master it in the classroom. After a conversation with Julia, Beth starts using the same step-by-step approach at home. Eventually, everyone hopes, Gabby will be able to wait more successfully there as well.

Outside Work: Supporting Energy Regulation While Celebrating Speed

Gabby loves to run. Many of our Tiggers do. Often, we're so pleased that these kids can take off with freedom once they are outside that we leave them be. That is a good idea some of the time. But outdoor and gym times offer many playful opportunities for helping kids with the skills of cueing in and slowing down. And although Gabby's team does some of this skills-based work with her, it is another child whose situation illustrates that work best.

A few years ago, I headed to a program where one of my supervisees was particularly concerned about a high-energy five-year-old. Marcus was a second-language learner, had some processing challenges, and was experiencing hard times at home as well. To make things even more complicated, he was a bona fide Tigger: a bouncy, energy-filled, speed king of a child. Marcus's teachers had lost patience with him, and my supervisee was at a loss as to how to help them see things differently.

Once I arrived and took a look, I found that my role would need to include noting how often Marcus was trying valiantly to do well. It also would involve offering some concrete strategies to support growth. One of those strategies concerned playground time. Like Gabby, this boy thoroughly enjoyed being on the move. He spent his time outside racing from here to there, clambering up and down the playground structure, and tooling around on his favorite tricycle. His teachers were so relieved that he did well outside that they weren't concerned that he rarely stopped for even a moment. Unfortunately, that meant they were losing the opportunity to work on skill development in the place he was the happiest. I decided, with their permission, to give some new ideas a try.

After spending some time connecting with Marcus inside, I hoped that he would be willing to join me in some fun outdoors. As he tore around the playground, I started waving to him as he zoomed by the spot where I was standing. After his third circle round, I called out. "Stop and see me next time, Marcus . . . I have something to tell you!" During his next circuit, I stepped in front of him as he headed my way, put out my hand as a stop sign, and smiled at him encouragingly. I wanted him to understand that what I had in mind wouldn't involve criticism. He stopped, red faced and out of breath.

"Wow, Marcus! You're amazingly fast! Can I count to see how many seconds it takes you to go around again? You can stop and I'll tell you, okay?" Marcus thought that getting a speed check was a fine idea. Thus began a stop-start game. My goal was to help him go from fast to slow and from slow to a cued-in state of responsiveness. And there wasn't a moment that didn't involve play. Interestingly, when it was time for the group to exit the playground, Marcus was far more able to slow down by its fence, have a connected back-and-forth with me, and plan out what he'd do when he got inside. It was easier for him to calm down for lunch as well. His teachers took note. They could see there was something to build on.

Strengthening Connectedness and Changing Patterns: The 90–10 Rule

All of the skill-building work just described—with Gabby, with Marcus, and even with Lizzie's class—is infused with two more elements from this chapter's focus on five. The first involves work to strengthen connectedness. The second involves seeking interactive patterns that lead to fewer, rather than more, behaviors of concern. I focus on these two elements together here for a reason. Kids like Gabby and Marcus get nagged a lot, and adults get frustrated with them a lot, too. Over time, they often begin feeling like they're not just *acting* badly but *are* bad. Sometimes, they appear to decide that they might as well behave poorly right from the start. At least then they'll have some control over the fact that things usually turn sour— even when they have tried for another outcome.

Often, in addition to behaving in problematic ways, high-energy children stop listening to requests for attention. That makes sense: frequently what they hear when they *do* attend is unpleasant to them. The adult end of this patterning occurs for a sensible reason. It is so hard to grab the attention of an inattentive child that adults tend to ask for that attention only when they feel they need it. What this means is that adults end up requesting a high-energy child's attention in one of two scenarios: either she is doing something she shouldn't do and a course correction is required, or she needs to stop something that is fun (like building with blocks) to do something that isn't so enjoyable (for example, brushing her teeth).

Here is where seeding the day with connection comes into our work with wiggly kids. The ever-helpful rule—connect before you correct or redirect—does too. Both of these core strategies relate to a guideline that I call the "90–10 rule." Imagine that in the case of a child like Gabby, adult requests for attention are followed by something unwelcome about 90 percent of the time. That leaves only 10 percent of the time in which that youngster attends and is rewarded with a pleasurable back-and-forth. The 90–10 rule invites adults to flip those percentages on their head. Now, unlike before, they will seed the day with connection so that nine out of ten times their requests for this child's attention are followed by entirely upbeat interchanges.

I came up with the 90–10 rule years back and have offered it to teachers many times since. Of all the strategies this chapter suggests, it may be the one that is the easiest to carry out and has the most powerful impact, both in school and at home.

Keeping the Big Picture in Mind . . . Including Life at Home

There is a lot to keep in mind here. That is all the more true when we consider that our support of high-energy kids requires both artistry and patience. When Julia, for example, sees that Gabby doesn't want a quiet corner break, takes her to the big room's wall to preview what's next, and then suggests cutting some hay to help her slow down further, you can see a master teacher at work. Even with such a gifted teacher on board, however, kids like Gabby often change slowly. One reason for this is that their hard wiring frequently has a role to play in what is going on. Another is that their families often need help in learning how to foster self-regulation at home. Providing help to families is the final area of focus on this chapter's list of five.

The nature of such family-focused work is partly featured in chapter 1, which describes some of Julia's and my conversations with Gabby's mother, Beth. Another aspect of this work, offering the kind of guidance parents need to set effective expectations at home, is highlighted in chapter 16. As recounted in chapter 1, Julia and I meet with Beth regularly through the year. Beth needs encouragement to find a friendly but firm voice of authority with her daughter and works hard to do so. Her finding that voice helps to a degree, and her learning family-friendly versions of strategies the team uses to support skill development in school contributes to Gabby's progress as well. But Beth's growth—just like Gabby's—takes time. That is often true in the case of our wiggly ones and their families.

Slow improvement, however, doesn't mean no improvement. Whatever the journey ahead, Gabby leaves for kindergarten a far more skilled girl than she was when she started her last year of preschool. She listens better, shares more, and shows up for group time with lots to say. She has friends that enjoy her and activities at which she perseveres. And she rarely does things that set her teachers running out of fear that one of their kids is about to get hurt. Beth takes great pleasure in what her daughter has accomplished. Julia and her team are proud of Gabby too, even as they worry about how she will fare in elementary school. I make sure to ask them if they are proud of themselves as well—they have been a stellar teaching team for a wonderful but challenging child.

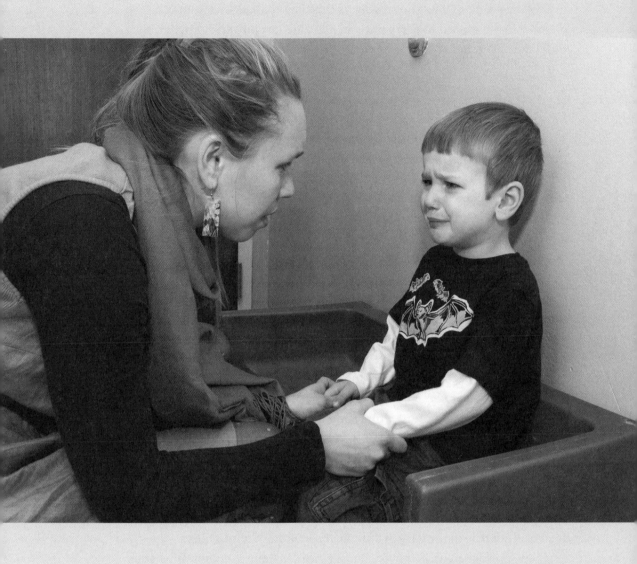

14 Getting to Work with Brian
Helping an Easily Frustrated Child

I have just walked into Lillian's mixed-age classroom fifteen minutes after the start of the morning's free-play period. Four-year-old Brian is sitting on the carpeted bench that serves as a boundary for circle-time activities. During free play, that same bench defines the edge of a multipurpose space where kids give puppet shows, make large block constructions, engage in storytelling, and more. Right now, though, children are giving the bench—and Brian—a wide berth. They probably sense the same thing I do: Brian is dangerously close to exploding. Lillian, who clearly shares that concern, is sitting by Brian's side.

"Brian, which one?" Lillian asks calmly. She's showing him a laminated sheet that is divided down the middle with a bold, blue line. On the top of the sheet's left side is written, "I'm Brian!" That statement is accompanied by a photo of Brian smiling. Nearer to the bottom of that same side the sheet says, "Sometimes, I feel mad." Those words rest next to a photo of this boy scowling. To the right of the bold line are more words: "When I'm mad, I can . . ." Underneath them are two simply drawn pictures. One depicts a daisy with clearly outlined petals. The other shows a child blowing up a balloon.

Brian has not answered Lillian's question. It is clear that he doesn't want to. "I know it's hard, Brian, but you can do it, I know you can!" she says. She looks at her student with warmth. "Which one?" she asks again. "Should we do the daisy or the balloon?" Brian jabs the flower. He picks up a pretend daisy, angrily plucks one of its petals, takes a deep breath, and blows the petal into the air. Lillian does the same thing at the same time. She nods at Brian encouragingly. He plucks another and blows it as well. So does his teacher. Then they do the same to three more. Five petals, five big breaths, and one somewhat calmer boy.

" Okay, Brian! Let's sit here for a minute and relax. Can I put my arm around your shoulder now?" Brian shakes his head. He's not ready for comfort just yet. Lillian speaks with a few kids who have come to ask if she'll help them get some fresh paint for the easel. She will, she tells them, but in a few minutes. She's helping Brian right now. What colors have run out, she asks?

Lillian is taking her time before turning her attention back to Brian. She's probably doing so on purpose: he seems to be using the break to calm down further. Soon, however, she faces his way. "Brian, something made you feel mad. Can you tell me what happened?" Brian proceeds to complain about his friend Andy, who took the blue racing car he, Brian, wanted to use. "Would you like some help making a plan with Andy?" she inquires. He would. They head over to the area where Andy is playing. With support, the boys come up with a plan for who will get the blue car and when it will be passed along. Lillian signals her colleague Joe to help the painters get the supplies they need. The boys have solved their difficulty. But if she leaves before they settle into playing, she's probably thinking, Brian will get frustrated again within seconds.

Understanding Easily Frustrated Children

Many years ago, I worked with a first-grader who had an amazing way with words. As he, his parents, and I talked about how hard things had become at home, he said something that I have never forgotten: "I know what the problem is. I just don't know what to do about it. *My big feelings get really big really fast and they stay big for a long time.*" I have used this description with many children since. They almost always understand what I am saying. It is the most child-friendly way I have found to frame what the problem is for kids who have trouble regulating strong emotion. But this boy wasn't just clear about the nature of his problem. He also communicated that he didn't know what to do about it. That is almost always true for kids in his situation. Or, better said, such children may know what they *should* do. However, they can't figure out how to do it. Our job, of course, is to come up with a chunked-down approach that helps them master the skills they're lacking, one step at a time.

Children like this first-grade boy hit a small "bump" and have a large and quickly escalating reaction. Sometimes their family members and teachers feel as though there is no trigger for their intense upset. Sometimes, as is usually the case with Brian, a particular trigger is apparent, but there's little time for those adults to offer help before the youngster's emotions have risen dramatically. Either way, these kids are notably hard to reach once they're highly frustrated. The first-grader I just described had words for this phenomenon, too. A few weeks after his "big feelings" declaration, he looked at his mother as she began yet another lecture about his unacceptable behavior. "Be careful, Mom," he said pleadingly, "I'm about to be stranded on the island of agitation."

The reasons children are propelled onto this lonely island vary widely. Some have experienced inconsistent limit setting. Some came into the world with high-intensity temperaments or processing vulnerabilities that have made the daily experience of living especially challenging. Some have been exposed to scary violence in their families or communities or have experienced physical or sexual abuse. Some have siblings who boss them around a lot. Then there are the kids who never get enough sleep and are left without the reserves they need to manage frustration. There are other possibilities too—far more than can be listed here. Often, there is a mix of factors behind what is going on. In situations that involve children who carry around a heavy load of emotional distress, we are left with a tricky question. How do we help emotionally overloaded kids build the skills they need to manage strong feelings while also attending to the feelings themselves?

This chapter and the next address this question, along with a host of others that speak to how we help "big feelings" kids. As a way of setting the stage for these explorations, it is worth considering a few important points. Most are based on the influential work of Ross Greene, author of *The Explosive Child* (2010).

When Big Feelings Get Very Big Very Fast: Ideas to Keep in Mind

- Children who have trouble managing strong feelings often get stuck in problematic patterns in their families. A child starts losing control. His parent threatens consequences. The child's behavior gets worse. At some point, the parent loses her temper—screaming at the youngster to stop what she, the parent, is now doing as well.

- It's not uncommon for family members and teachers to change their expectations midstream if an easily frustrated child looks like he is about to unravel. As a result, though it's no one's intention, the child ends up being reinforced for the very behaviors those adults hope will stop.

- Kids who have gone beyond a certain emotional threshold can't think clearly enough to engage in sensible problem solving.

- Past this "point of no return," they have probably also lost their ability to take into account how badly they will feel about an outburst after they have calmed down.

- However, children in a state of emotional overload often appear to make sense. As a result, adults sometimes continue trying to help them see reason long after such efforts only make a situation worse.

- Once a child is in such a state, his only job should be to regain a feeling of calm. Once he does, problem-solving help may be useful.

- Children who lose control frequently usually have marginal problem-solving skills. Even though sensible limits may help reduce their explosive behaviors, they also need assistance in learning to come up with reasonable solutions when situations aren't working out to their liking.

- Easily frustrated youngsters are hard to be around, and they know it. They often begin to see themselves as not only unpleasant but unloved.

- Research suggests that children's exposure to on-screen fighting and violence and to aggressively themed toy choices can increase aggressive behavior. That is why some of our work with families may involve talking about what their kids see and play with. (See appendix C for more on this important topic.)

There are a few additional points worth making in conjunction with this list. Some children who are easily frustrated undoubtedly have a great deal to feel angry about. Frequently they don't know what to do with their upset feelings other than to let them take over. In addition to learning how to regulate their emotions, these youngsters often need two more kinds of support. First, they need help in expressing and working through their troubling feelings. Second, if ongoing circumstances are contributing to these feelings, they need some of the adults who care for them to work on making their living situations better. That can include attention to physical or emotional abuse, help with intense sibling issues, a place to sort through family conflict, and much more. Sometimes a referral for child or family therapy—or other supportive services—is in order.

Targeting a Range of Issues; Goals for the Work Ahead

It is clear: if we want to help an easily frustrated child like Brian, we will have to address a number of issues. We'll need to promote behavioral and developmental mastery in areas where he is lagging. We'll have to offer support for emotional well-being and attention to emotional distress. A focus on frayed relationships, problematic patterning, and life at home will be important too. As always, to consider those overall goals in child-specific form, it helps to have a clear picture of a youngster's situation—to understand the story behind his behaviors and feelings. In Brian's case, I gain a lot of information about that story about three weeks before the petal-blowing intervention that opens this chapter.

Brian's Story

Lillian has asked for some floor time during her program's lead teacher "drop-in" group. It is the same group attended by Gabby's teacher, Julia, in chapter 1—a place where lead teachers know they can get support and do some brainstorming when they're stuck. Lillian needs some new ideas about how to help Brian, she tells those of us in attendance. This child has been exploding frequently and without a lot of warning. Kids are getting hurt and becoming uneasy about playing with him. It's not that Brian is disliked, she notes. During his calm moments—and there are many—he is an eager, enjoyable playmate. But Brian's days are long, his temper is short, and it feels to Lillian as if things have been heading in a worrisome direction.

Brian's life at home is not easy, we hear. He is much loved. But he has two teenage half brothers who are on the hard-to-manage side. Their father and mother had a tempestuous relationship when these boys were young, and they witnessed some scarily intense arguments. Brian's mother eventually left her first husband. However, her older sons appear to carry some emotional scars from their early years. They are easily frustrated and at times quite rebellious. That said, they adore their little brother, and sometimes they let him tag along when they are out and about. Lillian senses from things Brian has said that his brothers let him watch some of the violence-saturated movies and TV shows they like. She wonders if Brian has gotten overwhelmed by the teenage activity he has seen and the images he has witnessed on-screen.

Lillian experiences Brian's family as both committed and caring. Brian's mother met his father over eight years ago. This man is a good provider, and loves not only his wife and biological son but also his stepsons. It's clear that Brian's mom loves her boys as well. Lillian senses, however, that Grace feels overwhelmed by the challenges of parenting. Making things even harder, her husband's work schedule is grueling, and she is often home as the only adult. Lillian has the feeling that Grace ends up tiptoeing around all three kids so as not to set any one of them off. She can only guess that such tiptoeing makes what is going on at home harder for everyone. Maybe, Lillian says as she finishes her initial presentation to our group, she can offer Grace some ideas about how to be more in charge when she is home alone. But she's worried. Grace seems to feel quite bad already, and Lillian doesn't want her to think she is being judged.

Lillian has given our drop-in group a lot of information in a very short time. Brian's ability to manage frustration is strikingly low and is affecting his play and his friendships. He appears to be carrying a load of emotional distress that likely stems from issues at home. Some of those issues connect to his siblings' early experiences of domestic violence and the way the emotional aftermath of those experiences still takes a toll on family life. Some may result from exposure to violent media content. Patterns between him and other kids—and him and his mom—have gotten worrisome: kids are becoming afraid of him, while his mother may be avoiding conflict with him (and his brothers) in a way that only makes things worse. In the midst of all of this, Brian is well loved by his family and well liked by his classmates at school.

Lillian and her team's goals for Brian, then, parallel the goals already listed for so many big-feelings kids: they'll need to target developmental skill, emotional well-being, interactive patterning, and life at home. The way in which they approach the first element, developmental skill, is featured through the rest of this chapter, which also offers additional possibilities for intervention—options that Brian's team doesn't choose to use with him but that can be employed with kids much like him.

Crumpling or Coping? Three Core Skills

Kids like Brian seem to crumple or explode in the face of seemingly minor frustrations. They need to learn three skills. First, to calm down when they are upset. Second, to stop and think before they act inappropriately. And third, to find solutions to the many frustrating situations they run into each day. In other words, they must learn to *regulate their feelings, control their impulses, and engage in successful problem solving*. We know that kids who have these skills are more resilient in the face of life's challenges than those who don't: they cope better in the short term and fare better in the long term. That makes our job of fostering each one all the more important. They're undoubtedly interrelated skills, too, which makes intervention easier. But even though the approaches we use to support their development are equally interrelated, the strategies underlying those approaches are best examined separately.

Learning to Self-Soothe

Easily frustrated children don't just need to learn how to calm down. They must also begin noticing when they are starting to get upset in the first place. What strategies help us support mastery in these areas? In Brian's case, Lillian has already tried to foster self-soothing wherever he happens to be when he starts getting triggered. But that approach hasn't been too successful. Unless she is playing alongside him—and often even then—he gets angry so fast that he lashes out before she can help out. That is why she and her team decide that once Brian has started to escalate, they'll try only briefly to give him a hand. If that doesn't work quickly, they will have him temporarily leave where he is. He'll be directed to the same place each time and get a consistent version of support for moving through a set of steps to regain composure. Some of those steps involve physical actions accompanied by slow breathing. In addition—and this is often a plus for kids—the steps are illustrated by a visual aid.

Lillian has argued for using the bench as the place for this work. Brian's level of shame around his lack of self-control is already high. Thus, she feels that wherever he is removed to and whatever she and her team do there should feel as upbeat and nonpunitive as possible. On the bench, she hopes, he won't feel he is being ostracized the way he might if he had to retreat to the room's more isolated "cozy corner," where other kids often go to calm down.

The tool the team develops for Brian is simple and friendly. It offers choices too: "Should we do the daisy or the balloon?" Lillian asks. This tool is just one of many we can use when children need assistance in identifying feelings and learning to self-soothe; a number of additional options are listed below. Choosing which specific tool or tools we use (they can be mixed and matched) depends both on the child and the teacher—they have to work for both. Options that are starred, both on this list and in the narrative that follows, are also listed in appendix C, along with additional information about where to learn more about how they work.

Tools of the Trade: Helping Children Recognize and Modulate Feelings

- *The emotional thermometer*: Introducing the "colors of emotions" during group time, we help children identify a certain color (perhaps red) with being really angry. Another color represents moderate frustration (maybe orange). Two others stand in for either mild grumpiness (purple) or total calm (blue). Those colors get put on a chart or "emotional thermometer" with pictures of suitably characterized faces next to each one. Then we play games and do role plays that help kids practice how to go from one color—and one emotional state—to another. Eventually, those colors and calm-down strategies can be used as needed throughout a child's day.

- *The turtle technique*:* This technique is a widely used feature of the CSEFEL program and is illustrated through a downloadable story, *Tucker Turtle Takes Time to Tuck and Think.* The Tucker story offers children four steps that help them (1) notice that they are getting upset, (2) "pull into their shells," (3) calm down, and (4) figure out what to do next. Once we have taught and practiced these steps, we can support their use when a youngster needs help calming down and thinking clearly.

- *Choice-focused key chains or boxes:* We offer a "Things I Can Do When I'm Upset" key chain that kids can carry in their pockets or clip on their belts. Alternatively, we provide a box children can go to filled with similar, visually depicted options*: I can take a deep breath and count to ten. I can share with my friend. I can go to my peaceful corner. I can read a book. I can find my teacher. I can play at the water table.

- *Books about feelings*: The Chocolate-Covered-Cookie Tantrum* (Deborah Blumenthal) and *When Sophie Gets Angry—Really, Really Angry* (Molly Bang) are just two of many options.

- *Calming places and spaces*:* We set up a pillow house, a peaceful corner, or a safe space—whatever we and our children want to call the spot, where they can retreat when they need time to regroup. Sometimes we model using that spot by occasionally going there ourselves.

- *Feelings charts*:* "Oh my goodness, your face tells me you're feeling something strong! Come here and show me on the chart which feeling it is. Mad? Oh, okay . . . Now let's have Tommy show us what *his* feeling is. Disappointed? I see. Now let's think about what happened . . ."

- *Sensory activities:* We offer water or sand table play and/or other sensory activities as soothers. Alternatively, we provide "calming bottles,"* squeezable toys, drawing journals, and other options that promote self-soothing.

- *Yoga and meditation:* We teach kids some simple yoga exercises and/or child-friendly meditation exercises, and offer to do them together when feelings are rising.

- *Puppets, role plays, scripted stories,* and more:* We use puppet-based instruction, do individualized and group-based role plays, tell stories about ourselves, write scripted stories, and/or do group problem solving about what kids can do when they're upset.

Bringing Solutions Alive: Puppets, Scripted Stories, and More

As seen in chapter 13, puppets are a compelling option for teaching and supporting new skills—in this case, the skills of self-soothing and frustration tolerance. A puppet character who knows what it is like to get swamped by strong feelings might be just the thing for a child like Brian. That puppet's help might involve some engaging storytelling at circle time, some child-friendly descriptions of self-soothing, and some practical techniques the puppet character learned to use when he was about to lose control. It might include an emphasis on how proud his family members and teachers were when he was successful, and some circle-time practice of the skills he has learned. To offer additional support and practice time, the puppet character would most likely return for a number of visits to the classroom. Perhaps those visits would include his spending time with the particular child needing extra help in this area—becoming that child's special ally in learning and practicing the skills of self-control.

Our own storytelling can serve a similar function, and children's literature can as well. The latter is especially useful if we don't just read children a story but invite them to talk about it, act it out, and share their own experiences related to its theme. Scripted stories can also play an important role in fostering mastery. Sometimes referred to by teachers and specialists as "social stories," based on the influential work of Carol Gray, scripted stories can be written with a specific youngster in mind and provide a child-friendly frame for the skill development they support.

Scripted stories are presented in simple language and begin, over a number of pages, by offering a clear and nonjudgmental description of the problem at hand. (*"My name is Marianna. I like to play with my friends. We have fun! But sometimes I feel really mad when my friends are using the toy I want! Sometimes I grab that toy! My friends don't like that."*) Then, they describe a child-friendly alternative kids can try when they're in danger of getting stuck. (*"When my friends have a toy I want, I can say, 'Can I have a turn soon?' I can wait for my turn!"*). Scripted stories always end with an affirmation. (*"When I ask for a turn, my teachers will be proud of me. I will feel proud too! And my friends and I will have fun playing!"*)

CSEFEL offers a number of such stories on their website. One is titled *I Can Be a Super Friend.* * I have seen a classroom take a ride on that story with a fancifully sequined "super friend" cape that a teacher proudly delivers—with the ring of a bell—when an easily riled child has shared, waited, or controlled her temper. (Of course that cape is also offered to other kids, so the youngster in question doesn't feel singled out.)

Breaking Down the Steps of Impulse Control

Brian needs to learn to self-soothe, and clearly he and Lillian are working toward that goal as they pluck imaginary petals and blow them to the wind. The second skill-based goal the team has in mind is for him to learn how to manage his impulses. After all, for Brian to be able to stay put when he is upset, he has to be able to stop himself from hurting one of his buddies. Only then will he be able to start reasoning his way through what is bothering him and have a chance to play or talk with his friends successfully. I like to picture impulse control as the space between what a person *feels* like doing and the *act of doing it*. In the middle comes thinking: What will happen if I do that? Will my friend get hurt? Will my teacher get mad? Will I get in trouble? What could I do instead?

As always, steps are helpful. One version of teaching impulse control—though not one Brian's team chooses to use—involves the **S-T-A-R** progression*: **S**top. **T**hink. **A**sk yourself what will happen if you do what you feel like doing. **R**espond in a way that will make you and the people around you proud. These steps can be taught at circle time, with the help of puppets, children's literature, posters, or friendly conversation. Practice is essential as well. At first, such practice works best if it takes place at a time *when the targeted child is doing well, not poorly.*

Whatever the method, posting the steps of impulse control on a wall is often useful. In addition, having a visible way of celebrating children's success can be a wonderful motivator. A "Who stopped and thought this week?" sticky-note collection, a "We did it!" bulletin board, or a "We're all S-T-A-Rs" jar with pompoms representing moments of self-control are a few possibilities for celebration. Having a puppet "teacher" come back for a party when the members of a group are demonstrating greater self-control is a great option too.

Working on Problem Solving

The team's third skill-based goal for Brian involves problem solving. Kids often embrace a child-friendly language to describe what needs to happen when they have gotten stuck and need to think out solutions to the dilemma they're facing: "Oh . . . it's problem-solution time!" one of my favorite teachers tells her students. "Hey boys, it looks like it's a work-it-out moment!" says another. I learned yet a third possibility from a child I worked with earlier in my career. A girl whose thinking got rigid as quickly as her emotions got big, five-year-old Sandra told me that her problem was that her mind "froze up" when she was frustrated. Now my colleagues and I sometimes say to kids, "Are you in 'brain freeze'? Why don't you take some time to unfreeze? Then we can figure out what you can do . . ."

Problem solving involves a set of steps and is frequently paired with our work on self-soothing. In fact, the first step of problem solving *almost always involves self-soothing*. Lillian engages in this pairing regularly with Brian, and in the previous vignette she can be seen offering problem-solving assistance as soon as he's calmed down on the classroom's bench. ("Would you like some help making a plan with Andy?" she asks.) One of the teachers I consult with regularly has a poster on her wall that outlines the steps involved in problem solving. Here is her list:

How to Solve a Problem!

1. We **bring our feelings down**, from red to orange to green to blue.
2. We **say the problem.**
3. We **think of some solutions**.
4. We **pick one** and try it.
5. We **try again** if the first solution doesn't work.
6. We **give ourselves a pat** when we figure out what to do!

This list is just one of many that teachers can use, whether self-generated, as in this case, or found in a prepackaged social skills curriculum. One example of the latter can be found on the CSEFEL website, whose child-friendly "problem-solving steps" and "solution kits" are worth a close look.*

From Goal Setting to Intervention: Embedding Support in the Life of the Classroom

The many ideas just outlined probably sound reasonable, and they do help teachers remember to be proactive (not reactive) in their work with easily frustrated kids. But classroom life is full of bustling activity, and with a child or two like Brian in the mix, things can heat up in seconds. That's why it can help staff to have responses ready for three possible scenarios, as Brian's teachers learn to do. These scenarios are particularly relevant to free play and outdoor time but pertain to other periods as well.

Envisioning and Preparing for Difficulties: Three Scenarios

There is no doubt that, in general, Brian has trouble managing his feelings once he is frustrated. More specifically, his teachers have noted that there are certain kids he gets particularly frustrated with. Andy, his protagonist in the "blue racing car" incident, is one. His good buddy Samantha, with whom he has a love-hate relationship, is another. When Brian heads off to play with one of these two kids, teachers know that trouble often follows. That situation is an example of scenario one: *A problem will happen if no adult is present.* Scenario two, *a problem is starting to happen,* takes place when Brian—or a child like him—is beginning to get upset. There is a "window" during which support and problem-solving assistance might be welcome, but it's small. The third scenario is the easiest to notice but can be the hardest to deal with: *A significant problem has already occurred.* A child has gotten punched. A heavy toy has been thrown with the intent to hurt. A youngster's cherished block tower has been deliberately knocked to the floor, and he is both inconsolable and enraged.

Effective intervention requires having a proactive stance in regard to all three scenarios. One aspect of such proactive practice involves a mix of "zone defense," problem-solving assistance, and play support. Strategies that support this mix are explored here, using Brian as a case in point. (Another aspect of this kind of proactive practice—connected to the third scenario only—involves safety planning. That is covered in the next chapter.)

Zone Defense

It is now several months after the team started using Brian's calm-down plan. He is making real progress: he's just had a trouble-free stretch of drawing with Samantha at the art table. Not only did he stay calm and friendly with Sam, but he didn't get frustrated by his inability to draw a house the way he wanted to. Lillian, who is standing nearby, sees that Brian is now preparing for a change of venue. She heads over and chats with him about his drawing. "Where are you going now?" she then inquires. "To the blocks. I want to play cars with Andy," Brian replies.

Lillian glances across the room to the block corner. Sure enough, there's Andy. And if she is not mistaken, he has the police car that has been a recent bone of contention between the two boys. Joe, one of Lillian's co-teachers, is at that end of the room. "Brian, stay here one sec!" Lillian requests. "Let's call to Joe and tell him you're done here and are going to blocks!" That is just what they do. Joe, who is supervising a group of kids at the water table, looks up and nods. As Brian heads toward Andy, Joe asks him to come over for a moment. "Let me know if you need anything," he tells Brian. "I'm right here!"

Lillian's "heads-up" and Joe's response are part of their action plan. They are doing what Kathryn LeLaurin and Todd Risley described years ago as "zone defense" (LeLaurin and Risley 1972, 226). That is, staff in the room try to position themselves so that there isn't a "zone" in which Brian might play where there won't be a teacher relatively nearby. If Brian leaves the zone where one teacher has been keeping an unobtrusive eye on him—ready to zoom in with support when needed—that teacher cues the adult in the zone to which he is heading. Joe's nod to Lillian tells her that he knows it is his turn to be on duty. His "I'm here if you need anything" to Brian partly reminds Brian that he can ask for help when he needs it. (That has been a target for skill building of late.) But it also puts Brian on notice: someone will be watching what he is doing. As a result, Brian knows that if he crosses the line of what is acceptable, it will be attended to. That fact probably serves both as a comfort and a warning. The comfort element may allow Brian to stay calmer a bit longer than usual. The warning element may help him to stop and think before he lashes out.

"Use Your Words!" (What Words?)

Zone defense is almost always coupled with problem-solving support in the case of kids like Brian. For example, Joe is with a group of children at the water table but may need to head to Brian quickly in situations involving scenario two. Brian, he knows, still struggles with inflexibility, still feels he is going to miss out if he doesn't grab, and still needs help with the "how abouts."

I use puppets to teach the "how abouts." You may not. But even without the help of a furry friend, they are a great tool. "*How about* you be the mom and I'll be the baby?" we teach kids to ask as they're playing with a buddy. "*How about* I get the police car first and you get the fire truck?" Starting a sentence with this phrase allows kids to begin a negotiation rather than declare war. That negotiation may need to be supported from start to finish at the beginning of our work with easily frustrated kids, but it's a start.

The "how abouts" are one piece of the problem-solving assistance we offer children like Brian. In the case of zone defense, when we're not right next to a child as a problem emerges, we offer the use of these words as a way to de-escalate a situation that has already started to intensify. Then we help kids begin the process of working out whatever conflict of interest is at hand. When we are already by a child's side helping her play or converse with her peers, we can support the use of a "how about" *before* things have headed in a stressful direction. These words then become one aspect of how we support and model what successful interchanges can look and feel like.

It is important to note here that most early childhood teachers encourage kids to "use their words." Alternatively, if a child has come seeking help with a situation about which she is unhappy, those same adults may ask, "Did you use your words?" But what words? The words kids tend to use when they are mad often get them in trouble. "I hate you!" they say. "You can't come to my birthday party." "You're dumb." The point here is that we often need to offer *larger sets of words* in order to foster growth. And rather than using the words ourselves, we need to help unskilled kids learn to do the asking and then contend successfully with whatever they hear in response.

Brian and Andy are starting to play, and Joe has decided to join them. The kids at the water table are doing well, he feels, and know where to find him if they want help. He settles in. Unsurprisingly, Brian is already getting upset that Andy has the police car. "Brian," Joe says. "You *want* that police car, don't you! And Andy is using it. That feels *bad*!"

Brian is in full agreement. "You can say, 'I want that, can I have it?'" Joe suggests. Brian repeats Joe's words verbatim. Andy's answer, however, is a definitive "no." Brian is crushed. Joe jumps in quickly. "Oh Brian, he said *no*! You're *disappointed*!" Brian looks like he is either going to grab the police car or throw the red one he's holding at his friend. Joe puts his arm on his student's shoulder. "Brian, you can say, 'Can I have it when you're done, Andy?' Why don't you try that?" Brian does, once again repeating what he has heard.

Andy isn't being cooperative, and Joe now moves in to do some negotiating himself. "Andy, I think it's fair that Brian gets a turn. How many minutes?" ("How many minutes?" is a well-known question in this class, and kids understand that their job is to give a number.) "Five," Andy replies.

"Hey, Brian, Andy said you can have it in five minutes! That's not so long to wait!" Joe's voice is full of enthusiasm. "You can say, 'Thanks, Andy!'" Brian mumbles his thanks, and Joe makes sure Andy responds with a friendly "You're welcome." "Andy is being a good friend, Brian!" Joe says with obvious pleasure.

"And you were a good friend to him yesterday when you let him use the police car after you'd had a turn! Now . . . what's going to happen next, boys? Brian, what car will you use for now?"

Joe's work here relies on several now familiar aspects of intervention. One is "compassionate emphasis," first described in chapter 9. "That feels *bad*," he says with warmth. "You're *disappointed*." This use of compassionate emphasis helps Brian hang in for the duration. Joe uses the same strategy again when he frames the waiting as "not so long" and later remarks on what good friends these boys are learning to be to each other. He hopes that Brian can embrace the frame of friendship rather than one of deprivation.

Joe also provides some lend-an-ally play support (see chapter 6) and shows great skill in sensing when Brian has hit the outer edge of his ability to tolerate frustration. At that point, he stops asking Brian to do the work of negotiating and takes it on himself by giving Andy a prompt that tells him he is going to need to bend. Once Andy does, Joe shifts back to having the children engage in the end stage of the problem-solving process themselves. Having helped the children solve their conflict of interest, Joe begins looking forward. "What's going to happen next, boys?" he asks. He wants to help them move beyond conflict to constructive play.

When I suggest offering support like this, teachers sometimes tell me that it sounds very labor intensive. It is. However, I have become aware over the years that such work is often far less draining than what happens in its absence. It usually takes less time and energy to get in "up front" and help kids avoid a meltdown than it does to pick up the pieces after one occurs. In addition, this kind of work undoubtedly helps children build skill. And as they gain skill, they begin needing less adult assistance.

Leverage for Learning: Come Early and Stay Late

I have a motto for lend-an-ally play support: "Come early and stay late." Joining children even before they begin to play gives us leverage for learning. We can be there as they come up with a play theme. We can offer ourselves as a "wise child" and provide ideas and alternatives when it looks like something frustrating is emerging. We can help kids use their words in a way that really works. Then we can stick around for a while to help them extend and deepen their experiences of success. This is exactly what Joe proceeds to do.

An eager wise-child participant in Andy and Brian's police car scenario, Joe offers some ideas of his own and gets excited as he and the boys play out a story of danger and rescue. He assumes the role of adult coach, too, to help them envision possibilities when the wise child isn't able to do that work himself. Later, Joe picks up the adult coach mantle again as he encourages Brian to ask for his turn with the police car when Andy's five minutes are up. By that time, the boys have agreed that another car can serve as a police car too, so Andy isn't too upset by handing the real one over.

As the play continues, Joe moves to an aspect of lend-an-ally work that can be particularly important (and delicate): he offers Brian a short opportunity to try out his slowly growing skills without adult help. Seeing that the boys are doing well, he excuses himself to check out what is happening at the water table.

"I'll be back shortly, boys," Joe declares as he gives Brian a pat. "I want to see if the people in the car crash are doing okay at the hospital. Do you think the policemen need to get themselves some food? They've been working hard!"

When kids are first learning to interact without losing control, such short periods of unsupervised peer play may work best. For particularly explosive kids, we also need to think about what to do if the adult offering play support needs to move on. Then it may be time for some solo play or play at a community table with well-defined spaces and materials. That is true as well if no adult is available for play support in the first place. It's not fair to leave kids in situations where we know they are going to fail. That said, it is also unfair to separate easily frustrated kids much of the time. If we do that, they will never learn the skills they need to succeed.

Skill Development Is Crucial . . . but Not Sufficient

Brian's story is not yet complete: the team's work on skill development, after all, is only one aspect of the help he needs. That is also true, of course, for almost all easily frustrated children. The next chapter highlights other elements of intervention for such kids. In addition, it takes a look at another set of children who struggle with self-regulation—those who get swamped with anxiety.

15 Getting to Work on "Big Feelings"
Helping Children Who Get Swamped by Anger or Anxiety

Even though Brian struggles mightily to control his frustration, he never gets so out of control that he begins trashing his classroom, knocking over tables, or throwing chairs. Furthermore, although he doesn't like being guided to his calm-down bench, he always goes. He gets there without hurting someone on the way, too. The teachers in a classroom across the hall face an even more challenging situation. Their group includes Tina, a just four-year-old whose rage spikes so quickly and intensely that things can become worrisomely unsafe.

Tina has been playing with Mei-Zhen in the doll corner, where they often enjoy spending time together. As usual, Tina is being the mother while Mei-Zhen manages a number of babies. Tina is issuing numerous instructions about what those babies must do. But Mei-Zhen, who is generally very accommodating, doesn't sound happy about her marching orders.

Mei-Zhen's ability to protest is new and represents progress; the teachers, worried about her timidity, have been trying to help her learn to assert herself. But Mei-Zhen's asserting her needs with Tina may turn sour if she doesn't have an ally. Cate, the classroom's lead teacher, heads over as quickly as she can. Not quickly enough, however. As Cate is en route, Tina starts screaming. She kicks Mei-Zhen's leg, then aims another infuriated kick at one of the doll cribs.

Brian doesn't need a safety plan. Tina does. Her story is featured here because no exploration of our work with big-feelings kids would be complete without a look at how to develop plans for challenging behavior that continues to occur even after a scaffolding- and support-filled action plan is in place. I call that kind of behavior "breakthrough behavior"—it breaks through teachers' efforts to promote skill building and avoid explosions. There is no doubt that such proactive efforts lie at the heart of any action plan for an easily frustrated or angered child. The more intense that child's behavior, in fact, the more important it is to seed the day with connection and to move in quickly to support mastery whenever possible. However, for youngsters like Tina, even the most proactive plan works only some of the time. For others, like Alain (in chapters 2–6), unsafe behavior occurs so often that we need a way to diminish its frequency in order to have the opportunity to foster growth.

Clearly, then, there are times when safety considerations are of prime importance, and this chapter first looks at how to proceed when that is the case. Then it explores ways to offer extra support to emotionally overloaded kids and to partner with their (sometimes equally overloaded) families. Finally, it examines how some of the ideas that inform work with easily frustrated children can shed light on how to help kids who get flooded with anxiety.

Plans for "Breakthrough Behavior"

How do we respond when a child explodes in a way that is not only scary to other children but also is unsafe for all concerned? The answer to this question has significant implications: without a team-wide approach to such moments, our work is often far less successful than it would be otherwise. Coming up with such an approach requires thinking about when to "lean in" and when to "lean out," a balance first discussed in chapter 6. In general, we lean in with emotional support and skill-building assistance all through children's days in the classroom. But if a particular youngster is easily frustrated, as Tina so often is, she needs to know that when she hits to hurt, kicks or bites, hurls toys or chairs, we will lean out. In the latter case, *we respond with comfortable authority and do so in a similar way each time.* The particular combination of leaning in and leaning out for kids like this shouldn't be a "sloppy mix." We offer support with warmth, not judgment. We set expectations with clarity, not confusion. We follow through with calm assurance. And we keep our own frustration out of the way as much as we can.

Cate makes it to the doll corner at the same time that her coteacher Laurie does. Laurie crouches down by Mei-Zhen, who is crying. She rolls up Mei-Zhen's pants and looks at her leg. "Let's get some ice," she says warmly. "That looks like it hurts! It's not okay to let your mad out like Tina did. Cate will help Tina get safe. Then you can talk with her."

Cate, in the meantime, has positioned herself between Tina and Mei-Zhen. She doesn't look straight at her student, nor does she attempt to take her arm.

She speaks quietly yet with undeniable firmness. "We have safe feet in our class, Tina. Mei-Zhen got hurt. It's time for a break." Tina is still screaming but appears to know that she has to accompany Cate. She seems to know where she needs to go, too: to the classroom's "yoga corner." There, she will find a mat that is reserved for just such occasions, along with a few comfortable pillows. Some photos of Tina doing the classroom's much-practiced breathing exercises are posted on the yoga corner's wall.

Tina plops down with her back against that same wall, folds her hands across her chest, and glares at Cate. "It's okay, Tina," Cate says gently. "Your feet forgot to stay safe. They'll learn!" She stands back and stays silent as Tina lets out a big "no." Many more "nos" echo through the room as Cate remains quietly nearby. Once again, she doesn't look straight at her student.

A few minutes later, after this child appears to be slightly calmer, Cate moves in closer and offers to roll out the yoga mat. Tina responds with a barely perceptible nod. Yet another minute or two passes before Cate and Tina begin doing some breathing together. Cate doesn't appear to be in a hurry to help Tina reconnect with Mei-Zhen, who is back in the doll corner playing. Tina, she is probably thinking, isn't yet ready to show caring or remorse toward the friend she has hurt, nor is she ready to engage in constructive problem solving. Both will be important, but not until the right time.

When? Why? What Happens Next? Doing an ABC Analysis

In her interactions with Tina, Cate finds a sensible (and "clean") mix of leaning in and leaning out. She leans out first, with clear expectations of what is and isn't allowed and what Tina needs to do as a result of having been unsafe. Leaning in comes next, with Cate's "It's okay Tina, your feet forgot to be safe," her rolling out the yoga mat, and her helping Tina to calm down by doing some deep breathing alongside her. What doesn't show up in this brief exchange are the many other ways in which Cate and Laurie's action plan for Tina includes large doses of leaning in—plenty of seeding the day with connection, play-based support, and slow work on the steps of problem solving, to name just a few. Even if the wisdom of that plan is apparent, however, a question may remain: if a child loses her composure frequently, how do teachers know when to offer support and when to respond with firmness?

The answer to this question isn't simple. Often, the first step to figuring it out involves looking at the events surrounding that child's behavior and doing the kind of ABC behavioral analysis explored in chapter 4. When does the child act this way? What are the triggers? Can at least some of those be addressed? How do adults respond to what she does? Is there a chance that as a result of her behaviors, she *gets* something she wants or *avoids* something she doesn't want? Can her world be organized so that she is neither getting set off in predictable ways nor being reinforced in dysfunctional ways?

If this child always falls apart before nap, for example, why? Is there something about going to sleep that scares or overwhelms her? Is she mostly looking for attention? Or is she trying to avoid the difficult-to-manage task of having to slow down before sleep? If the first, how can we help her feel less overwhelmed? If the second, how can we give her the attention she craves in a way that doesn't reinforce the behavior she uses to get it? If the third, what does she need to learn in order to slow down in the middle of the day?

Cate and Tina have already taken an ABC-style look at Tina's difficulties as part of their work to understand her. It yielded some interesting data: Tina's explosions don't always have an obvious trigger, but they often seem to occur when she is having trouble finding the language she needs to express what she has in mind.

Tina's language processing issues have been apparent to everyone for a while, and she has been getting services from her local school system. Cate and her team have been offering plenty of language-based support too. But they know they can't be with Tina all the time. Furthermore, they believe that there is another piece to what is going on. While processing issues may be what starts fueling Tina's explosions, she appears to have learned that if she looks like she is about to explode, kids often back off from insisting on what *they* want and let her have her way. That appears to be true with adults at home, as well.

As a result of this analysis, Cate and the team have a number of goals in mind. They want to support continuing growth in the area of communication. They want to help Tina learn the skills of give-and-take—skills she is sorely lacking. But they also want to target the way she is seeking to achieve what she wants through behavior that is neither acceptable nor good for her. This is where the nuances of leaning in and leaning out "cleanly" come in. Cate doesn't want Tina to feel bad about herself. But neither does she want to reinforce Tina's behavior with the kind of acquiescent responses that have been a feature of her relationships both at home and in school. She doesn't want to reinforce that behavior with negative attention, either. That is why she stands near Tina without saying much. It is also why she doesn't look directly at Tina when she's the most upset.

The ABC analysis made clear that when teachers have done the latter in the past, Tina's behavior has escalated.

Considering Classroom-Wide Change

Changes that emerge from an ABC analysis are undoubtedly useful. But sometimes we put undue focus on a particular child rather than thinking about classroom routines and overall classroom tone. If a classroom has one or more kids who have trouble with self-regulation, it is often useful to ask whether there is a way to run a particular period of the day differently and better. It's also worth considering whether a feeling of mild chaos or group contagion has taken hold in the room. Do things get noisy or wild in a way that is hard to rein in? Do children generally listen well? Do they usually treat each other and other adults with respect? Do they treat the classroom's materials respectfully too? These questions lead back to the idea, discussed in chapter 13, that *classrooms can get unregulated, not just kids*. In Tina's case, the classroom as a whole is generally organized and calm. Earlier in the year, however, the transition from free play to group time had been dicey for everyone. As a result, Tina almost always got set off. Tightening up that transition—and being sure Tina had a job early on and knew where her place would be when it was done—made a big difference.

If you are concerned about classroom-wide issues, it can help to have a colleague or supervisor come in, take a look, and then do some brainstorming with you. On occasion, what's needed is some work on finding a comfortable voice of authority that you can use when you need it. When other, routine-focused changes are in order, you may want to think about approaching them proactively and teaching their steps encouragingly. Otherwise, you may get stuck issuing innumerable stern or frustrated reminders. That can make things worse rather than better.

Support and Scaffolding or Expectations and Limits?

Once the results of an ABC analysis and any classroom-wide issues have been addressed, it's time to focus on setting effective expectations. My teaching colleagues and I often start by making a list of the behaviors about which we are most concerned. Then we decide which ones will be ignored, which will result in extra support, and which will be responded to with a firm limit. We ask ourselves what actions will lead to immediate removal, too, and figure out where the child in question will go. Sometimes we decide that if that child hits a peer, but on the gentler side, it will still qualify as a moment for quickly offered problem-solving assistance. Sometimes we agree that hitting of all sorts will result in a temporary break. Sometimes we decide that if a youngster persists in screaming loudly, she will be asked to leave what she is doing to regroup elsewhere. In the case of a child who has been lashing out physically, however, this same behavior may be a step forward. Then we may plan to offer her additional support instead.

It is probably apparent from reading about Cate and Laurie's teamwork that there is a clear plan in place for Tina. The team knows to stay close at hand, to provide zone defense (see chapter 14), and to be ready for breakthrough behavior. When that behavior occurs, they have a seamless approach to helping out. Laurie generally goes to the child that's hurt. Cate immediately offers firm but kind containment. Addressing what has gone wrong, how to make amends, and how to move forward comes only after Tina has regained composure.

The problem is that for any particular child, it can be hard to know what is called for. In that situation, the only option is to make a "best guess" decision and stay steady for a while to see what happens. For children who need clear limits in order to learn better coping skills, we may agree that unsafe behaviors will result in an immediate removal. "We have safe hands in our class! Let's go to the cozy corner," we might declare. Or we may frame things differently. "Oh! Your hands forgot to be safe," we might remark calmly. "They need some time to remember so they can learn!"

For kids who are emotionally troubled, who have witnessed domestic violence, or who have been victims of abuse, a softer approach may be in order. In those cases, we may decide to ask other children to leave an area as we offer the youngster in question a gentle "stop message" accompanied by quiet support. "My job is to keep you and the other children safe," we might say. "It's not okay to hit. Let's sit here together until you feel better inside." Alternatively, we may guide that child to a classroom's "safe space" and give her a blanket or favorite stuffed animal as she calms down. Part of what we try to do in cases like this is to offer responses that are what the field now calls "trauma-informed." (See Kathleen Fitzgerald Rice and Betsy McAlister Grove's wonderful publication *Hope and Healing: A Caregiver's Guide to Helping Young Children Affected by Trauma* for further information about what such responses look like.)

Whatever the plan, consistency is crucial. With that in place, children learn what they will be allowed and not be allowed to do. They may need to keep testing out the edges of their control for a while. But, not infrequently, they will begin to feel steadier as they see those edges remain the same day after day. In fact, I have been struck over the years with just how much out-of-control kids crave such boundaries, even though it doesn't always look that way on the surface. *You can handle me,* they begin to think. *I don't scare or intimidate you like I do the others.*

The Twenty-One-Day Plan: Staying Steady in the Face of Unsteadiness

When you are trying to help a child feel like this, and you know that consistency is going to be important, it can help to consider the idea of a "twenty-one-day plan." I wish I could credit the person who came up with this idea; all I know is that I heard it early in my career and have relied on it many times since. The idea is this: once you have a "best guess" plan for what to do differently with a particular child, you need to stick with it for at least twenty-one days. If you carry it out for only three or seven or seventeen—or if you shift gears every hour or two—you won't give her a chance to steady out. This child may need to test out your new way of responding to her, perhaps many times over. As a result, things may look quite messy at first. Perhaps they will even get worse for a while. (The latter was the case with Tina.) It is at that point when you will be most in danger of trying something different.

If you can stay steady through all of this, though, the child will eventually trust the kinds of responses she can count on from you. It's only then that you will be able to tell if your new approach holds some promise. It is not that you can't tweak things along the way if your instinct says you can do something slightly differently and better. You can. In addition, there may be times when you become quite sure that what you are doing is harmful in some way. In that case, you will know to bail on the plan entirely and start over. Such a situation aside, though, after twenty-one days you should have a strong sense of how things are going. At that point you can decide whether you are on the right track. If you aren't, it's back to the drawing board. If you are, it is a good time to stop and reflect about what interventions to add or remove.

Details Matter: Who Does What? How Do They Do It?

Consistency is important. To provide it, there are always details to work out. When there are multiple staff on hand, for example, it may be that one individual feels the most comfortable taking charge when a child has lost control. Another may be too frightened to have the calming influence that the youngster needs. The problem in such a case, of course, is that sometimes the go-to person is sick or unavailable, or feels that being asked to play that role constantly takes her attention away from other children too often. The team needs to have a clear plan in place for such situations. Will the less comfortable staff person—or people—step up when needed? If so, how will they learn to do so? Will the program director or a supervisor come in? If not, who can serve as backup if things aren't going well?

The answers to these questions will vary. But the logic behind them does not: once kids feel that the world of their classroom is organized to help them stay safe, even when their steadiest anchor isn't available, they often begin doing better. When adults seem overwhelmed by over-the-top behavior and responses to that behavior vary widely, those same children often feel less steady inside themselves and act less safely as a result.

It is interesting to think about the qualities that "anchor teachers" share, qualities that Cate is known for. What do teachers like Cate offer kids that others do not? I have known teachers like this who are very soft-spoken and those who are rather gruff. I have known some who are utterly rigid about expectations and those who are more flexible. The common factor seems to be that they broadcast both care and clarity—and that they don't convey fear. These teachers know what they want and believe they can get it. They don't move in so quickly or intrusively that kids feel overwhelmed and triggered. But neither do they tiptoe around children's difficulties. In addition, they seem to have "eyes in the back of their heads." They tune in quickly when feelings are rising and get to work offering support or setting limits as soon as needed. In addition, in the middle of a child's upset and any limits that follow, they convey that she is still cared for and still good at heart.

Having Program-Wide Clarity

There is another piece to this puzzle of when to do what. It involves program-wide clarity about what is permissible when safety is a concern. Are you allowed to take a child's arm, place your hand behind his back, and gently guide him to a safe spot? If you are, but the child won't go without the possibility of you or him getting hurt, what then? Are there instances during which moving an out-of-control youngster or holding a child physically—though not oppressively—is allowed? If so, does your program offer guidance on how to do this safely for all, and does it require a "debriefing" meeting that ensures that any time this happens staff later ask whether there were alternatives available that could be tried the next time around?

My experience is that once there is clarity about expectations, a sensible plan, and consistent follow through, it is the rare child who doesn't begin to fare better. This is especially true if teachers are sure the plan doesn't involve attention that unwittingly reinforces poor behavior, and does involve large doses of connection and skill-building support. It is not that these easily triggered children stop getting upset entirely. They often don't. However, those upsets usually diminish in intensity and frequency.

I would be remiss if I didn't emphasize one last point here. A small number of kids need far more help than a non-specialized program can provide. If you sense that this holds true for a child in your classroom, it may be time to consider alternative options. Before you do, however, finding an early childhood mental health consultant to lend a hand may be useful. I can think of numerous cases when I have been called in about a child who is seemingly uncontrollable. With a fresh look at what is happening, some team-based brainstorming, and a comprehensive plan of action, things have often improved dramatically.

It is several months after the doll corner incident, and Tina and Mei-Zhen are playing there once again. Tina's language has been improving slowly. So has Mei-Zhen's ability to be assertive. Laurie, sitting with a group of children nearby, knows she is the one providing zone defense at the moment. She can see that, as is often the case, Tina is being on the bossy side.

Mei-Zhen begins asserting herself. Tina puts her fist up in the air, her face radiating fury. It looks like yet another journey to the yoga corner may be coming, and very soon. But then Tina glances at Laurie. Laurie gives her a "don't do it" look that is both firm and loving. Tina balls up her fist, puts her hand behind her back, and stamps her foot. Then she lets out a loud "ugh!" She looks back at Laurie. As this teacher heads over to lend a hand, she gives Tina a big thumbs-up. "Tina, that was *amazing*!" she says as she arrives in the doll corner. "You did that just like we practiced! You made a fist and put it behind your back. And you stamped and made a big noise. Wow! Let's tell Cate later, okay?"

It is, indeed, a moment worth celebrating—one filled with new learning. The team's combination of leaning in with warmth and skill-building support and leaning out with firmness is working. And as Tina listens to Laurie's glowing words, she may feel a sense of pride and accomplishment. She should. She is learning to express strong feelings without exploding, to wait for the help she needs in order to use words not fists, and to please the people who love her, all wrapped up in one.

Supporting Emotional Expression and Healing

Some children who struggle with big feelings need a safety plan in place. Many more need help with some of the emotions that plague them. Brian is in the latter category. And like so many easily frustrated kids, his family could use some help as well. In the previous chapter, Brian's team worked on the skill-focused elements of his plan. Here these other elements come center stage. The first has to do with supporting Brian as he works through some of the feelings that trouble him so deeply. The second involves partnering with his parents so that changes at home allow those feelings to diminish in intensity.

Chapter 9 touched on the importance of helping children "embed" their troubling feelings in play narratives rather than being stuck acting out those feelings in their daily lives. It also introduced the idea of offering emotionally fragile youngsters a "curricular bridge" to support growth and healing. These two concepts have great relevance for easily frustrated children. They are connected to the notion that when a child exhibits worrisome behaviors on the surface, emotions are often rumbling around underneath. Finding ways to help children express and work through those emotions is a crucial part of our job.

Some teachers and parents believe that supporting children in their efforts to sort through their experiences and confusions through play is solely the job of play therapists. But the truth is that teachers can do a great deal in their classrooms to help with this all important work. Because if we tune into children's play, the themes they're working on are often clear. Then, by offering ourselves either as witnesses from outside the play or as "wise child" partners from within it, we can help them find opportunities for emotional expression and healing. In chapter 9, for example, Claudia and Nancy support Hannah's cat- and lion-inspired play—play that helps this traumatized child experience the softness of connection and the power of feline strength. In chapter 11, these same teachers set up a "caring place" so that Isabel can play out some of her confusion about her abuela's frightening illness. These are just two examples of using play-based support not just as a tool for developmental skill building but for emotional healing as well.

One more example of this kind of therapeutic play support comes in the previous chapter, as Joe joins Brian and Andy in their stories of danger and rescue. On one level, Joe is helping Brian with play skills. But he knows that Brian feels confused about issues connected to power and vulnerability and that he carries within himself easily ignited feelings of anger and hurt. Police, fire, and hospital themes often surface for children like Brian, and Joe and the other teachers are alert to the ways in which these themes can be used to promote healing. The team is also aware of the potential for building one or more "curricular bridges" that will help this boy sort through some of his troubling feelings.

Escaping Zombie Land: A Curricular Bridge

In January, a new theme invades Brian's classroom: zombies. Lillian and Joe know the theme began with some things Brian started talking and playing about after he had spent time with his stepbrothers one weekend. They guess he had seen a zombie-focused TV show or movie with those older boys, perhaps even more than one. That is a concern in its own right. But now his disturbing experiences have taken hold in their room, with a number of their more active and aggressive children catching a ride on the theme's intriguing possibilities. Within days, it seems, zombies and monsters creep into play both indoors and out. It is a significant problem: other kids are getting frightened by what a small group of boys and girls are playing and talking about. They are not the only ones feeling overwhelmed though. The play's instigators seem compelled to continue, even as they are increasingly unnerved.

Brian has a particularly hard time as the theme takes hold both in his brain and in the classroom. He starts talking only about zombies. He prowls around the classroom as if he *is* a zombie. And he stops being able to fall asleep at naptime because he is afraid of having nightmares about being attacked by zombies. (It seems, from what he says, that he has had such nightmares at home a few times and isn't sleeping well there either.) Lillian and Joe sit down for a team meeting—they know they need a plan.

The next day, they start off circle time talking about how everyone can feel scared on occasion. And how, sometimes, we even have nightmares about things that frighten us. Lillian asks whether the children know what a nightmare is. They do. Then she inquires about whether nightmares are real. They aren't, the children agree, but they can feel as if they are. Monsters and zombies aren't real either, they admit, but can seem disturbingly real and scary too. Lillian reads *There's a Nightmare in My Closet* by Mercer Meyer. Then the teachers invite children to draw their nightmares on large pieces of white paper.

The first day, kids are asked to draw their nightmares in light pencil. Lillian hopes that this will help their illustrations feel dreamlike—and less frightening. Throughout the week, the children begin filling out their pictures with color.

Over the same period, there are a number of circle-time conversations about how it's okay to feel afraid or scared. The kids also discuss what it means to be brave and brainstorm about the meaning of the word *courage*. Then they talk about times that they remember being brave or courageous. Eventually they dictate some lines about those moments, and one of the teachers records what they say at the bottom of their nightmare pictures. All the pictures end up on a wall with the header "There's a Nightmare in My Closet."

The teachers ask whether the children feel okay about "turning off their brain's television set" when their interest in monsters is getting the better of them. With a palpable sense of relief, the kids agree to try. They also make a pact that it's okay to tell their classmates when they don't want to hear any more—or play anymore—about scary things. Thankfully, over the course of two weeks, zombie play in the classroom dies down. Just as importantly, Brian's obsession starts dying down too. Napping eventually becomes, once again, a comfortable option. A curricular bridge has been built and emotional well-being slowly restored.

Can We Talk? Problem Solving with Parents

During this same period, Lillian initiates an important conversation with Brian's parents. Zombie movies and shows are, she suggests, more than their son can handle, and other violently themed movies and shows probably are as well. These parents take a while to get on board. It's going to be hard to shield their youngest from the interests of his older siblings, they note. Especially since he wants nothing more than to feel a part of the "big boy" crowd. After a friendly exchange of questions and ideas, however, Brian's parents agree to see what they can do. Lillian wonders what that will mean, but it feels like a start.

A start is just what the conversation turns out to be. Brian's mother, Grace, seems to feel that a friendly door has been opened, and she begins requesting occasional meetings with Lillian to discuss life at home. Brian's dad, she explains, won't be able to make it to these meetings because of his work schedule. She will, however, fill him in on the content of what is discussed. That content ranges widely. Some of it concerns a firmer and more consistent way of setting expectations in the midst of family life with all three boys. Some has to do with fostering Brian's self-soothing and problem-solving skills. (Lillian gives Grace a copy of the "daisy or balloon" calm-down sheet described in the previous chapter, and it turns out to be a big help.)

Lillian and Grace also discuss the possibility of getting therapeutic support for her older boys. They have never had a chance to talk about or work through the hard times they experienced when they were young. If they are less reactive, these adults agree, things may be easier for Brian as well. Overall, it appears that Grace has been desperate for some parenting advice and is eager to make changes. It's not easy—with three intense boys and her own soft-spoken nature, Grace has her work cut out for her. Eventually, Lillian convinces Grace to join a parenting group at a local community center and to get some counseling for herself as well.

Conversations like those Lillian has with Grace often unfold slowly. We start by forging a warm partnership with parents and other family caregivers. We invite them to collaborate with us and tell us what they know—rather than only the reverse. Then we explore how we can create a home-school "net" that will help an easily frustrated child begin to thrive. For some kids, creating such a net is relatively easy. Parents have been confused but are eager to collaborate with us. For others, it is far harder. Things at home are chaotic, unhappy, or full of tension. There is little time and little energy to focus on home dynamics. (That may even be why the child we are worrying about is struggling so intensely in the first place.) In such cases, we keep trying to reach out. Perhaps small changes will lead to increased energy for bigger ones. Perhaps the help we are offering in school will begin making a difference at home, and as a result, partnering with a particular family will be easier down the road.

Brian and Tina: Lessons Learned

Brian and Tina are two very different children. Brian has had a complicated and chaotic experience at home and needs not only skill-building help but emotional support. In addition, life at home needs to become a significant focus if things are going to move forward. By the end of his prekindergarten year he is doing far better. Then in early summer, just months before he is to head off for elementary school, Brian takes a tumble. He starts to have tantrums the likes of which teachers haven't seen since he first arrived in the program. He doesn't explode with rage that is frighteningly unsafe, but he seems deeply unhappy and troubled once again.

It takes a while for everyone to understand what is going on. Many of Brian's friends have already left the program in preparation for going to their next school, and a number of new kids have taken their place. Brian, we realize, is feeling confused and bereft. Lillian and Joe imagine that he is scared about the upcoming change, too. They guess that he is asking himself an unsettling question: *Will I be okay when I'm not here anymore, where people know and love me even when I do the wrong thing?* It is time for another curricular bridge, this one about changes, about growing up, and about staying connected after you say good-bye to people who have cared for you. Brian rallies. But it is poignant to see just how much he feels that his success is connected to a place and its people, not to something he holds within himself and can bring along wherever he goes.

Tina is a different story. Her growth is both slower and steadier than Brian's. Tina's team agrees that, at heart, her difficulties stem from language processing challenges. They are convinced, too, that some problematic patterning emerged in response to Tina's frustration at not being able to make herself understood. (That patterning has played a role at home as well, and there has been a family piece to the team's work that isn't explored in this chapter.) As Tina's language has improved and that patterning has been attended to, her level of explosiveness has diminished. What has taken its place as a central concern is how much this child needs to be in control, and how rigid and constricted her play is. Both may be connected to language processing issues as well—it is still hard for Tina to make herself understood and to put together longer sequences of language and play. She has another year in the program and will be assigned to Lillian and Joe's prekindergarten class in the fall. They are ready for her. They know they will need to scaffold language, support deepening play possibilities, and foster flexibility and friendships in the classroom. They will continue to work with Tina's parents as well, to be sure this child is getting plenty of support but not too much negative power at home.

Supporting Children Whose Anxieties Run High

Tina and Brian's slow progress in learning to self-regulate involves feelings of frustration and anger. But struggles with self-regulation can involve other feelings as well—including, quite commonly, feelings of intense anxiety.

Down the hall from Brian's and Tina's rooms is a class of mostly three-year-olds. Two children in that group had significantly more trouble than their classmates separating from their parents when they began attending the program in September. Now one of them, Maia, has become so afraid of the program's occasional fire drills that she asks many times a day whether one is going to take place. Reassurance doesn't seem to help for long. This is true even though she now understands that since fire drills frighten her, she'll not only be warned before one occurs but have someone to be with as soon as it begins.

Maia's classmate James is anxious too. Recently, he experienced an intense windstorm that knocked down a large tree limb near his house. No one was hurt. However, he no longer wants to go outside if there is even a hint of wind. He doesn't like to hear wind banging against the classroom's windows either. In fact, he goes running for a teacher in an almost full-blown panic when there is the slightest clatter. Reassurance doesn't seem to help him any more than it helps Maia.

As far as their teachers can tell, neither of these children has experienced either a hard start or hard times. Instead, they both appear to come from families where there is a history of anxiety. As a result they may have an extra dose of anxiety built into their hard wiring. In addition, it is very possible that this anxiety has led to some interactive patterning frequently seen between anxious kids and their caregivers.

Two Common Patterns, Two Related Approaches

The patterning these children are experiencing connects to the question of self-soothing. Maia doesn't explode like Brian or Tina in the face of big feelings. That is because her big feelings involve not anger or frustration but instead fear and worry. That said, she doesn't know how to calm herself down any more than Brian and Tina do at the beginning of their experiences being in school. If Maia could soothe herself when she gets anxious, she wouldn't keep seeking reassurance. If James could do the same, he wouldn't insist that he doesn't want to go outside when it is even mildly breezy. These two patterns are worth describing clearly and knowing well:

- *Pattern one—reassurance seeking:* A child feels anxious. She turns to someone else, usually an adult, for reassurance. That adult offers the reassurance requested. As kids get older, it often involves words that explain why the child doesn't need to worry. Whatever its form, this reassurance may temporarily work. But *because the child can't reassure herself, her anxiety pops up again, and often fairly soon*. At that point, more reassurance is requested and given. However, little if any capacity for self-soothing grows, leading to increased reassurance seeking. The child and the adults around her end up in what we might call an "amplifying loop."

- *Pattern two—avoidance:* A child feels anxious. There is something he doesn't like dealing with, whether a dog, a particular store, an elevator, or even (as in James's case) wind. *The child does everything he can to avoid the thing about which he is worried.* He refuses to go to the store that makes him nervous or to get in an elevator that leaves him feeling closed in and frightened. He crosses the street at the mere thought of encountering a dog. He won't go outside for fear of the wind blowing. Whatever the trigger, the more he avoids the thing that concerns him, the more unimaginably awful it seems to become. He is not learning to self-soothe any more than a reassurance-seeking child is, and the loop he's engaging in may be amplifying just as much.

Addressing Reassurance Seeking

While some anxious kids engage mainly in one of these patterns, many alternate between them. Either way, there are some relatively simple strategies we can use to help out. I call the first, *"meet and greet, cap and contain."* It aims to increase self-soothing while slowly reducing reassurance seeking. What does it look like? Here is what Maia's teacher Brenda now does in response to this child's fire drill worries:

Maia has been asking about fire alarms many times a day. Since a team meeting in which her reassurance seeking was discussed, lead teacher Brenda and her team have a new plan. The first time Maia approaches Brenda with this worry, Brenda squats down and talks with her student warmly and at some length. "Oh, Maia, you're worried! What do you want to know?" Maia asks if there will be a fire drill, and Brenda calmly assures her that no drills are planned for that day. "Maia, let's go find your story about fire drills. We can read it together if you want to!" Brenda and Maia locate the laminated scripted story the team wrote just for her—it's in an easy-to-find spot in her cubby. The story reminds Maia that fire drills happen. It notes that some kids find them to be very loud. It emphasizes that fire alarms exist so that everyone knows what to do to stay safe. And it offers reassurance that someone will always be there to hold Maia's hand if she feels scared by the noise. The story also reminds her that school is a good place to have fun and that she can "put worry away and begin to play." She will be happy when she does this, it concludes. This last page includes a picture of Maia playing with friends and grinning.

This vignette illustrates the first part of "meet and greet." It involves leaning in and giving a child our full attention and support. A hug. An explanation. A scripted story if we are so inclined. Whatever it takes to calm the child down in the moment. Then comes cap and contain.

"Maia," Brenda says kindly after reading the scripted story as they snuggle on a pillow. "We're done talking about fire drills. Let's go see who's playing!" Now Brenda begins walking around the classroom with Maia by her side. She is seeking a group of children who are doing something that Maia might find engaging. Then, in "human glue" fashion, she works to help Maia experience enjoyment rather than worry. The next time Maia pops over with the same reassurance-seeking behavior, the meet and greet component is very short. "Oh, do you have a worried feeling? It will go away soon! Do you want to find a place to look at your story, or do you want to play some more?"

Maia is welcome to stay by Brenda's side this time, but Brenda won't offer specific reassurance about fire drills. Because now Maia has a job to do—the job of self-soothing. If Maia keeps pushing for reassurance, Brenda may place an arm around her shoulders or offer her a hand. But she will continue to focus on the fun happening throughout the classroom. Her goal, of course, is to cap reassurance seeking and help Maia learn (probably slowly) to contain her anxiety herself. Brenda is never unkind and never unavailable, but she clearly provides less fuel for the reassurance-seeking loop than she did earlier in the day. Furthermore, the team is working so that if Maia goes to yet another teacher to initiate a similar conversation, that teacher will remark that she knows Maia already talked with Brenda about fire drills. Does she want to get her story, or would she like to play?

Addressing Avoidance

Our approach to addressing patterns of avoidance has a somewhat different thrust. Its "meet and greet" element may look similar, as we invite kids to chat about what is worrying them and offer comforting words in response. But, in the case of avoidance, we then join children as we help them *gradually approach* what worries them.

As the rest of the class gets ready to exit the door to go outside with the room's assistant teacher, Brenda makes clear that she's going to take an extra minute with James. She squats down next to him. "Let's look and listen, James! Yes, there is some wind! Let's put our hands over our ears and then take them off. We'll count to three to see what it sounds like. Then we'll put our hands back on our ears!" James isn't happy about this idea. However, with Brenda crouched down by his side, he imitates what she is doing. "Now let's step outside and do it again," Brenda says. They do. Then it is time to head to the playground. "James, we'll join the class now. There is a little wind but it's safe here. We're all done talking about wind. You can stay with me until you're ready to play. Your friends are waiting for you!"

In a situation like this, we are asking children to begin the work of self-soothing by providing a gentle push that counteracts the tendency toward avoidance that keeps them from doing that work. And without being unkind, we are also removing attention from their way of seeking us out to talk and fret. They can be by our side. Their worry may still plague them. But with our comforting presence and seeming disinterest in their intense anxiety, they may slowly begin to find some strategies that allow them more inner freedom.

When Anxiety Has Complex Roots

The approaches just described can be very useful. However, they don't work with all kids. How could they? Some children are anxious due to truly difficult experiences—in the past, in the present, or both. Many of those youngsters will benefit from a therapeutic context in which to express and work through their feelings. I recently supervised a Head Start–based mental health specialist who had some questions about a suddenly anxious child who had recently witnessed his aunt having a heart attack. This woman got treated quickly and was doing well, but her nephew had become frozen with panic. He seemed plagued by some troubling questions: Could this happen to anyone who appeared to be healthy? His teachers? His parents? His siblings? His friends?

Six weeks of short-term therapy were enormously helpful to this boy. For youngsters who have experienced ongoing trauma, who have dealt with severe loss, or who have undergone invasive medical treatment, such help may be beneficial as well. In those cases, however, it may take longer for children to experience the healing and relief they need. In short, there are no easy answers to helping out when anxiety looms large and the reasons are complex. If you would like to learn more about working with anxiety in general, and traumatized, anxious children in particular, there are some good resources listed in appendix C. Those resources include a few books to recommend to families. They may be worth having on hand because in the face of children's anxiety, it is always a plus when we and adult family members are on the same page. In particular, it helps if we offer similar approaches to providing both support and containment at home and in school.

It Is Hard to Be Little in a Big World

The previous two chapters have scratched only the surface of how we work with children who have trouble regulating emotions. Youngsters like this, whose big feelings get really big really fast, need our help desperately. If they can learn to live with those feelings yet not become hijacked by them, they will have a far easier time as they move beyond their preschool years. Sometimes we find that we have given such children great gifts as they go on their way. That is certainly true for Brian. It will likely be true for Tina, Maia, and James as well—although these three have at least another year in their program before heading to kindergarten. Big-feelings kids give us gifts too. They help us learn patience. They remind us that even the most surly child has a desire to be loved lurking just under the surface of a strong need to push us away. And they help us remember how hard it can be to be little in a big and overpowering world.

16 Spotlight on Parenting
Helping Families Set Effective Expectations at Home

I am sitting at the head of a long, rectangular table. Five mothers, three fathers, an aunt, and a grandmother are seated there as well. Some have left their children at home with a partner or babysitter. Others have dropped off their kids in a room down the hall where free child care has been provided. It is dinnertime, and pizza, salad, and cold drinks have been put out in both rooms. In five minutes or so, one of the program's regularly scheduled family support sessions will begin.

The program in question runs six preschool sites spread out across a midsized city. Amina, one of its teacher-directors, is sitting by my side—she and I will run the meeting together. The subject of the evening involves setting sensible expectations and knowing how to back them up. This will be the first of four meetings on the same topic. That's because when the program's families are asked what they most want to talk about, their answers often have to do with managing difficult behaviors more successfully at home. Learning how to change what is happening in that regard usually requires more than just one conversation.

The room is abuzz with chatter. Except for the experience of one mother who is nursing an infant, it is a rare moment of child-free dinnertime conversation for many who have walked in the door. Some of them are talking about a stomach virus that has been making the rounds or the cheapest place to get diapers. Some are discussing a new soccer program they have just discovered or the stress of balancing kids and work. The room is abuzz, in other words, with the details of family life in the twenty-first century.

"We're All in This Together": Engaging Hard-to-Reach Parents

I have been an early childhood consultant and teacher trainer in this program for years, and we have always offered parent meetings like this one. What we found early on, however, was that the adults who showed up for such meetings included mainly our easiest-to-reach parents. It's not that we didn't enjoy partnering with those adults. But we wanted to reach our most stressed and harder-to-help parents as well. We spent some time brainstorming about this dilemma. As a result, we have started featuring the topic of our evening's session later in each school year. Early every fall, we begin thinking about which families could use some extra guidance about life at home. And we consider which of those families might need additional encouragement to show up for our support groups.

As part of this attempt to attract a broader group of participants, we now provide dinner and child care. That helps. But there is more. Starting in October, we begin "talking up" these groups, though they don't begin until January. During informal conversations and formal family conferences alike, teachers slowly begin bringing up some of the issues they are seeing. And they start mentioning how "You might love talking with other adults about this. It can feel so good to share stories."

There is something else we have started doing as well. Some of our parents are second- or third-year veterans of the program—and of these meetings. Perhaps they started out struggling with limit setting at home and were rather inconsistent in their responses to their children's difficult behaviors. Maybe they got some one-on-one help from a teacher or teacher-director and also attended some of these parent sessions. Now they're feeling much more successful in dealing with difficulties as they arise. We invite some of these adults to join us as parent mentors. And we encourage them to reach out to caregivers who are on the earlier end of this learning curve. That has been a real boon, both to the veterans (who feel empowered in their new role) and to the caregivers they support. It has also helped us in creating a feeling that each preschool site is, in its way, a family—that "we're all in this together." That's a feeling that many of our families need and appreciate. We like it too.

When Life at Home Is Challenging: Offering Guidance and Support

As a teacher, you are usually aware of which children and parents are struggling in intense ways at home. You see it at drop-off time. You notice it at pickup time. You hear about it in conversations with caregivers that take place on the fly and in regularly scheduled parent conferences. Often, the difficulties kids are having at home seep into your classrooms in the form of less-than-welcome behaviors. And, as you know, those behaviors can be hard to change at school if they are a big piece of life elsewhere. With all of this in mind, you and your colleagues probably end up wondering how to help some of these stress-filled families find new ways to be together.

This chapter explores some of the ideas we can invite such families to consider. It also provides a look at one option in which they can do so: parenting groups. There is no doubt that parent trainings and support groups can be useful and efficient when you have a number of families who are struggling. However, not all programs have the resources to run such groups, and not all have enough parents who are interested, either. Luckily, the ideas anchoring Amina's and my group-based efforts at mentoring and supporting parents can easily be woven into one-on-one family meetings. It also helps to have a list of books to recommend to families who like to access the help they need through reading—or at least want to start there. Some good resources to suggest in such cases can be found in appendix C.

However you choose to reach out to parents in need of guidance, being able to share easy-to-understand principles and easy-to-use strategies makes a big difference. It is important to keep in mind, too, that the time you spend supporting and mentoring such parents is often like gold in the bank as far as children's growth and well-being is concerned . . . even though that time can be hard to come by.

Hopes for the Long Haul, Problems Right Now

After welcoming everyone, Amina and I frame the topic of the evening. Acknowledging that we will be talking about things that aren't going well at home, we pose an initial question to the adults in the room: *If you imagine your child (or grandchild, niece, or nephew) as a teenager and then an adult, what are your hopes for him or her? Do you have some deeply felt wishes for what he or she will be like?*

Amina and I are asking these questions on a particular evening, but the answers we get back feel like many we've heard before. We want her to be kind, we hear, to care about others and take their needs into account. We want him to be patient but also to be able to advocate for himself. We hope she'll learn to roll with the punches, to deal with whatever life may bring. We want him to have things he's passionate about and to be able to persevere when something is hard. We'd like her to be curious about the world and love learning. We want him to listen well and to be polite—to have good friends and be a good friend. We want her to feel successful, confident, and proud.

Many of those present are nodding in agreement as others share their seemingly universal hopes for their kids. And a feeling of common purpose begins to fill the room even though the adults at its large table come from widely varying backgrounds and cultures. Now Amina and I move on to caregivers' worries, asking about what kinds of unwelcome behaviors leave these adults feeling uneasy or helpless. In response, we begin hearing about whining, tantrums, and lengthy arguments about what's fair. Children's troubles listening to what's being asked of them—and responding willingly—come up frequently too. So do difficulties managing frustration and being flexible when things change unexpectedly. We hear about children's resistance to eating when it's time to eat, sleeping when it's time to sleep, and leaving for school when it's time to get going. Eating what is served and wearing what is available come up quite a bit as well.

Limit Setting Isn't an End in Itself—It's a Teaching Tool

As we always do after such opening conversation, Amina and I will create a bridge from the sharing of hopes and worries to the role of limit setting. We want our participants to see that while limit setting isn't an end in itself, it does play an important role in supporting children's development. In our eyes, we'll tell them, it is one of many tools parents can use to help their kids master skills essential to their well-being. To make that point clear, we will highlight some of those skills, which are also listed in a set of handouts we distributed before the meeting began. Setting and following through on sensible expectations, one of those handouts says, helps kids learn:

- to be flexible
- to manage their strong feelings when something doesn't go the way they wish it would
- to tolerate other people's ideas and agendas—to be able to "go with the flow" when adults ask them to make a shift or do something they'd rather not do
- to have empathy for other people's feelings and needs
- to be able to do what is asked if it is reasonable, and to wait even when it's hard
- to be able to control their impulses and their tempers

Amina and I glance at each other. It feels like our parents are with us. I ask them whether what we've said about the role of limits in development make sense. It seems to. Our participants can see the link between enforcing what they expect and helping their kids become more mature, cooperative, and caring. We have an important point to add before moving ahead, though. *Setting limits in a way that leaves kids feeling cared for rather than judged makes all the difference. Keeping in mind who a particular child is and how she is "built" does too.* That's why, Amina remarks, we sometimes give these conversations a headline: "Parenting with Love and Limits."

Familiar Stories, Underlying Patterns

The next step in helping parents explore what is going on at home involves looking at the interactive patterns that lie behind some of the things they're worrying about. Asking for concrete examples of what takes place in the midst of family life often gets at those patterns quite quickly.

Amina looks around, her face radiating encouragement. She has a question, she tells the group, one she knows may be a little awkward to answer: Would some of those present consider sharing a story of family life when things aren't going so well? What she's talking about, she goes on, would involve one of those "here we go again" moments that every parent can experience. A mother begins talking about trying to get her child out the door in the morning, and the disastrous yelling that often ensues. A father jumps in to describe his feeling of helplessness each night that he's "on" for bath time. As more stories emerge, others at the table begin to nod. It's that bedtime nonsense, Amina and I can see them thinking. It's the dinnertime thing, or the "I won't and you can't make me" mess. More adults jump in with examples. Each time, either Amina or I take a few minutes to ask questions about how things start, what the child does, what the adults on hand do in response, and what happens next.

Soon, the two of us start sketching out some of the common patterns adult caregivers may have fallen into when children aren't doing well. As we do this, we first notice what the pattern is. Then we ask those present to brainstorm about what their children are learning when such interchanges take place repeatedly. Eventually, we stop the storytelling in order to take a closer look at four common patterns that have come up in the course of our conversation. We tease out what children learn from each one. Then we consider what these caregivers can do differently to support the behaviors and skill development they would like to see.

Those patterns and the learning that grows out of them are listed on the following pages alongside ideas for more effective adult responses. In fact, what you see on the next two pages is a verbatim handout from our family support sessions—that's why there is some introductory text at its beginning. You are welcome to use it with your families, as well, if you think it will be helpful.

Patterns and Problems
A Few Common Mistakes That Make Things Worse over Time

It's easy to fall into patterns with our children that, despite our best intentions, lead to more of the very behaviors we're concerned about. Here are just a few. Keeping them in mind—and knowing how to avoid them—can make a big difference. Changing them can be hard at first though!

Pattern 1

You make a request, then repeat it three or four times. Still not getting what you're asking for, you issue a threat. You repeat that a few times too. Finally, you go to the "big bang" stage. (That's when you might yell, stamp your foot, or lose your temper entirely.) After the big bang, your child finally does what you've been asking.

What is your child learning? To continue on through all the nagging and threats until the "big bang."

What can you do instead? Don't set expectations you won't have the energy to carry through with! Once you decide to go ahead with a request, (1) get your child's attention, (2) set your expectation, and (3) give him a little time to comply. Then, if he doesn't do what you've asked, (4) respond with whatever limit-setting approach you have chosen for follow-through.

Pattern 2

You call your child's name and don't get an answer, call it again and still don't get a response. You say it once or twice more. Nothing doing. Finally, in frustration, you yell it in a way that would be very hard to ignore. At that point, she looks up.

What is your child learning? To wait until you yell her name with irritation before responding to your cue for attention.

What can you do instead? Go over to her. Tap her shoulder if it will help. Call her name. Wait for at least five seconds. Try again if needed. Offer some warm pleasure when she "pops up" to find out what you have to say. (If you find this rarely works, come up with an enjoyable plan that helps her practice popping up to pay attention after she hears her name called.)

Pattern 3

Your child asks for something and you say "no." He repeats his request, whines, or stomps his feet. You say "no" again. He keeps protesting. Eventually, you give in.

What is your child learning? To keep on trying to get you to change your mind, rather than to take "no" for an answer.

What can you do instead? If you're going to give in, do it right at the start. If you say "no," then hold the line.

Pattern 4

Your child isn't very good at paying attention. So, for the most part, you end up asking for her attention only when you really want it. That's usually when she's doing something you don't want her to do, or when you want her to stop what she's doing and enjoying (playing with her toys, for example) to do something less interesting (like taking a bath).

What is your child learning? When I pay attention, I'm going to hear something I'm not crazy about.

What can you do instead? Start noticing when your child is happily involved in something she enjoys doing. Get her attention, and then have a cheerful back-and-forth about what she's up to or about a topic *that will feel good and connected to both of you.* Think of this as "seeding your child's day" with moments of attention and pleasure. Then, when you need her attention for something that's less fun on her end, start by getting her attention. After you can tell she's focused on what's to come, "connect before you correct . . . or redirect!"

Can You Help Us Make the Change? The Nuts and Bolts of Parent Support

Supporting parents in beginning to see these patterns is the first step toward change. Helping them learn what it takes to alter them is the second. That usually takes more than just a handout—some in-depth exploration is often needed as well. One example of this kind of exploration involves the "big bang pattern." The big bang, as noted on the handout, is my phrase for what occurs after an adult caregiver issues a series of reminders followed by some repeated threats. It is the cue for kids that they'd better get it together *and fast* before something really bad happens. (Because now that adult truly means business.) The question for teachers is how to describe this pattern to parents, and how to help them find a more effective way of dealing with misbehavior.

Mapping Out Difficulties, Planning Out Alternatives

The big bang pattern is so common and so important for parents to understand that I sometimes draw a visual representation of how it unfolds. (I learned to do this from the work of Russell Barkley, author of *Your Defiant Child*. See Barkley 2013, page 42.) But whether or not I offer a sketched-out "map" of how it works, I emphasize one important thing: any repeated nagging and threatening is extra "noise," not effective limit setting. As the "Patterns and Problems" handout highlights, that noise teaches a child to wait for the big bang.

This picture usually makes sense to family members. Furthermore, it turns out that once they hear about the pattern, or see it sketched out, they usually recognize if they're repeatedly engaging in it. They can describe what their personal version of the big bang looks like, too. In our program's family sessions, there is often a lot of rueful laughter as those descriptions are embarrassedly shared.

The next step is envisioning an alternative scenario. What you need, Amina and I tell parents, is an *exit strategy*. And that strategy, we emphasize, needs to come right after you have issued your request. You need a plan for what you will do if you don't get what you've asked for, and you have to be ready to follow it when necessary. So if you aren't sure you want to follow through, don't issue your request in the first place. That means, we note, that you have to give yourselves a minute to think before asking your children to do (or not do) something. Be both "softer and harder." If you're going to give in, *do it with a smile right up front.* If you're going to ask for something, *hang on for the ride.*

Parents and other caregivers usually grasp this overall idea. It is doing it that's challenging. That is where Amina's and my support and "cheerleading" come in—and where the support and cheerleading of fellow group members can play such a powerful role. Some written material helps support our suggestions, too. Here is another handout Amina and I provide at our meetings. You are welcome to use this one too.

Setting Effective Expectations at Home

If you feel that your children aren't behaving well, you may end up yelling, lecturing, or even hitting far more than you'd like. You may also be getting so sick of battling things out at home that you say "no" a lot and then, eventually, give in. The following tips can help you move things in a better direction.

- ***Only set limits that you're completely sure you want to back up.*** Any time you have a hunch that you are going to give in eventually, don't say "no" in the first place.

- ***Be both softer and harder.*** Say "yes" cheerfully on all the little stuff that you sense you'll eventually cave in about, then hold the line on the really important, big things. And be sure that a "no" stays a "no," and a "yes" stays a "yes." Don't worry, later you can become more flexible again.

- ***Find a simple, core strategy for disciplining that works for you.*** There are many methods that work well. Thomas Phelan's book *1-2-3 Magic* (2010) offers one option. Lynn Clark's *SOS Help for Parents* (2005) provides some others. Ask your child's teachers if you'd like additional recommendations.

- ***Keep words to a minimum and emotions at bay.*** As you find a set of limit-setting strategies that work for you, *try not to use too many words, and stay as calm as you can*—focus on behavior and consequences instead of morals and disappointment. And feel free to have a mix of limit-setting strategies on hand. "Active ignoring" (see *SOS Help for Parents*), time-outs, if-then consequences, and "time away" when kids are getting grumpy and can't seem to turn themselves around all work together well.

- ***Don't rely just on limits.*** Limits on their own don't help kids learn to behave reasonably. If a child has only one way of reacting to stress and frustration—which is to get mad and lash out—limits will certainly help him get himself under better control. But he will also need ongoing support in learning how to calm down and solve problems as well. He'll need to feel that you enjoy and cherish him too!

From *When Young Children Need Help: Understanding and Addressing Emotional, Behavioral, and Developmental Challenges* by Deborah Hirschland, © 2015. Published by Redleaf Press, www.redleafpress.org. This page may be reproduced for program use only.

Finding a Voice of Authority—An Essential Ingredient

Even when armed with the best of strategies, many parents need help in learning how to issue calm and clear instructions about what they expect. In our parent meetings, Amina and I often ask for volunteers to try out what we call a friendly but firm "voice of authority." Many of our parents find that either their voices are noticeably angry by the time they have gotten serious about what they want, or they discover that their voices are not nearly forceful enough in tone.

As mentioned earlier, our groups often include veterans from previous years' trainings, adults whom we have invited to join us as experienced "parent mentors." These mentors frequently speak up about their experiences trying to find a voice of authority when they first took on the task of changing patterns at home. They describe what they probably sounded like before they got started, and share what they learned to do differently. Depending on the evening (and my willingness to feel embarrassed), this topic may lead me to talk about my first job after college. I was hired to run a residence for very challenging boys whose intense behaviors (and difficult family situations) made it impossible for them to live at home—at least for a while. My first week on that job, I tell group participants, I yelled so much that I lost my voice for a week.

I share this story for a reason. I want participants to know what I eventually learned: that as a rather soft-spoken young woman, my voice of authority turned out to be lower and quieter than the one I usually use—not higher and louder, as I had thought it needed to be. But quiet as it was, I emphasize, I found a way to give that voice an "iron rod" right down its middle. And I model what that voice sounds like to this day: it's low, quiet, and a bit stern without being mean. It doesn't sound angry (at least when I'm at my best), just utterly and completely clear. I tend to speak a little more slowly than usual when I use it, too, which gives whatever message I'm delivering a little extra oomph. Now, I tell our groups, I use that voice of authority in preschool classrooms when I feel a child needs the comfort of knowing who is in charge—me, not him. It doesn't always work, of course. But almost forty years after that first job post-college, I am still surprised at how often such a child stops short, listens, and does what I ask.

Helping Kids to Listen to and Comply with Basic Requests

Once parents develop a feel for their own voice of authority—and what works for each individual will differ—we can help them get a sense of how to use it. Amina and I often tease out what is involved, which is summarized in the list that follows. The ideas on this list come from Lynn Clark's phenomenally helpful *SOS Help for Parents* (2005, 17–19), a book I recommend to family members more often than any other.

First . . .

- Find a voice of authority—one that communicates that you are in charge and expect to be listened to. It doesn't have to be loud and shouldn't be unfriendly, but it does need to have an "I mean business" quality.

- Remind yourself before you start not to frame your request as a question. That means not ending your request with, "Okay?"

Then, once you have these principles in mind . . .

1. Move close to your child.

2. Call his or her name.

3. Get and maintain eye contact.

4. Use a firm tone of voice.

5. Give a direct, simple, and clear command.

6. Be prepared to back up your command with a limit if you don't get the response you are looking for.

(Quoted and adapted from Clark 2005, 19)

Parents Contribute to Patterning . . . but Children Do Too

Changes in the direction just outlined, and the many others offered in this chapter, can have a profound and positive impact on children's behavior. But the explorations to this point may make it sound like parents carry the full load of responsibility for what unfolds between them and their kids. In a way, they do. They're the grown-ups in their families just as you are in your classrooms. But as you know from your own experiences with kids you're trying to help, children can be powerful participants in problematic patterns. Their temperaments, developmental vulnerabilities, even their troubles sleeping well can have a lot to do with what goes on. I often hear evidence of children's contributions to interactive patterning in my conversations with parents. I've talked with many who have managed to set effective expectations with a number of their kids but have had difficulty figuring out how to get it right with one in particular. *This one*, I might hear, has always been intense emotionally, has always had a hard time focusing, or is by nature inflexible and hard to move along. *This one* has us stumped.

It is abundantly clear: hard wiring looms large in children's parts of these patterns, and developmental vulnerabilities and skill deficits do too. Hard times may as well. Sometimes there is so much going on in a family that the basics get lost. As a result, kids' behaviors—and the interactive patterning that ensues—take an understandable turn for the worse.

Some Final Thoughts

Given how complex families can be—and how children differ one from the other—helping adult family members learn to set effective expectations can't be a matter of presenting a one-size-fits-all template for making things better. Instead, it often involves understanding a child's unique hard wiring and a family's particular situation. That idea leads to a final list, one that offers overall ideas for inviting parents into the work of changing patterns at home. These ideas don't just apply to the kind of work Amina and I so enjoy doing during our parenting groups. They offer possibilities for almost any context in which you and your colleagues help families learn to set effective expectations at home:

- Consider starting with interest rather than solutions. Open the door to exploration and learning by being curious about parents' hopes and worries, experiences, and stories. Share your own stories, too, if you have some and don't mind. Let the humanness of these dilemmas fill the room you're in so that parents feel how common their difficulties really are.

- Offer a hope-filled picture of growth and the reasons behind making a change.

- Explore the power of patterning and the specific (and problematic) patterns that may be going on. Use visuals, handouts, anything that helps parents see these interactive loops and begin to recognize when they're in the midst of one. That is the first step toward change.

- Offer simple language that explains what has been "messy," and simple ideas for making things better.

- Explore alternatives. Help parents make a step-by-step plan for what they can try to do differently.

- Follow up. Support is almost always necessary for the journey ahead!

- And if it works in your situation, think about the possibility of group-based conversations and learning. Parents feel better when they see others in the same boat. Sometimes they're more able to make slow changes when they see others working to make such changes too.

There's one last point, which I want to separate from all the others because it's perhaps the most important of all. *Reach out, reach out, and reach out again. Many of our hard-to-engage parents need our help the most, just like our hard-to-reach kids do.*

Putting It All Together

4

How can the many strategies already described in this book be combined when a child doesn't fit neatly into one category or another? After all, many of our most puzzling and challenging kids don't. One youngster has language-processing issues and is easily frustrated as well. Another is a "wiggly one" but also strikingly anxious. A third holds back with deep reserve and has notably poor problem-solving skills. In situations like this, figuring out how to provide a mix of approaches in child-specific ways is a crucial aspect of intervention.

Chapter 17 addresses this all-important topic through the story of Sam, a bright and creative boy who was born with a subtle mix of hard-wired vulnerabilities. It includes a letter written to Sam's teachers and parents in which I offer a friendly look at what is going on, along with some ideas about how to support growth. The letter intentionally avoids giving Sam a diagnosis. Instead, it paints the kind of child-specific portrait that fuels the work teachers do with all the children in this book.

My hope in including this letter is to accomplish two goals. One is to provide some perspective on children whose hard wiring makes it difficult for them to be flexible learners, friends, and family members. The other is to offer an integrative picture of how we describe and approach intervention for all children who need extra support and help from the adults who care for them—youngsters who puzzle us, worry us, and challenge us to be thoughtful and creative problem solvers. With that picture setting the stage, the book's final chapter reflects on the journey of keeping those kids company.

17 A Letter about Sam
Helping a Child with Multiple Challenges

On a chilly mid-October day, Linda and Peter sit in my office for a first visit. As they begin describing their three-year-old son Sam, I hear about a boy who is "wonderful, lovable, and hard." Sam is bright, curious, and full of energy, they relate. He loves to build things and to explore the natural world. A child who is especially interested in trains and dinosaurs, he likes to expound on both—as best he can, that is, given his struggles to communicate.

Sam can be cuddly and loving, these parents tell me. It is hard for him to go with the flow, however, and to make it through each day without huge upsets. He has trouble playing with their friends' children without upsets too. These difficulties have been a regular part of family life for quite a while. Peter thinks that Sam needs more firmness and more time to grow up in order to behave reasonably. Linda agrees that they haven't found a way to parent Sam with consistency and that he may manage himself far better in another year or so. He has already matured a lot, she notes. But she also feels that there is "something different" about her son in a way that is hard to understand.

Based on Linda's concerns, these parents had Sam evaluated by their town's early childhood program last spring. He qualified for a spot in its integrated preschool program. That program is attended by a mix of "typically developing" kids and kids with challenges. Sam is in the latter group based, in part, on his language delays. Now, six weeks into the start of school, Linda and Peter are worried. Sam's entry into the program has been terribly difficult. He has been having lengthy tantrums each morning when he arrives at school. He falls apart regularly throughout the day, throwing toys, kicking other kids, or trying to run out of the classroom. In addition, he once bit a teacher so badly that she had to leave school to seek medical help.

Sam isn't toilet trained yet. He has been so resistant to the idea that, after a number of tries, Linda and Peter have decided to wait for a while longer. In school, he becomes like a caged animal when asked to go to the bathroom for a diaper change after he has soiled the one he is wearing. Most recently, staff have been calling Linda to come in and lend a hand at such times. Luckily, she works from home and can show up as needed. She hopes, though, that she won't have to continue doing this through the year—it is taking a considerable toll on her professional life.

The program isn't giving up on Sam, Linda and Peter emphasize. But its director has suggested that they get some consultation about home-based issues. The director has also asked whether I might come in to observe Sam in his classroom and then collaborate with his teaching team. I have worked with this town's early childhood program before, offering additional guidance to parents when staff can't provide all that is needed. The program is much respected in the community and for good reason: its staff members are committed, skilled, and wonderfully supportive of kids and families. The fact that its director would like me to offer "an extra set of eyes"—something she rarely requests and her staff rarely need—suggests that Linda is right about Sam being hard to understand.

Linda and Peter sent along a thick packet of reports in advance of our meeting. Sam has been evaluated by the program's behavioral consultant, speech and language specialist, occupational therapist, and psychologist. Thus, I have now read about (and these are direct quotes) Sam's "variable attention," his "sensory processing challenges," and his "profile of reduced language and visual/perceptual reasoning skills." One report notes concerns involving Sam's ability "to inhibit impulsive responses, adapt to changes in routine, modulate his emotions, sustain working memory, and engage in the planning and organizing of problem-solving approaches." That report concludes that "although Sam is young, his profile is consistent with a diagnosis of Attention Deficit Hyperactivity Disorder with associated executive function deficits." I can only imagine how Linda and Peter feel after reading these detailed and problem-focused write-ups. I find them overwhelming, and I encounter such descriptions regularly.

Now we are sitting together and chatting. As I hear about the intelligent and cheerful yet challenging child these parents describe, I decide that going into the program to see him in action does indeed make sense.

On the Continent of "Difference"

From the reports just cited, it is clear that Sam has a mix of difficulties. If there is one category he fits into most easily, it's that of "developmental difference." As you may know from your experience, the children who fit this description have wide-ranging ways of being. Some face significant hurdles in regard to a number of developmental issues, while others have mild difficulties that respond quickly to specialized help. Some will have ongoing challenges throughout their years in elementary and secondary school, while others will eventually look very much like the more "typically developing" children in their classrooms. Developmental difference, in fact, often feels less like a unified category than a continent full of unique and fascinating countries, each with a culture all its own.

Some of the children living on this interesting continent may eventually get a diagnosis—Asperger's syndrome, Nonverbal Learning Disability, Pervasive Developmental Disorder, Social Communication Disorder, and the like. Others will be diagnosed in this way along with language processing issues and/or ADHD. Many may be best described as "quirky" (Klass and Costello 2004), "offbeat," or "gifted but rigid" (Hirschland 2008, 229). However we label them, such youngsters can be tricky to understand and to parent and teach.

Deep Tracking: A Unifying Concept

My job as clinician and consultant has brought me into contact with many such children. A good number of them have trouble relating to others with interest and flexibility, just as Sam does. Sam gets deeply compelled by what he is playing with, discussing, or learning about. It is truly difficult for him to pop out of his inner world to listen to someone else's ideas. It is hard for him to share the materials or toys he is using at a particular moment, too. And it is challenging for him to shift mental sets—to change what he is doing in response to another person's agenda. At moments when he is asked to do one of these things, he tends to fall apart. Screaming, biting, hitting, and running away often ensue.

Some theorists describe children like Sam as having difficulty engaging in a state of "joint attention," a state in which two people *notice and respond to each other's presence*. It can also help to think of such kids as "deep tracked," a phrase I came up with a number of years ago. When I describe deep tracking to teachers or family members, I say something like this:

"Have you ever seen the luge competition in the Olympics? It's truly odd to watch. The athletes get on a sled lying backwards. Then they race down a frozen track with high sides—it fits just one sled, goes one way, and ends up in one place. These children spend much of their time in a similarly narrow and high-sided track. They know where that track is heading, and its destination is the only place they want to go. It's really hard for them to *widen the track* so another person can be in there with them. It's even harder for them to *change tracks*—to go in a different direction entirely. Helping them learn to do both is important. But we have to understand how. Often, we start by *joining them in their track,* just the way it is. That way *we use our interest in their interests to help them feel connected to us*—not just to themselves and the content that compels them. Then we work, one step at a time, to help them experience what it is like to engage in a mutually pleasurable back-and-forth. We target developing flexibility as well—though work on that issue often comes a little way down the road. It takes a while to reach these goals because of how deep-tracked kids are built."

Deep Tracking and Problematic Patterns

Deep-tracked children frequently pull parents and teachers into worrisome patterns, and understandably so. Trying to engage these children in the kind of back-and-forth just described is frustrating, as is insisting that they bend in the face of others' needs. They sometimes appear to fend off most invitations for connection and exchange. They can have a seemingly endless need for control, too. Thus, after many attempts to move things in a more engaged and interactive direction, the adults who care for such a youngster may become unhappily resigned. "I'll just leave her be," they may start thinking. "She seems fine on her own . . . and when I ask her to come my way, things get ugly." Children can have similar reactions. Sometimes, they leave a deep-tracked peer to her own devices. Sometimes—and this occurs especially if that peer has interesting play ideas—they cave into her need for control.

Whether adult-to-child or child-to-child, these common patterns have an unfortunate outcome: they amplify a youngster's natural tendencies. As a result, we start seeing even more moments of deep tracking, more rigidity, and more upset in the face of demands for flexibility. Some of our goals for intervention, then, must address the nature of ongoing interactions. That is certainly true in the work I do with Sam's parents, and is probably why his program's director encouraged them to seek help. As Linda and Peter have both noted, it is hard for them to be consistent in the face of their son's intensity. Like many family members of deep-tracked kids, they need help learning what such consistency should look like given his unique challenges. (See Hirschland 2008, 229–50, for more on parent-focused work with these children.)

Deep Tracking and Diagnostic Puzzles

Children with developmental differences can be notoriously hard to diagnose. That's because their brains work in unique ways. As a result, they often experience multiple and intertwined challenges. Diagnostic labels aren't great at capturing such complexity. Perri Klass and Ellen Costello, the authors of *Quirky Kids*, offer a chapter that they call "Specialists, Labels, and Alphabet Soup: Arriving at a Diagnosis" (2004, 31–62). There, they emphasize how the same "quirky" child might end up being seen and diagnosed in strikingly different ways by different specialists. This dilemma brings me back to the idea of individualized portraits. Such portraits are always useful, and never more than when they help us understand the fullness of a "developmentally different" youngster's experience. In developing them, we work to address a set of questions: What is hard for the child in question? What is easier? What strikes her interest? What input can she tolerate? Which part of what we see involves her temperament? Which aspects have to do with her ability to process information? Finally, how should we factor in life at home and in school?

Looking and Learning

I have many of these questions in mind as I enter Sam's classroom on a November morning. He hasn't yet arrived. I am prepared for a big scene when he does because, as far as I know, transitioning from home is still a challenge for him. I'm happy to discover that I'm wrong.

Sam comes into the room holding Linda's hand and gets a warm greeting from Phyllis, the classroom's lead teacher. He signs in willingly, separates from his mother with a couple of hugs, then snuggles next to Phyllis as she reads a book about dinosaurs. His eyes are riveted on pictures he appears to have seen many times before, and he chants parts of the book's text as she reads it. When Phyllis asks him a question about one of the dinosaurs they are looking at together, he mumbles a half-sentence answer. I begin to see why the reports I've read suggest that communication is an area of vulnerability.

Book complete, Sam accompanies Phyllis as she locates his choice board. Sam decides he'll play with the classroom's trains and attaches a laminated train picture to the board. After that, he agrees, he will find either Phyllis or one of his other teachers to make another choice. Sam appears only marginally willing to go along with this choice board routine: his eyes are unfocused and his body is restless. Phyllis is working hard not to lose her now-tenuous connection with him. Even so, they make it to the train table relatively easily.

Sam doesn't interact with the other children who are playing at that table once he arrives. In a few instances, he tries telling those kids what he is doing. However he doesn't wait to get their attention before speaking. Furthermore, he starts talking as if he is in the middle of an idea—he doesn't seem to understand how to bring his listeners along. Sam doesn't appear to mind, or perhaps even notice, when no one at the table responds to what he has said.

The morning unfolds with numerous difficulties. Sam refuses to join the circle and isn't willing to find something quiet to do instead. As he begins getting wilder and angrier, one of the assistant teachers tries guiding him to a place where he can play. He hurls a pillow at her and starts screaming. None of the adults on hand pays much attention to the commotion. The other children pay it little mind as well—I suspect that they have gotten accustomed to his upsets. Eventually, Sam settles down.

On the group's trip out to the playground, more problems emerge. Sam doesn't want to stand in line, doesn't want to wait until the rest of the children are ready to go out, and doesn't want to follow the rules once he gets outside. He lobs a ball out of the playground's fenced-in area and then makes a valiant (and almost successful) effort to go get it. He won't share the ball once he gets it back. Later, he refuses to return indoors, and it takes Phyllis almost five minutes to coax him along.

There are other notable elements to the morning too. As I have been told happens daily, Sam has great difficulty managing himself when he has soiled his diaper. He sits at the playdough table with little ability to get children's attention when he wants them to see what he's doing. And he squirms his way through the ending circle before it is time to go home. Overall, I sense that Sam has settled into the classroom's routines and isn't balking as much as he used to. But he isn't yet participating in much of what is going on beyond beginning to follow the classroom's routines . . . he doesn't seem to know how.

Later the same day, I sit down not only with Sam's teaching team but with the program's specialists. We have a wide-ranging conversation about who he is, why life can be such a challenge for him, and how to support his growth. As the group's outside consultant, I try to offer a cohesive picture that pulls together information from the different reports I've read and the range of behaviors I've observed. I also facilitate conversation about how what the team does in school can support work at home—and vice versa.

A few days after that meeting I write the team a letter, one that I will send to Sam's parents too. Rather than providing a formal assessment or set of diagnoses, it sketches out an individualized portrait of Sam. Then it offers goals for growth and some strategies for achieving them. Some of the letter's content repeats ideas from earlier chapters in this book, and there are a few ideas from this chapter as well. I offer this letter in just the form I wrote it, with such repetition included and its see→think→do progression clearly in evidence. That way, it can illustrate how the concepts encountered throughout these pages can live and breathe in the world of a classroom—and be used by families as well.

A Letter about Sam

Hi everyone—

It was a pleasure to observe Sam and then to meet together on Tuesday. I was so impressed with your program, and it was wonderful to see the phenomenal progress Sam has made. I know I saw him on a stellar day, but the fact that he could have such a day is terrific. His growth is a tribute to all of the skillful support you've offered him at school and to the hard and loving work Linda and Peter have been doing at home. It's also a tribute to Sam himself, who has been working hard in both places.

It's great that we all seem to be on the same page as we think about next steps. I thought it might be useful for me to write down a few of the things we discussed—both how we picture what's "driving" Sam's difficulties and where we see ourselves intervention-wise. I write letters like this from time to time as an alternative to working up a formal report. They help me clarify my thinking after a productive meeting like the one we had. Sometimes, they also serve as a guidepost for the work a home-school team undertakes as they help a child begin to thrive. So, with the latter aim in mind, here are a few questions about Sam and some tentative answers that may help in our work moving forward.

What is driving Sam's behavior?

In our meeting, I mentioned that the ADHD diagnosis feels "off" in terms of the best frame for thinking about Sam. It's not that it's wrong exactly . . . his behavior does tally, at least some of the time, with the criteria that go along with this diagnosis. But the more I see and hear about him, the more I picture his profile as one that involves delays across a set of developmental systems, with the two central areas of challenge involving communication (both receptive and expressive) and the capacity for mutual engagement. The latter, as you know, has to do with the comfortable back-and-forth that allows kids to register and take in other people's input and then respond to what they have seen or heard.

My guess is that Sam's inattention and impulsivity flow from these two areas of challenge. (That's why, although both are important in their own right, I don't see them as the primary issues diagnostically.) In addition, Sam seems to have some sensory issues, some motor planning issues (getting his body to do what his mind envisions), and difficulties in managing strong emotion. This sounds like a long list of challenges and it is. But as those of us who have been working with children for a long time know well, with good help, lots of kids who start out with these sorts of developmental lags end up doing just wonderfully in the long run.

What are some of the things we need to keep in mind, no matter what Sam's diagnosis?

- Sam has made a lot of progress but still struggles to note and respond to people's requests for contact and attention. Even when he does "cue in," he doesn't always respond in a way that matches the input he has gotten. So, as we all know, he still needs significant help in order to tune in to the world of others . . . their questions, their ideas, their interest in him, and their needs for a change of behavior or a change of activity. This is what some people call the ability to engage in a state of "joint attention." Challenges in this area can really hold kids back, both in their learning and in their socializing. That's why we'll put work on this ability center stage as we think about how to help Sam.

  In our meeting, I mentioned that I like to think of kids like Sam as "deep tracked." That's just another way of describing difficulties with engaging in this state of joint attention. It's as if this group of children live inside a deep track with high sides . . . they know where they want to go and how they want to get there, and they barrel ahead with enthusiasm. But they don't always feel at ease letting other individuals "join their track," nor do they know how to "widen the track" to include other people's ideas and needs. In addition, it can be very hard for them to "change tracks" when the world around them requires them to make a shift in what they're up to or what they have in mind.

  This picture might help us make sense out of how Sam thrives once he settles into routines (which itself takes a while) but can balk when there are small changes in schedule or activities. It also illuminates why he doesn't always answer when called, or why the responses he does make to others' input don't always follow the question he's been asked or the comment someone has made. In addition, it may help us understand why, even though he is now a lot less troublesome to other kids behavior-wise, he isn't yet highly sought after as a playmate in the classroom: currently, he just doesn't have enough skill in the give-and-take of play and friendship to be a fully successful buddy.

- Sam also has a hard time using words to expand on ideas. The things he says can be pretty simple in linguistic construction. And, at times, he repeats basic thoughts over and over again. This would fit with the communication challenges outlined earlier . . . he may not yet be able to come up with one "idea bubble" and link it to another and then yet another, thus coming up with increasingly longer stories, play narratives, descriptions of his interests of the moment, etc.

  I was really struck by this when, the day I observed, Sam kept repeating (while holding up some playdough), "This is a birthday cupcake!" Not only was he talking to the air—which is connected to his not totally "getting" the give-and-take of relationships and communication—but when he finally did vary what he had to say, he merely shifted to "This is pizza." Not much of a story line for such a bright, verbal boy! My guess is that the ideas are all there and then some, but that organizing and sequencing those ideas, inviting the attention of the person with whom he'd like to communicate, getting his ideas out, and then hanging in to take that person's response—only to go through the whole thing all over again—is a tall order for him right now.

- Flowing from these issues—troubles with communication and tunneling into his "deep track"—we see some difficulties attending and some real delays in the ability to be flexible. Sam isn't exploding as much as he used to, which is so wonderful for him and everyone who cares for him! But he still has his moments, and he has a way to go before he is really skilled at handling the frustration of not getting what he wants just when he wants it.

- Then there is the sensory piece. Sam's mind-body connection seems, at times, a bit off. He has great coordination in some ways, but can appear out of touch with where he is in space or a little off-balance in how he moves. And he appears to need a fair amount of sensory input to feel comfortable in his body. (As we have all seen before, this grouping of challenges isn't uncommon for kids who have Sam's profile of vulnerabilities across developmental systems.) It is these mind-body/ sensory issues—coupled with Sam's inflexibility and his not being tuned in and responsive to adults' everyday expectations—that probably account for the difficulties we've seen with toileting.

- Toileting, of course, is a big focus right now. Everyone seems to agree that Sam's confusion/hesitancy about pooping is getting in the way of his feeling at ease, and that when he begins to feel the discomfort of needing to go at school, his behavior heads downhill quickly.

- Finally, there is all the wonderful stuff. Sam's curiosity. His intelligence. His creativity. His good humor. His willingness to take help. The great thing is that the more of that help Sam gets, and the more he progresses developmentally, the more these wonderful qualities have begun to shine.

What are our goals at this stage?

- *More experiences of and success with joint attention:* Sam will get better at noticing and responding to adult requests for attention and the invitations both adults and kids make for contact, conversation, or play.

- *Continuing growth in relationship to going with the flow:* Sam will become better able to tolerate and follow rules, to be flexible in the face of changes, and to comfortably manage routines and expectations both at home and in school.

- *Increasing ability to stick with conversational back-and-forth:* Sam will get better at both initiating and responding to overtures for connection and conversation, and at throwing the "conversational ball" back and forth successfully. Part of this increased ability for conversational back-and-forth will include Sam's getting better at framing his ideas successfully, at sticking with a topic of conversation or play, and at elaborating on ideas with more depth and complexity (see the next bullet).

- *Increasing ability to string together sequences of ideas, or to expand on the ideas he has in mind:* This goal includes Sam getting better at starting at the beginning of a thought (rather than halfway through, which he does sometimes!), putting his ideas in order, and hanging in there as he tries to offer more information and more depth of thinking. He is a very creative child, but he can't always give us (or even himself) a full picture of his rich inner life.

- *Success in toileting both at home and in school:* This goal targets not only Sam's ability to read his body's signals and then to use the toilet, but also his feeling increasingly relaxed in regard to toileting.

- *More pleasurable, mutually satisfying experiences with peers at home and in school, including the beginning of shared narrative play.*

And what approaches and strategies can we use to get from here to there, both at home and in school?

Most of the strategies on this list involve things all of you are already doing. So the ideas here are by way of a reminder and tweaking of what is already in place...

Goal:
To support joint attention and help Sam stretch his ability to engage in the back-and-forth of communication and play.

Strategies:

- We talked in the meeting about putting some very gentle "muscle" into helping Sam tune in to requests for attention and contact. When he's talking to the air, adults can help him direct himself to someone in particular. When someone asks him a question, they can help him orient and respond.

- Just as importantly, we can focus even more fully now—since Sam has made so many gains in other areas—on offering adult scaffolding of his connections and communication with other kids, thus helping him throw the conversational (and narrative play) ball back and forth. He is right on the cusp of being able to do this but can't yet manage it on his own all that often. The good thing is that as he gets better and better at following routines and directions, Sam is going to need less help targeting basic behavioral compliance, so there will be more time for this kind of friendly assistance.

  The developmental psychiatrist Stanley Greenspan has a great image for this business of throwing the conversational ball back and forth: he talks about opening and closing "circles of communication." Greenspan's idea is that one person initiates or opens contact, often with both words and gestures. The next person responds, and then the first person closes the loop. As kids head toward kindergarten, we want them to be able to open and close many of these circles at a time. Right now Sam can only open and close a few rounds on his good days. The scaffolding we're talking about here will help him not only engage in these circles more often but do so through lengthier exchanges.

I've come to call this scaffolding "lend an ally" work, as a way of describing how parents and teachers join a child in his areas of interest (whether in conversation or play), do some of the work of gluing together connection and conversation with the child's peers, and then slowly support the child in taking full control as he becomes more skilled. In Sam's case, the time and patience needed for such lend-an-ally support seem well worth it. Because my sense is that he'll be a willing partner in what goes on, and that offering scaffolding for play and connection will be a pleasure for everyone.

Goal:
To help Sam organize, sequence, and expand on his ideas.

Strategies:

- Work on this goal will also involve adult scaffolding as we help Sam stick with a topic, start from the beginning, ask questions to deepen and expand content, and eventually go from single "bubbles of ideas" to multiple units of content that he connects up with interest and pleasure. Sam is showing a lot of emergent skill in this area, and my guess is that he'll comfortably join us in this endeavor, as long as when he reaches his limit and tuckers out, he can take a break.

Goal:
To help Sam have increasing success at meeting basic expectations and going with the flow.

Strategies:

- The classroom routines and expectations are helping enormously with this goal, and previewing any anticipated changes or expectations—including your use of visual schedules, etc.—will continue to support Sam at school. In fact, my guess is that this goal mostly needs a bit more attention at home—families often find it harder to be predictable and consistent than schools do. That said, Linda and Peter and I have talked a lot about previewing expectations, keeping things simple, friendly, and firm (including not getting highly frustrated with Sam . . . letting the "limits do the work"), and then showing real pleasure when Sam is able to be a flexible, responsible family citizen. We'll keep discussing this in our family meetings—it's an ongoing process.

Goal:
To help Sam feel comfortable and successful in using the toilet when he needs to.

Strategies:

- Linda is going to send out an e-mail on the specifics of this one. She, Peter, and I came up with a sensible plan for moving the toileting issue forward, and they're going to start that plan shortly. Toileting has obviously been a real struggle for Sam, but my guess is that he is now more ready than he realizes, and a consistent, friendly approach at home may work this time around. Linda and Peter know they're going to need to stick with the plan and have some good language to use when they introduce it to Sam. They intend to stay firm but very friendly and supportive, and are willing to make carrying out this plan a top priority—including changing their preferred schedules for a few weeks if necessary. That way, they'll make sure the routine stays steady while Sam gains the mastery that will leave him feeling much more competent and relaxed.

That's it for now. I hope what I have written here offers an outline for the work to come. I'm going to e-mail a copy of this letter to Linda and Peter as well as to everyone on the school team, in an effort to provide us with a shared language to describe Sam's challenges and a shared picture of what we're up to. I do hope you'll think of this as a work in progress, add to it as you see fit, and change whatever seems off. But until I'm back in touch with you or you with me, I hope you know that I feel very fortunate to be working with such a gifted school team and such a loving set of parents. And to have the opportunity to watch Sam take flight!

Warm regards to all—Deborah

The Story Goes On

This letter provides a snapshot of a moment in time—one full of both concern and hope. In the months that follow, Sam makes remarkable progress. By the end of the year, he is no longer thought of as his classroom's most difficult child. Instead, he has become one of its striking success stories. He can follow routines successfully and contribute simple ideas at group time. He is able to play successfully with his peers, at least for short stretches. And he is toilet trained, a huge relief to him and the adults who care for him. This wonderful progress doesn't lead either Sam's teachers or his parents to believe that he will cruise his way through his final year of preschool. Children with developmental differences don't suddenly change their genetics, and these adults are well aware that there are more challenges ahead.

I have been fortunate to stay in touch with Sam's parents over the past few years—he is about to enter fourth grade. They have hung in there by his side, with tremendous affection, regular doses of frustration, and a deep commitment to offering him the help he needs. These parents aren't just committed to their son's growth. They also feel strongly about helping parents and teachers who want to support other children whose issues parallel his. When I asked them if I could use the letter you just read in some teacher trainings I planned to run, the answer was, "Of course. Whatever we can do to help people understand kids like Sam is well worth it." More recently, when I e-mailed to ask whether I might include the letter in this book, the reply was another resounding "yes." The note Linda wrote to accompany that "yes" was a poignant one, and it continues Sam's story in the next chapter.

Some Unanswered Questions

No book can cover all topics equally. What I have offered here is a comprehensive way of thinking accompanied by a detailed look at approaches to intervention for a range of difficulties. I haven't explored what you can do when you feel your teaching team is not functioning as well as it might. Though left unanswered here, that is an important question—especially since tough children can splinter a team, and a splintered team can lead to kids being tough. I also haven't written about how teachers can most effectively collaborate with specialists, nor how home-school partners can consider thorny questions related to pharmacological intervention.

This last question deserves extensive thought. That is true generally but especially in early childhood, when children's brains are developing rapidly and we often don't know just how medications affect that development. For the most part I believe in waiting, just as Peter and Linda did, and if warranted, considering the option of medication in the elementary school years. Even then, I am on the conservative side concerning the use of medication. I sometimes feel it is a good choice if other kinds of intervention and support have been tried fully and the child in question can still use an extra boost. Even then, as you see reflected in Linda's e-mail, medication is almost never a "magic bullet." Instead, it occasionally allows children to more easily use the help they are getting.

There is one more area I have only touched upon. That is the way in which each of us carries our full self into our work with young children. We aren't blank slates any more than the youngsters we care for are. They bring their histories and temperaments to us, and we bring ours to them. They can get to us, bother us, make us feel things we have felt before and never want to feel again. Sometimes we become overprotective. Sometimes we get disturbingly angry. And sometimes a particular child leaves us feeling chronically annoyed or even profoundly disengaged. There are always reasons for these inner experiences, and they are worth attending to.

In Conclusion

As an author and practitioner, I find it hard to leave such issues unaddressed. But this book can't explore everything, and other content has taken precedence. I hope that reading these pages has resulted in rekindled energy and inspiration for the work of supporting hard-to-help children and partnering with their often overwhelmed parents. I'd like to believe, as well, that I have offered a realistic picture of how kids learn and grow. Anyone who presents children's progress as magically quick or seamless is tying things up far too prettily. Children make progress, then take tumbles. Or they move forward encouragingly, then hit a seemingly endless plateau. Families rarely grow with a uniformly upward trajectory either. How many times have you seen parents learn to support their kids with more skill and then lose their way as their energy flags, their distractibility grows, or they hit tough times?

Linda once put words to the feelings you may have when things get bumpy in one of these ways. It was Sam's second year of preschool—a full year after she, Peter, and I first began talking. Peter couldn't make one of our appointments, but Linda came anyway. The last time I'd seen these parents, Sam had been doing very well. It had been an amazing pleasure to Linda that she could take him to a playground or community event and feel—for the first time—that no one was staring at her judgmentally as Sam fell apart. Now he was going through a difficult stretch, and she was profoundly discouraged. Why wasn't Sam okay, she fretted? Why couldn't he handle himself like other kids? And why wasn't she able to be the consistently supportive parent she wished to be in the face of his struggles? We talked about the journey to date and the journey ahead, about going back down the ladder when Sam was slipping and meeting him on the "rung" to which he had descended. As she found her bearings once again—a challenging task with a child like Sam—Linda had some insightful things to say:

"When things have been good and then your kid slips, it's harder to remember the techniques that work. Because since things started getting better, you haven't had to use them consistently. And you lose patience more quickly. You get frustrated because you feel like you've made progress and now you're going backwards. You feel like you've lost ground. Even though you haven't. Then everyone suffers. . . . You have to ask yourself: 'What is your definition of success?'"

Perhaps, through reading this book, your definition of success has shifted slightly. Perhaps the content I've offered will allow you to add a few more tools to your toolbox, and to remember that big changes always start with small steps. I hope so. I hope, too, that the importance of the job you do each day shines through the stories and ideas I have shared. The work of teaching and caring for young children is as meaningful and influential as any work one can do. The journey with some of those children can be long and taxing. But the impact you have on their lives, and the lives of their families, can be life changing.

Appendix A:
Seeking Clarity—Useful Forms

Questions for Team-Based Discussion and Action Planning

Child's Name: _____

Child's Age: _____

Gathering Observations and Information: What Do We See?

What are the behaviors and issues we're worried about?

What are some of the child's strengths? What do we enjoy about him or her?

Where and when do behaviors and issues of concern show up? What do we see then?

How do any challenges we've noted "play out in play," both what the child *does* during play that we worry about, and what he or she *doesn't do* that we'd like to see? How do this youngster's strengths show up in play as well?

What do we notice about times and situations when the child does better? What is worth noting about periods when he or she is struggling?

Have we done an ABC analysis (**A**ntecedents → **B**ehaviors → **C**onsequences) of what is going on? If we haven't, should we? If we have, what have we discovered about the ABC progression? Are there things this child *gets* or *avoids* as a result of his or her behavior?

What have we noticed about the quality of our connection with this child? Is there a feeling of warm engagement running between us? Are the behaviors we're seeing leading us (or some of us) to feel irritable and/or frustrated with him or her? Do we know if there are worrisome tensions present in relationships at home?

Understanding the Child's Behaviors and Feelings: What Do We Think?

What is our understanding of this child's ability to engage in warm, trusting relationships?

What areas of developmental/behavioral mastery are less far along than we would like to see given this child's age? Check areas that will benefit from skill-building support:

- ❑ communicating successfully
- ❑ being cue responsive
- ❑ focusing and sustaining attention
- ❑ managing energy
- ❑ managing strong feelings like frustration, anger, sadness, and anxiety
- ❑ changing tracks and being flexible
- ❑ sharing space, ideas, and materials
- ❑ engaging in give-and-take with friends
- ❑ controlling impulses
- ❑ waiting
- ❑ problem solving
- ❑ engaging in age-appropriate play, including developing stories in play
- ❑ other _____

What is our sense of how this child is doing emotionally: his or her experience of self, feelings about the world, and/or confidence about handling life's ups and downs?

What do we understand about this child's hard wiring, both in regard to temperament and to capacities for language and information processing? Do there appear to be some sensory issues at play in what is going on?

Do we know whether this child had a particularly "hard start" during his or her first few years? If so, what do we know about what went on?

Do we have information about whether this child has experienced some hard times at home? Does life in the family seem to involve significant stress? If so, what do we know about the cause of that stress? Are there financial or housing issues? Sibling or marital issues? Mental health or substance abuse issues? Other family-related situations of note?

Where were this child's parents born? What cultural norms lie at the heart of family life? Do the child's parents speak English at home? Is he or she a second-language learner? Are there issues having to do with immigration that may be making life particularly stressful for everyone in the family?

Is there any known trauma or domestic violence in the child's history? Has he or she been removed from the home at any point?

Developing an Action Plan: What Should We Do?

Step One: Setting Goals

I. Goals for enhancing adult-child relationships and connectedness:

II. Goals for developmental mastery:

III. Goals for emotional well-being:

IV. Goals for changing problematic "interactive patterning":

V. Goals for clarity and consistency of response when this child is behaving unacceptably or unsafely:

VI. Goals for partnering with and supporting this child's family:

VII. Goals for accessing evaluations and additional supports and services for this child and/or family:

Step Two: Refining Our Objectives, Choosing Our Strategies, and Creating an Action Plan

Strategies for Supporting Warm Connection, Developmental Mastery, and Emotional Well-Being:

Goal _____

Classroom-wide strategies:

Individually focused strategies:

Goal _____

Classroom-wide strategies:

Individually focused strategies:

Goal _____

Classroom-wide strategies:

Individually focused strategies:

Goal _____

Classroom-wide strategies:

Individually focused strategies:

Goal _____

Classroom-wide strategies:

Individually focused strategies:

Additional Notes Connected to Goals and Strategies, Including Those Related to Interactive Patterning:

Team-based plan for calm, consistent, and unified response to unacceptable or unsafe behavior when prevention/skill-building strategies are not sufficient:

Plan for reaching out to and partnering with this child's family:

Plan for accessing evaluations and/or additional services if appropriate:

Step Three: Asking and Answering a Final Set of Questions

How can we get on the same page as a team? Who is going to do what?

What is our time frame? How long should we take before we check in again?

Date of Meeting: _____

Team Members Attending:

_____   _____

_____   _____

_____   _____

Preview to Creating an Action Plan: Areas for Consideration

Check areas that may apply to the work ahead, and review possibilities.

_____ ***Seeding the day with connection:*** How will we do it? What will work for this child? What will help him or her to feel cherished, noticed, and enjoyed in a steady way?

_____ ***Clear, reasonable, and consistent expectations on behavior:*** What should be done in the whole group so that kids know what is expected in a positive, clear, and friendly way? What should be done in a fashion that targets this particular child? How can we be sure that any time we can prevent behavior or support skill development rather than set a limit, we do so? How can we set our expectations so that all children know consequences in advance, and then how might we let our limits "do the talking" for this particular youngster? How can we make sure that he or she feels welcomed back to the group once any consequences we have to set are over?

_____ ***Child-friendly routines, transitions, and classroom structure:*** How can we make our classroom routines and schedule predictable, consistent, and reassuring? Do we need to post some easy-to-see visuals that remind kids of what happens when? Are our circles and/or group-instruction periods happening at a time that is predictable? Is content engaging for this child, especially if English is a second language, or if he or she has trouble processing information or has difficulties staying focused? If our group instruction time is longer than this youngster can tolerate, is there a child-friendly plan that includes a spot for him or her to take a break *before* challenging behavior becomes an issue? Does this child need a personalized set of visuals or an extra way of being reminded of what's coming up? Something to hold during group time? A special job to get him or her through transition times? A special chair/place to sit that offers extra support for his or her body? An "I need a break" card?

_____ ***Work in support of cue-responsive behavior:*** Do we need a classroom-wide or individually based "cue" to work with? Will it help us to remember the 90–10 rule? How can we support cue responsiveness through positive interactions?

_____ ***Work on communication and supported conversation:*** What assistance might this child need in order to understand others more fully and communicate with more success?

_____ ***Group/individual work on understanding and expressing feelings:*** How can we help this child feel seen and understood, and support him or her in finding reasonable ways to express feelings and/or embed them in play? Can we make use of emotional thermometers, children's literature, curricular bridges, scripted stories, puppet work, feelings charts, and/or role plays? Are there any other feelings-related tools that may be particularly useful for this child?

_____ ***Group/individual work on managing strong feelings:*** What skill-building tools might we use to help our whole group learn to "wrap up" strong feelings and move on? What kinds of step-by-step strategies and visual aids will help this particular child develop the self-soothing skills he or she needs to thrive? Do we need to adapt our usual style of relating to kids to help this youngster tolerate our support and use our help? Can a puppet serve as an ally, can scripted stories offer guidance, and/or can children's literature provide comfort as this child works to gain self-control?

_____ ***Group/individual work on controlling impulses:*** How might we break impulse control down into its parts for our whole group? Can we use a Stop→Think→Ask→Respond progression to initiate learning? Might puppet work help explain and reinforce these steps? How about role playing? How can we support impulse control proactively so we have to set limits less often? And how can we keep things positive and encouraging as this child's skills increase and his or her behavior slowly improves?

_____ ***Group/individual work on being part of a community:*** How can we create a child-friendly classroom environment that leaves everyone committed to contributing to the whole group's well-being? Can we do this in a way that allows our kids to embrace the idea of doing their share, and to feel good about following directions because doing so helps everyone out? Will sticky notes on a "we're a great team" wall help? Jelly beans in a jelly bean jar that, when full, leads to a celebration? A place for pictures of kids sharing and helping out—pictures that are highlighted at group time? How can we follow through on group work about being a positive part of a whole, with an emphasis on pride and pleasure when this particular child chips in to make things better for everyone?

_____ ***Group/individual work on waiting:*** How can we break down what waiting is in a step-by-step fashion, and then offer a child-friendly way to lay out what its steps look like? How can we work on the skill of waiting in the whole group and support its mastery in individual interactions?

_____ ***Group/individual work or follow-through on sharing:*** How do we break sharing down into its parts? How can we teach it in a child-friendly way? How might we work on it, talk about it, explore it in the whole group, and then support it in individual and small-group interactions? What scripted stories, children's literature, role playing, and/or puppet work might help?

_____ ***Group work and/or individual work or follow-through on the steps of problem solving:*** Do we need a story, a chart, a puppet, a plan, and/or classroom-wide language like "problem-solution time"? What does this child need in order to stop exploding and start looking for reasonable solutions?

_____ ***Small group and/or individualized work on supported play:*** Where is this child developmentally in regard to play skills? Does he or she know the basics of play? If not, where do we start? Does this child need help creating and expanding on stories?

_____ ***Team-based plan for unacceptable behavior:*** What should happen if all of our proactive/preventive strategies don't work and this child acts out in an unacceptable way? Where will we draw the line that determines when we'll offer skill-building support and when we'll set a limit? What will we do if the child becomes out of control or unsafe? What will we do if he or she refuses to follow our directions and can't be redirected? (And who, in particular, will do what in that case?) How will we help this child reenter the group when he or she regains composure? When will outside supports be called in? When will parents be notified?

Appendix B:
Staying on Track—
Principles for Intervention

Principles for Intervention

When a particular child is especially puzzling or challenging, it can help to remind ourselves of the overall principles that guide intervention for all kids. More often than not, reconnecting with those principles—and the compassion-filled reflection and intervention they promote—allows us to discover a pathway to growth when things have been hard.

Seeking Partners and Perspective

- ***Reaching out to parents:*** The work of collaborating with parents—sharing information with them, learning from them, and offering them support and guidance—can be an essential ingredient in moving things forward.

- ***Partnering up for change:*** We aim for approaches that can be shared by family members, teachers, and any specialists on the scene. When kids experience similar strategies in different places, change happens more quickly and more fully.

- ***Getting specific before getting to work:*** Before coming up with ideas about how to help a child, we have to develop the clearest picture we can of what is causing his difficulties.

- ***Setting overall goals for development:*** Once we feel comfortable with our "best guess" picture of what is going on, we use it as a springboard for developing a set of long-term goals.

Building on the Power of Connection and the Centrality of Relationships

- ***Keeping in mind the importance of connection:*** No matter what our goals—and the strategies we will use to meet them—we remind ourselves that children's experiences of warm and loving connections with the adults who care for them are the most important element of intervention.

- ***Remembering to connect before we correct . . . or redirect:*** Even when we need to help kids stop what they're doing in order to do something more acceptable, it is important to remember that our input works best when it starts off with warm connection.

- ***Relating at eye level when possible:*** Getting down on a child's level—so we can meet her eyes easily—can increase her experience of connectedness and increase the power of whatever help or support we have to offer too.

"Chunking Down" Expectations for Growth

- ***Beginning where a child is, not where we want him to be:*** We begin working where a child is on a particular developmental "ladder" and build from there in a "rung-by-rung" way—rather than setting expectations that fit with where we would like him to be given his age.

- ***Choosing a small number of target areas at a time:*** In addition, we don't target too many behaviors and developmental agendas at once. Doing that tends to backfire. Instead, we let some of our overall goals go for a while, and get back to them after the child shows signs of mastery in areas we've worked on first.

- ***Working step-by-step to achieve behavioral goals:*** We break down expectations for change into little bits. That way, both the child and the adults who care for him can feel successful.

Cultivating a Stance of Readiness

- ***Having the "basics" in place:*** We rely on good room design, well-taught and steadily run routines, sensible rules for acceptable behavior, and an overall focus on respect for others to promote a feeling of calm and kindness in our classrooms. These classroom-wide basics help to prevent some of the problematic behaviors and "group contagion" issues that make life difficult for kids and teachers alike.

- ***Thinking in advance so we are ready in response:*** We expect worrisome behaviors to occur and have strategies ready for when they do. And if we're quite sure that a child will have trouble handling an upcoming situation, we work with her before she gets stuck, offering the skill-building and problem-solving help that will allow her to succeed. In other words, we are "proactive, not reactive."

- ***Knowing when to lean in and when to lean out:*** We shoot for a combination of emotional support and skill-building assistance (leaning in) and clear expectations for behavior (leaning out). Aiming for a mix that is "clean" rather than "sloppy," we stay patient and friendly as we provide a child with the skill-building help she needs much of the time, while setting limits calmly and firmly when needed.

- **Seeking the "biggest bang for the buck":** Whenever possible, we rely on approaches that target more than one goal at a time, thus making our work easier and our impact on growth stronger.

Using a Mix of Approaches to Support Mastery

- **Lending an ally to support learning:** Targeting one or more areas of mastery, we join the child in enjoyable activities, both one-on-one and when he is with his buddies. Then, while offering him our friendly company, we provide any skill-building support and scaffolding needed for the slow development of competency in areas of challenge.

- **Relying on the power and pleasures of play:** Remembering that play is a wonderful medium for intervention, we consider how a child's challenges "play out in play." Then, with our goals for growth in mind, we offer play-based support from a position outside of the play (as a play observer or play coach) or from the inside (as "wise child").

- **Using a child's strengths to work on any challenges:** When a child's motivation is high, he is more likely to be a willing partner in our efforts to foster growth in areas of difficulty. That is why, whenever we can, we build on his interests and strengths, slipping in skill-building support in a way that feels good to him.

- **Encouraging the safe and healthy expression of feelings:** If we are expecting a child to behave more reasonably in the face of difficult feelings, we also help him find safe places to express and work through those feelings. For some youngsters, this assistance may include regular time with a therapist. For many others, it can be offered solely at home and in school.

- **Supporting opportunities for steady practice:** Children who face behavioral, emotional, and developmental challenges take longer than others to learn the skills that are the hardest for them. That's why we seek out many low-key opportunities for a child to practice the skills he lacks—it is this practice that helps kids grow.

Monitoring and Changing Behavioral Feedback Loops

- **Supporting mastery, not difficulty:** We "look for the gold," the small signs of mastery that show us that a child is beginning to get on track. Then, seeing those signs, we react with warmth and pleasure. At the same time, we watch to make sure that the negative attention a child gets for her misbehavior isn't functioning—despite everyone's best intentions—to reinforce that misbehavior.

- **_Shooting for an upbeat, friendly tone:_** When a child experiences adults as easily irritated, angry, or critical, she is less likely to want to please. So when we notice that a youngster has gotten "under our skin," we work to be just as positive and upbeat as we can. That can be a challenge, and sometimes takes some extra support from compassionate friends or colleagues. But getting emotional reactivity out of the way on our end can make a big difference for everyone.

Tracking and Modifying Our Approach

- **_Paying close attention to both successes and failures:_** Once we have landed on an approach, we watch carefully to see what's working and what isn't. And when necessary, we use what we notice about the child's increasing successes and continuing difficulties to figure out how to tweak, change, or add to what we're doing.

- **_Making sure that strategies are tailored to the people involved:_** Strategies don't come in a one-size-fits-all package. That's why, though it is important to find an approach that meshes with our understanding, the specific techniques we use need to be comfortable for everyone involved.

- **_Seeking further consultation, testing, and/or services:_** Sometimes the help parents and teachers have to offer isn't enough to support a child's growth. At any step along the way, testing, additional consultation, and/or direct services from specialists may be useful. If so, finding outside specialists who fit that child's and that family's style (as well as the family's financial and logistical needs) is really important.

- **_Accessing additional family support:_** Therapeutic support or increased services can be enormously useful when families are burdened with traumatic histories, domestic violence, or significant conflict. The same is true when parents are emotionally overwhelmed, struggling with substance abuse, dealing with significant medical issues, or facing serious financial and housing pressures. Supporting families in accessing such services can sometimes be an important part of our job.

Taking Care of Ourselves

- ***Finding time for reflection:*** Creating space for conversation, reflection, and support helps us stay on track. Teachers almost always do better in supporting a challenging child when they have a net of connection and knowledge to buoy them up along the way.

- ***Seeking opportunities to get away, have fun, and regain our sense of humor:*** Teachers sometimes feel that they need a break, and rightly so. (Parents do too.) Finding time to rest, have fun, and reconnect with other adults can offer a real boost to anyone dealing with a worrisome youngster.

(Adapted from Hirschland 2008, 98–102)

Appendix C:
Learning More—
Tools and Resources

Topic-Based Tools and Resources

Children's "Hard Wiring"

Books Highlighting Temperament

- *The Challenging Child: Understanding, Raising, and Enjoying the Five "Difficult" Types of Children,* Stanley Greenspan with Jacqueline Salmon (Da Capo Press, 1996)

- *The Difficult Child: Understanding and Managing Hard-to-Raise Children,* Stanley Turecki with Leslie Tonner (Bantam Books, 2000)

- *Temperament in the Classroom: Understanding Individual Differences,* Barbara Keogh (Brookes Publishing, 2002)

Books Including a Focus on Information Processing and/or Inclusion

- *The Child with Special Needs: Encouraging Intellectual and Emotional Growth,* Stanley Greenspan and Serena Wieder (Perseus Books, 1998)

- *Collaborative Intervention in Early Childhood: Consulting with Parents and Teachers of 3- to 7-Year-Olds,* Deborah Hirschland (Oxford University Press, 2008)

- *Including One, Including All: A Guide to Relationship-Based Early Childhood Inclusion,* Leslie Roffman and Todd Wanerman with Cassandra Britton (Redleaf Press, 2011)

- *A Mind at a Time,* Mel Levine (Simon and Schuster, 2002)

Books about Sensory-Processing Issues

- *Building Sensory Friendly Classrooms,* Rebecca Moyes (Sensory World, 2010)

- *The Out-Of-Sync Child Has Fun: Activities for Kids with Sensory Integration Dysfunction,* Carol Stock Kranovitz (Perigree, 2003)

- *The Out-Of-Sync Child: Recognizing and Coping with Sensory Integration Dysfunction,* Carol Stock Kranovitz (Perigree, 2006)

- *Sensory Integration: A Guide for Preschool Teachers,* Christy Isbell and Rebecca Isbell (Gryphon House, 2009)

Proactive Teaching Practice

- *Creating the School Family: Bully-Proofing Classrooms through Emotional Intelligence,* Becky Bailey (Loving Guidance, 2011)

- Center for the Social and Emotional Foundations of Early Learning (CSEFEL): csefel.vanderbilt.edu. (See, in particular, the home page sidebar that links to CSEFEL's "What Works Briefs." Included are briefs on routines and schedules, transition time supports, and environmental strategies, among others.)

- *Designs for Living and Learning: Transforming Early Childhood Environments,* Deb Curtis and Margie Carter (Redleaf Press, 2003)

- *Inspiring Spaces for Young Children,* Jessica DeViney, Sandra Duncan, Sara Harris, Mary Ann Rody, and Lois Rosenberry (Gryphon House, 2010)

- *Transition Magician: Strategies for Guiding Young Children in Early Childhood Programs,* Nola Larson, Mary Henthorne, and Barbara Plum (Redleaf Press, 2002)

Play and Play Support

- *A Child's Work: The Importance of Fantasy Play,* Vivian Gussin Paley (University of Chicago Press, 2004)

- *The House of Make Believe: Children's Play and the Developing Imagination,* Dorothy and Jerome Singer (Harvard University Press, 1990)

- *Magic Capes, Amazing Powers: Transforming Superhero Play in the Classroom,* Eric Hoffman (Redleaf Press, 2004)

- *Play: The Pathway from Theory to Practice,* Sandra Heidemann and Deborah Hewitt (Redleaf Press, 2010)

- *The Play's the Thing: Teachers Roles in Children's Play,* Elizabeth Jones and Gretchen Reynolds (Teachers College Press, 2011)

- *The Power of Play: Learning What Comes Naturally,* David Elkind (Da Capo Press, 2007)

Self-Regulation

Books and Manuals

- *Beyond Behavior Management: The Six Life Skills Kids Need,* Jenna Bilmes (Redleaf Press, 2012)

- *Challenging Behavior in Young Children: Understanding, Preventing, and Responding Effectively,* Barbara Kaiser and Judy Sklar Rasminsky (Pearson, 2012)

- *The Explosive Child: A New Approach for Understanding and Parenting Easily Frustrated, "Chronically Inflexible" Children,* Ross Greene (Harper Collins Publishers, 2010)
- *Freeing Your Child from Anxiety: Powerful, Practical Solutions to Overcome Your Child's Fears, Worries, and Phobias,* Tamar E. Chansky (Broadway Books, 2004)
- *Helping Your Anxious Child: A Step-by-Step Guide for Parents,* Ronald Rapee, Ann Wignall, Susan H. Spence, Vanessa Cobham, and Heidi Lyneham (New Harbinger Publications, 2008)
- *How Does Your Engine Run? A Leader's Guide to the Alert Program for Self-Regulation,* Mary Sue Williams and Sherry Shellenberger (TherapyWorks, 1996)
- *Lost at School: Why Our Kids with Behavioral Challenges are Falling through the Cracks and How We Can Help Them,* Ross Greene (Scribner, 2008)
- *Seven Steps to Help Your Child Worry Less: A Family Guide,* Sam Goldstein, Kristy Hagar, and Robert Brooks (Specialty Press, 2002)
- *Trouble in the Classroom: Managing the Behavior Problems of Young Children,* W. George Scarlett and Associates (Jossey-Bass, 1998)

Websites

- Center for Early Childhood Mental Health Consultation at Georgetown University: ecmhc.org (See, in particular, "Teaching Tools for Young Children.")
- Center for the Social and Emotional Foundations for Early Learning (CSEFEL): csefel.vanderbilt.edu. (See, in particular, the sidebar that links to a page titled "Practical Strategies.")

Tools to Promote Mastery

- Books about feelings: http://csefel.vanderbilt.edu/documents /booklist.pdf
- Calming bottle: http://creativesocialworker.tumblr.com /post/49310812693/calm-bottle-aka-glitter-jar-aka-mind-jar
- Emotional thermometer: www.do2learn.com/activities /SocialSkills/Stress/StressTriggers.html
- Feelings charts: http://csefel.vanderbilt.edu/modules/2006 /feelingchart.pdf

- Problem-solving steps and solution kits: http://csefel.vanderbilt.edu/resources/strategies.html#teachingskills
- Puppets: "Tips for Using Puppets to Promote Preschool Children's Social and Emotional Development" by Carolyn Webster-Stratton (The Incredible Years)
- Scripted stories for social situations, including *"Tucker Turtle Takes Time to Tuck and Think"* and *"I Can Be a Super Friend"*: http://csefel.vanderbilt.edu/resources/strategies.html#scriptedstories
- S-T-A-R Technique (adapted from the STAR Parenting Program): www.childtrends.org/?programs=star-stop-think-ask-respond-parenting-program

Managing Behaviors at Home

- *1-2-3 Magic: Effective Discipline for Children 2–12,* Thomas Phelan (Parent Magic, 2010)
- *Parenting the Strong-Willed Child,* Rex Forehand and Nicholas Long (McGraw Hill, 2010)
- *SOS Help for Parents: A Practical Guide for Handling Common Everyday Behavior Problems,* Lynn Clark (SOS Programs and Parents Press, 2005)

Screen Time Exposure (and Overexposure)

- *The Big Disconnect: Protecting Childhood and Family Relationships in the Digital Age,* Catherine Steiner-Adair with Teresa Barker (Harper Collins, 2013)
- *Imagination and Play in the Electronic Age,* Dorothy and Jerome Singer (Harvard University Press, 2005)
- *"Media and Children,"* Recommendations and Resources from the American Academy of Pediatrics: www.aap.org/en-us/advocacy-and-policy/aap-health-initiatives/Pages/Media-and-Children.aspx
- *Taking Back Childhood: Helping Your Kids Thrive in a Fast-Paced, Media-Saturated, Violence-Filled World,* Nancy Carlsson-Paige (Hudson Street Press, 2008)

Trauma and Domestic Violence

- *Children Who See Too Much: Lessons from the Child Witness to Violence Program,* Betsy McAlister Groves (Beacon Press, 2002)
- *Hope and Healing: A Caregiver's Guide to Helping Young Children Affected by Trauma,* Kathleen Fitzgerald Rice and Betsy McAlister Groves (Zero to Three Press, 2005)

References

Aber, J. Lawrence, Sara Pederson, Joshua L. Brown, Stephanie M. Jones, and Elizabeth T. Gershoff. 2003. *Changing Children's Trajectories of Development*. New York: National Center for Children in Poverty.

Ballenger, Cynthia. 1992. "Because You Like Us: The Language of Control." *Harvard Educational Review* 62, no. 2: 199–208.

Barkley, Russell A. 2013. *Your Defiant Child: Eight Steps to Better Behavior*. New York: Guilford Press.

Carlsson-Paige, Nancy. 2008. *Taking Back Childhood: Helping Your Kids Thrive in a Fast-Paced, Media-Saturated, Violence-Filled World*. New York: Hudson Street Press.

Clark, Lynn. 2005. *SOS Help for Parents: A Practical Guide for Handling Common Everyday Behavior Problems*. Bowling Green, KY: Parents Press.

Fonagy, Peter, György Gergely, Elliot L. Jurist, and Mary Target. 2002. *Affect Regulation, Mentalization, and the Development of Self*. New York: Other Press.

Gray, Carol, and Abbie Leigh White. 2006. *My Social Stories Book*. Philadelphia: Jessica Kingsley.

Greene, Ross W. 2008. *Lost at School: Why Our Kids with Behavioral Challenges Are Falling through the Cracks and How We Can Help Them*. New York: Scribner.

———. 2010. *The Explosive Child: A New Approach to Understanding and Helping Easily Frustrated, Chronically Inflexible Children*. New York: HarperCollins.

Greenspan, Stanley. 1992. *Infancy and Early Childhood: The Practice of Clinical Assessment and Intervention with Emotional and Developmental Challenges*. Madison, CT: International Universities Press.

Greenspan, Stanley, and Serena Wieder. 1998. *The Child with Special Needs: Encouraging Intellectual and Emotional Growth*. Reading, MA: Perseus Books.

Heidemann, Sandra, and Deborah Hewitt. 2010. *Play: The Pathway from Theory to Practice*. St. Paul, MN: Redleaf Press.

Hirschland, Deborah. 2008. *Collaborative Intervention in Early Childhood: Consulting with the Parents and Teachers of 3- to 7-Year-Olds.* New York: Oxford University Press.

Kagan, Jerome, and Nancy Snidman. 2004. *The Long Shadow of Temperament.* Cambridge, MA: Harvard University Press.

Klass, Perri, and Eileen Costello. 2004. *Quirky Kids: Understanding and Helping Your Child Who Doesn't Fit In.* New York: Ballantine Books.

Koplow, Lesley, ed. 1996. *Unsmiling Faces: How Preschools Can Heal.* New York: Teachers College Press.

Landy, Sarah. 2002. *Pathways to Competence: Encouraging Healthy Social and Emotional Development in Young Children.* Baltimore: Paul H. Brookes.

LeLaurin, Kathryn, and Todd R. Risley. 1972. "The Organization of Day-Care Environments: 'Zone' versus 'Man-to-Man' Staff Assignments." *Journal of Applied Behavioral Analysis* 5: 225–32.

Minahan, Jessica, and Nancy Rappaport. 2013. *The Behavior Code: A Practical Guide to Understanding and Teaching the Most Challenging Students.* Cambridge, MA: Harvard Education Press.

National Scientific Council on the Developing Child. 2005. "Excessive Stress Disrupts the Architecture of the Brain: Working Paper #3." Retrieved from www.developingchild.net.

Osofsky, Joy D., ed. 2004. *Young Children and Trauma: Intervention and Treatment.* New York: Guilford Press.

Rice, Kathleen Fitzgerald, and Betsy McAlister Groves. 2005. *Hope and Healing: A Caregiver's Guide to Helping Young Children Affected by Trauma.* Washington DC: Zero to Three Press.

Scarlett, W. George. 1998. *Trouble in the Classroom: Managing the Behavior Problems of Young Children.* San Francisco: Jossey-Bass.

Shonkoff, J., and Phillips, D. eds. 2000. *From Neurons to Neighborhoods: The Science of Early Childhood Development.* Washington, DC: National Academies Press.

Siegel, Daniel J. 2012. *The Developing Mind: How Relationships and the Brain Interact to Shape Who We Are.* 2nd ed. New York: Guilford Press.

Steiner-Adair, Catherine. 2013. *The Big Disconnect: Protecting Childhood and Family Relationships in the Digital Age.* New York: HarperCollins.

Tabors, Patton O. 2008. *One Child, Two Languages: A Guide for Early Childhood Educators of Children Learning English as a Second Language.* 3rd ed. Baltimore: Paul H. Brookes.

Thomas, Alexander, Stella Chess, and Herbert G. Birch. 1968. *Temperament and Behavior Disorders in Children.* New York: New York University Press.

Turecki, Stanley. 2000. *The Difficult Child.* New York: Bantam Books.

Vygotsky, Lev S. 1978. *Mind in Society: The Development of Higher Psychological Processes*. Cambridge, MA: Harvard University Press.

Williams, Mary Sue, and Sherry Shellenberger. 1996. *How Does Your Engine Run? A Leader's Guide to the Alert Program for Self-Regulation*. Albuquerque, NM: Therapy Works.

Zelazo, Philip D. 2014. "Executive Function Part One: What Is Executive Function?" Retrieved from www.aboutkidshealth.ca/En/News/Series /ExecutiveFunction

Index

ABCs of behavioral analysis
  described, 49
  use for "breakthrough behavior," 213–215
action, from reflection to, 5
action plan forms
  areas for consideration, 279–281
  discussion and planning
    gathering observations and information, 272–273
    setting plan goals, 276–278
    understanding child's behaviors and feelings, 274–275
adult-child connections
  in child-specific portraits, 57–58
  before correction or redirection, 76
  development of senses of security and of self, 101
  easily-frustrated child and, 57
  inconsistent adult responses and, 47
  in infancy, 88–90
  in three-part flip, 9
adult reactions. *See* interactive patterns
aggression
  connection as antidote to, 113–114
  on-screen violence and, 196
amplifying loop, reassurance of, 225
anger
  connection as antidote, 113–114
  expressing, 7
anxiety
  family history of, 225
  roots of, 225, 228–229
  See also high-anxiety children
assessments
  "storying" versus, 54
  See also child-specific portraits
attachment
  earliest relationships, 44
  understanding, 85–86
attention
  communication and engagement difficulties, 256

"love bombing" and, 113–114
  need for, 58–59
  negative, 70
  obtaining high-energy child's, 190
avoidance patterns, 226, 227–228

Bang, Molly, 200
behavior
  in child-specific portrait, 57
  energy regulation and, 11
  forms for understanding child's, 274–275
  of high-energy children, 174
  setting and enforcing expectations for, 178–181
  in "three-part flip," 8
  tools and resources for managing at home, 293
  See also breakthrough behavior; patterns; worrisome behavior
behavioral analysis ABCs, described, 49
best guesses, 216
"big bang pattern," 239–240
"big-feelings" children
  breakthrough behavior and
    described, 211
    plan development for, 213–215
    plan duration for, 217
    plan elements for, 212, 215–218, 220–222
    program-wide clarity about, 218–219
  importance of play-based support for, 220–222
Blumenthal, Deborah, 200
body language, 76
body-mind connection, 257–258
books about feelings, 200
brain
  early childhood stresses and attachment, 102, 103, 117
  executive functioning and, 175
  hard wiring and, 41
  information processing and, 42
  "light bulb of engagement" and, 142
  neural pathways and, 103, 117

breakthrough behavior
  described, 211
  plans for
    ABC analysis and, 213–215
    choices for scaffolding or limits in, 215–216
    classroom-wide change and, 215
    consistency of, 216–218
    importance of details in, 217–218
    safety concerns in, 212–213
    twenty-one day test in, 217
  program-wide clarity about, 218–219
breathing technique examples, 183, 199, 213
buttressing, 161

capableness, feelings of, as step on developmental ladder, 37
care as antidote to anger and aggression, 113–114
caring place, 152
Center on the Social and Emotional Foundations for Early Learning (CSEFEL), 178, 200, 201
charts, feeling, 200
child-specific portraits
  adult-child connections and, 57–58
  deep-tracked children and, 255–258
  developmental mastery and, 57
  easily frustrated children and, 197
  family culture and history in, 59, 60–61
  importance of, 53
  interactive patterning and, 58–59
  through "storying," 55–57
  triggers for difficulty and setups for success in, 59
  value of, 117
Child with Special Needs, The (Greenspan and Wieder), 41
Chocolate-Covered-Cookie Tantrum, The (Blumenthal), 200
choice-focused key chains or boxes, 200
circle of play, redrawing, 131–132
circles of communication
  enabling successful transition times and, 147
  opening and closing of, 259–260
  understanding of, 86
Clark, Lynn, 241, 243
colors to represent frustration levels, 199
communication
  ability, developmental importance of, 36
  buttressing of, 161
  circles of, 86
  impulse control and, 256
  during infancy, 88–90
  nonverbal, 76, 158–159
  scaffolding of connections and, 259

through presence, 92
  See also language processing
community rules, 178
compassionate emphasis, 119–120, 207
confidence, developmental importance of, 37
connection with others
  as antidote to anger and aggression, 113–114
  attachment and, 44, 85–86
  compassionate emphasis in support of, 119–120
  developmental importance of, 36, 83
  dances of engagement as vehicle for, 145
  fear of, 112
  fostering strategies for, 70
  as foundation of development, 83, 86
  "leaning in" as providing, 77
  nonverbal, 158–159
  "seeding the day" with connection strategy
    "gentle beaming," 114–115, 151
    "love bombing," 113–114, 151
    "slipping in warmth," 115–116
    turning on "light bulb of engagement," 117–119
    without asking for responses, 129
  signs of, 24
  See also adult-child connections; interactive patterns
consequences for unwanted behavior as reinforcement, 47
consistency
  in breakthrough behavior plans, 216–218
  deep-tracked child and, 252
  expectations of, 47
  responses of, 47
constitutional nature. See hard wiring
contribution of constitution. See hard wiring
Costello, Ellen, 253
cue responsiveness
  described, 87–88
  as foundational skill, 87
  nonverbal, 158–159
curricular bridges
  concept behind, 122
  examples of, 120–121, 135–136, 152
  play themes and, 220–221
  supporting emotional well-being with, 221–222

dances of engagement, 145
deep seeing
  described, 19–20
  as two-way street, 21
deep-tracked children
  characteristics of, 251–252, 256–258
  child-specific portrait, 255–258
  day of, described, 253–254

diagnosis and, 253
goals and strategies for
communication, 259–260
flexibility, 261
joint attention, 259–260
meeting expectations, 260
problematic interactive patterns, 252
deep tracking, 251–252
developmental difference, 250–251
developmental mastery
building blocks of, 33–34
in child-specific portrait, 57
climbing pathways/ladders
described, 35
meeting child on "rung" of difficulty, 90
uneven nature of progress, 148–149, 268
connection with others as foundation for, 36, 83
deficits and behavior, 5–6
goal development for, 62
profile of, 31–32, 36–37
in "three-part flip," 8
tools and resources, 292–293
diagnosis, limits of, 54, 253
Difficult Child, The (Turecki), 41
domestic violence, resources about, 294
"drop-in" groups
described, 3–5
discussions during, 11
three-step progression in, 5

easily frustrated children
adult-child connections and, 57
breakthrough behavior
plan development and, 213–215
plan duration and, 217
plan elements and, 212, 215–218, 220–222
program-wide clarity about, 218–219
safety issues and, 67, 212–213
causes of, 195
change and, 223–224
characteristics of, 195–196
importance of play-based support for, 220–222
intervention preparation
lending an ally, 207–208
"use your words," 205–207
zone defense, 204–205
intervention, timing of, 92
recognizing strengths, 69
regulating emotions, tools for
impulse control, steps, 202
problem solving, promotion of, 202–203
recognition and modulation, support for, 199–201

supports needed, 196
emergent learning, 185
emotional flatness
brain activation and, 117
development and, 102
engagement and, 100, 107
emotional thermometer, 199
emotional well-being
curricular bridges and, 121
in child-specific portrait, 57
goal development and, 62
in "three-part flip," 8
energy regulation
behavior and, 11
developmental importance of, 36
See also high-energy children
engagement
finding opportunities for, 144–145
hard starts and, 142
impulse control and, 256
nonverbal means to encourage, 158–159
turning on "light bulb of," 117–119, 142
executive functioning, 175–176, 185
exit strategies, development of, 239–240
expectations
importance of consistent, 47
previewing, 260
setting and following through on, 234
Explosive Child, The (Greene), 195
eye contact
in cue responsiveness, 88, 89
in "love bombing," 113

family culture and history
in child-specific portrait, 59, 60–61
effect on behaviors, 6
hard times and, 45
hard wiring of child and, 43–44
interactive patterning and, 27–28, 237–240
in "three-part flip," 9, 10
in tools and resources for managing behaviors, 293
underlying issues and, 13–14, 198
family partnership
and creating home-school net, 222–223
and dealing with easily frustrated child, 196
and dealing with high-energy child, 191
as goal, 63
and involvement in intervention, 164, 167
and reinforcing skill building, 187, 188
and scaffolding, 260–261
in tools and resources for managing behaviors, 293

feelings
    ability to regulate
        developmental importance of, 37
        in high-energy children, 174
    adult-child connections and, 57–58
    connection to behavior, 47–48
    forms for understanding child's, 274–275
    self-regulation mastery of
        impulse control, steps, 202
        problem solving, steps, 202–203
        tools for, 198–201
    See also big-feelings children
feelings charts, 200
flexibility
    developmental importance of, 37
    difficulties of deep-tracked children and, 251, 252, 257
    increasing child's, 261
focus, capacity for
    high-energy child and, 174, 176–177
    room design in support of, 177–178
    routines in support of, 177–178
focus on five
    overview, 176–177
    proactive teaching and, 177
    skill building
        focus on planning, 185
        multimodal approaches, 186–187
        90-10 rule, 190–191
        outdoor playtime as tool, 188–190
        pace, 191
        prompts, 183–184
        sensory-focused support, 185–186
        working on waiting, 187–188
Fonagy, Peter, 120
forms for action plan
    areas for consideration, 279–281
    discussion and planning
        gathering observations and information, 272–273
        setting plan goals, 276–278
        understanding child's behaviors and feelings, 274–275
From Neurons to Neighborhoods: The Science of Early Childhood Development (Shonkoff and Phillips), 31
frustration
    of adults, 125, 190, 268
    deep-tracked children and, 257
    difficulties expressing, 156
    leaning-out and, 77
    mastering
        impulse control, steps of, 202
        problem solving, steps of, 202–203
        developmental importance of, 35
        tools for, 198–201

    unsafe behavior and, 67
    using colors to represent levels, 199
    waiting ability and, 187
    See also easily frustrated children

"gentle beaming" strategy, 114–115
goals
    "chunking down," 72, 182, 188
    multifaceted intervention strategies for multifaceted, 65, 68–69
    in play-based support, 91, 93
    setting
        intervention preparation and, 204–208
        observation and, 8–11
        role in reflective process, 61–63
        using "storying," 143–144
Gray, Carol, 201
Greene, Ross, 195
Greenspan, Stanley, 35, 41, 86, 259–260

handouts
    Patterns and Problems, 237–238
    Setting Effective Expectations at Home, 241
hard starts
    communication, connection, and cue responsiveness, 90
    described, 44–45, 141–142
    healing from, 103
    toxic stress and, 102
hard times, 45, 149
hard-to-help children, described, xvii–xviii
hard-to-reach parents, 231–232, 245
hard wiring
    communication, connection and cue responsiveness, 90
    contribution to establishment of patterns, 244
    family situation and life experiences and, 6
    of high-energy child, 191
    information processing, 41, 42
    recognizing contribution of, 42–44
    temperament, 41–42
    tools and resources, 290–291
high-anxiety children
    common patterns, 225–226
    family history and, 225
    intervention strategies for, 226–228
    reasons for difficulties of, 225, 228–229
high-energy children
    behaviors, 174
    executive functioning, 175–176
    hard wiring, 191
    impulse control, 175
    language of "engine speed," 184

multimodal approaches for, 186–187
90-10 rule for, 190–191
self-monitoring, 184
sensory-focused support for, 185–186
"stop and look" prompt for, 183–184
transition times and, 182
working on waiting with, 187–188
home life. *See* family culture and history
home-school nets, 223
home situation. *See* family culture and history
"how abouts," 205–206
"human glue"
    described, 119, 122, 152
    double-focused version, 132
    teacher-supported play and, 166
    "wise child" as, 132–134
humor as intervention strategy, 116

I Can Be a Super Friend (CSEFEL), 201
impulse control
    communication and engagement difficulties
        and, 256
    easily frustrated children and, 202
    high-energy children and, 175
    self-observation and, 12
inconsistent adult responses, 47
"I need a break" cards, 187
infancy
    communication, connection and cue responsiveness
        in, 88–90
    development of senses of security and of self during,
        101
    hard starts during, 44–45, 90
information gathering
    forms, 272–273
    observation
        as first step, 5
        goal setting and action planning considerations,
            8–11
        importance of, 5
        impulse control and self-, 12
        linking to categories of importance and, 22
        as precursor to play-based support, 92
    as step one of three-step progression, 5
information processing, 41, 42
interactive patterns
    in child-specific portraits, 58–59
    circles of communication and, 86
    compassionate emphasis and, 120
    cultural norms and, 27–28
    effect on behavior, 6, 7, 40, 46, 195–196, 252
    feelings and, 48
    goal development for, 62

at home
    discussion at parenting groups, 235
    problems in and alternatives to, 237–240,
        244–245
    identifying, 106
    temperament and, 128
    in "three-part flip," 9
    See also family culture and history
intervention from outside play, 92
intervention from within play, 92, 94
intervention, principles
    building on power of connection and centrality of
        relationships, 284–285
    "chunking down" expectations for growth, 285
    cultivating state of readiness, 285–286
    monitoring and changing behavioral feedback loops,
        286–287
    seeking partners and perspective, 284
    taking care of ourselves, 288
    tracking and modifying our approach, 287
    using mix of approaches, 286
intervention, strategies
    building curricular bridges, 120–121
    children as co-facilitators, 94
    compassionate emphasis, 119–120
    connecting with the "spotlight" off, 129–131
    dances of engagement, 145
    family involvement, 136, 164, 167
    forms to aid in planning, 276–278
    fostering pleasurable connections, 70
    increasing play opportunities, 71
    increasing sensory input, 71
    playful obstruction, 145–146
    preparation for predictable difficulties, 74–75,
        204–205
    proactive support, 69, 74–75
    redrawing circle of play, 131–132
    safety considerations and, 66–68
    See also play-based support; seeding the day strategy

joint attention
    described, 256–257
    goals and strategies to support, 259–260

key chains, choice-focused, 200
kinesthetic reminders, 186–187
Klass, Perri, 253
Koplow, Lesley, 121

labels, limits of, 53–57
language processing
    expanding and extending language use, 161
    explosive behavior and, 214

expressing frustration and, 156
fostering, 163
help from specialists, 157
pace of improvement, 167
play and, 60
second-language learners and, 24
as source of frustration, 37, 47
strategies to develop competency, 160–161
leaning in–leaning out, 76–77, 214, 226–227
LeLaurin, Kathryn, 205
lending an ally, 73, 207–208
"light bulb of engagement," 117–119, 142
limit setting, 234, 235, 241
"love bombing" strategy, 113–114, 151

medication, 265, 267
meditation, 200
"meet and greet" strategy, 226–227
mind-body connection, 257–258
mirroring
nonverbal, 158, 160
in play-based support, 152
modeling responses, examples of, 119–120
"motherese," 144, 162
movement, reaction to levels of, 23

nature/nuture and worrisome behavior, 40
changing home situations and, 148
hard starts and, 44–45
hard wiring and, 41–44
90-10 rule, 190–191
nonverbal connections, 158–159, 160

observation
as first step in three-step progression, 5
forms for gathering, 272–273
goal setting/action planning considerations and, 8–11
importance of, 5
impulse control and self-, 12
linking to categories of importance, 22
as precursor to play-based support, 92
One Child, Two Languages (Tabor), 160–161
1-2-3 Magic (Phelan), 241
on-screen violence
aggressive behavior and, 196
fear and, 222
tools and resources, 293
outdoor playtimes, skills building during, 188–190

parent mentors, 242
parents
childhood of, 13
engaging hard-to-reach, 231–232, 245

feelings of, 48
role in establishing patterns, 243–244
supporting
changing problematic patterns, 237–240, 244–245
finding voice of authority, 242
in group sessions, 233–234
helping children comply with requests, 243
setting effective expectations, 241
setting limits, 234, 235
working with, 14, 136
See also family culture and history
patterns
hard wiring as contributing factor to, 244
of high-anxiety children, 225–226
parents' roles in, 243–244
as problem-solving attempts, 25
worrisome behavior and, 46–47
See also interactive patterns
pharmacological intervention, 265, 267
Phelan, Thomas, 241
Phillips, D., 31
planning boards, 146, 147, 187
play
age appropriate, 59
developmental abilities and, 90
goal development for, 63
language processing difficulties and, 60
themes, 220–221
tools and resources, 291
using outdoor, for skill building, 188–190
play-based support
child co-facilitators, 94
as cooperative effort, 93–94
described, 72–73, 91
goal setting for, 93
important for "big-feelings" and easily frustrated children, 220–222
increasing play opportunities, 71
lending-an-ally and, 73, 207–208
mirroring difficulties faced by child, 152, 220
redrawing circle of play, 131–132
roles of teachers in, 92–94, 152
steps of, 163–164
tools and resources, 291
playful obstruction, 145–146
praise, as reinforcement, 47
previewing support
to enhance transition times, 74, 146, 147
to go beyond eternal present, 185
to overcome fears, 136
to strengthen language processing, 166
primary caregivers